BISHOP'S
WALTHAM

A History

Detail from the 6 inches to the mile Ordnance Survey map of 1868.

BISHOP'S WALTHAM

A History

BARBARA BIDDELL

PHILLIMORE

2002

Published by
PHILLIMORE & CO. LTD
Shopwyke Manor Barn, Chichester, West Sussex

ISBN 1 86077 235 8

Printed and bound in Great Britain by
MPG BOOKS
Bodmin, Cornwall

Contents

List of Subscribers

Adrian Abbott
Margaret Abbott
William J. Aburrow
June Aitchison
Eileen Akehurst
Mr Ian & Mrs Lorna Allured
K.L. Anthony
Mary Antram
Keith Appleton
K. & D. Askew
Marc Askew
Aidan Oliver Baker
S.R. Baxter
K.R. Bearpark
Paul Bennett
Adrian & Veronique Biddell
Bridget Biddell
Mr & Mrs E.C. & Y.A. Birbeck
Mr P.H. Bird
Richard J. Blackburn
Barry Blake
Richard Blow
Martyn Blundell
Rebecca Blundell
Daniels G. Brame
Chris Breach
Mrs Maurveen Brown
Pamela Bruce
Lewis Buckwell
Norman Burchfell
Andy Burdon
Betty C. Burke
Sue & Peter Burkett
Jeff Burnige
Roger & Susan Burt
Tricia Burton
Georgina Busher
Elsa M. Buttress
Sue & Brian Cable
Mary Calvert
Tony Cauchi
Neville Chamberlain
Nigel Chamberlain
Kenneth F. Chandor
Philip Channon
Pat Chubb

David Chun
Mrs Rosemary Clark
Miss Gemma J. Clarke
Mr Reginald E.V. Cockle
Edward W. Colley
C.R. Conroy
Mrs S.J. Conway
Robert Cooper
John & Joan Cornell
Olivia Cotton
Mr & Mrs Dermot Cox
Barbara Crookes
Mr & Mrs Barry Cross
Angela E. Cruddas
W.R. Cullimore
Graham N. Curtis
Neil Curtis
Mrs Diane Daniels
John Dann
Denise Davies
H. Deries-Glaister
Ann Dilworth
A.E. & B. Dore
Trevor John Downer
Durley History Society
Mr M.O. Easton
Bob & Jill Edmunds
J.M. Edwards
Anne Elder
Tony & Jill Eley
David & Patricia Ellis-Jones
Edna Elmore (née Grossmith)
Evelyne Evans
Dennis Eyles
B.J. & A. Fairweather
Graham Fall
J. & C. Fewings
Edwin David Finch
Joanne Fletcher
Kate Fletcher
Trevor Fletcher
Jillian Elizabeth Flynn
Sandra & Peter Fowler
Priscilla Fryer
Mick Fuchs
D.R. & A. Fullerton

Christopher & Marilyn Gamblin
M.A. Gillies
M.D. Glaister
Malcolm Glaister
Charlie Jamie Golding
The Rev. Canon R.H. Granger
Hanna Gravestock
Martin & Amanda Grover
Mrs Rosemary Guest
Ann Gutsell
Lady Paulina Hadley
Kevan Halls
Mrs M.L. Hamilton
Jean Hammerton
Janet & John Hammond
Hampshire County Council
Ron & Shirley Harvey
Mr & Mrs J. Hayter
Jacqueline Hayward
Ernie & Denise Hazell
J.M. Henty
Elizabeth Hiscock
Roger & Lorna Hockin
Miss Sylvia Horlock
Gwen Houghton
Jean Houghton
Brian & Janet Hoult
Dr P.E. & Mrs A.M. Howden
Henry Howe
A.C.W. & D. Hunt
Bernard & Barbara Igra
Mark Johnston
Nicholas Jonas
E.D. & N.S. Jury
Josephine & Ronald Keat
Mrs Marie Patricia Kemp
Bryan King
Jaclyn Kippenberger
Tony Kippenberger
Hugh Knollys
Dr John Knowles
Dr Nick Lalor
Mr J.R. Lambert
Joyce Law
William F.J. & Sheila M. Lawton
James Laybourne

Helen Lennox
Adrian & Maggie Lightfoot
P.A. Lingard, CBE, JD
John Linter
Ray & Dawn Littlefield
Mrs C. Long
Alan & Virginia Lovell
Mr Bertram Loveridge
Mrs Kelvin A. Low
Susan Low
Ronald J. Lucas
Timothy Macleod-Clarke
The Reverend Mary MacVicar
Keith Marchant
Sheila Marshall
Nicolette Violet May
Charles & Maureen McAndrew
McGovern Family
McKenzie Family
John McLaughlin
William M.J. McNally
Jane Mears
J. Menendez
Dave Miles
Sally Miles
Richard J. Mills
Thomas L. Mills
Margaret Monier-Williams
Heather Moore
Martin Morris
Jackie Morrison
A.H. Mugridge
Gillian Mulley
Keith Munro
Oliver Murphy
Elizabeth Nelson
The Newman Family
Mr & Mrs D.M. Page
Iain Page
Oliver C. Parry
Stacey M. Parry
Nicholas Passingham
Rod & Cathy Passingham
Timothy Passingham

Revd. G.R. Paterson
Bob & Pam Pearson
Marion Pink
Michael & Elisabeth Plumridge
J.A. Pond
Mick & Barbara Pond
Peter Potts
John & Pauline Powell
Jennifer J. Pugsley
Mike & Eileen Rainey
Robert & Susan Rance
Dr F.W. Ratcliffe, CBE
Mrs Shirley Amita Ray
Fred & Margaret Richards
Janice W. Richards
John & Barbara Richman
Ridgemede Junior School
Amanda Roberts
Dawn Robinson
Audrey B.I. Rogers
Mr & Mrs J. Russell
Mr & Mrs N. Russell
Professor James Sambrook
Max Saunders
Lawrence & Caroline Sawers
Jonathan W. Scott
Mary Scott
Madeleine Selby
Sally Serridge
Mr & Mrs I.T. Shankland
Mr Raymond Sharp
Mrs P.A. Sheppard
Pam Simcock
Graham & Lucy Smith
Joan & Peter Sneath
Mr R. Spindloe
June & Bob Start
David Steel
Mrs D. Steele
T.W.M. Steele
Chris & Bob Stewart
Dr & Mrs Ian Stoddart
Barry, Miriam & Sophie Swann

Mr & Mrs R.S. Symes
Colin A.H. Tait
Susan Tatton-Brown
John Taylor
Joyce Thatcher
Mr J.H. & Mrs P.M. Thomas
Betty Thompson
Marjorie A. Thornton
Wendy Thorpe
Martin Tiller
Robert Toleman
Molly Townsend
Michael Tredré
Lady Troubridge
Janis Veck
Raymond Veck
Jane Vose
W.E. Walmsley
A.M. Ward
Mrs Pauline Ward
Frances Warren
Peter R. Watkins
Janet, Colin, Laura & Chris Watts
John Watts
Jean Weatherall
Harry Raymond West
Pauline West
Mrs R. Whiteside
Bill Wightman
The Revd. John F. Willard
Mr Kevin Williams
Mrs 'Timmy' Williamson
Mrs B.J. Willott
Terry Wilson
David Winsloe
Mrs Ronald Withers
Janet & Hans Wolf
P.C.G. Woolston
Nigel Wormald
Hugh & Jill Wright
John & Cheryl Young
Mrs Kay Young

Acknowledgements

I came to live at Bishop's Waltham in 1962, fortunate enough to live in the old rectory (now Longwood), where the house itself was a constant reminder of previous occupants, from the huge key which locked the great front door, the parish room set aside for the needs of parishioners, to the baize-covered servants' door which divided the back from the front of the house; green baize on the kitchen side, red on the drawing room side.

There were already two histories of the place, *The History of Bishop's Waltham* published in 1844 by the Revd Charles Walters, former curate and headmaster of the free grammar school, and *The Story of Bishop's Waltham Ancient and Modern* by the Revd Frank Sargeant, the rector from 1949 to 1962: a keen historian, he added to the collection of documents in the parish chest and wrote books on the palace and church: *The Story of the Bishop's Palace, Bishop's Waltham* and *The Story of the Church of St Peter, Bishop's Waltham*. I first worked on the poor law records; latterly with more time available I have studied other aspects. I have used the extensive notes (catalogued under HRO 5M/87) which Monica Martineau, devoted as she was to the welfare of the place, had made for a history of the town and John Bosworth's excellent pictorial histories, *Bishop's Waltham and Newtown: 25 Years of Change* and *Bishop's Waltham: A Pictorial Record*. John has supplied many of the illustrations for this book and has an invaluable knowledge of the history of the town. I am very grateful to the Trustees of Bishop's Waltham Museum for allowing me to use their illustrations. Ted Pitman's detailed history of the Clay Works, *Newtown and Clay*, has been most helpful. I have found articles by Edward Roberts on the Fish Ponds and Deer Parks of the bishops of Winchester, by Elizabeth Lewis on Excavations in Bishop's Waltham, by G.P. Hewlett and Jane Hassell on Bishop's Waltham Dikes, all printed in the Hampshire Field Club and Archaeological Society, invaluable. I have used J.N. Hare's article on the Palace produced in the *Archaeological Journal* and his guide *Bishop's Waltham Palace* published by English Heritage. I am grateful to the Warden and Fellows of Nuffield College, Oxford, for granting permission to quote from William Cobbett's notebook of wages (Nuffield XIII), which forms part of the College's substantial Cobbett collection. I am very much indebted to Professor James Sambrook who read a first draft of this book, for his very helpful ideas and suggestions and criticisms and encouragement; also to David Chun for his most pertinent suggestions, for pointing me to relevant articles and for allowing me to use his research on Waltham Chase. Dr Colin Haydon of King Alfred's College, Winchester, has guided me in research into Jacobite material, as has Professor Paul Monod of Middlebury College, Vermont, USA. I am most grateful to the Clerk of the Records of the House of Lords for allowing me to use their archive. The Staff of the Hampshire Record Office have been unfailingly helpful in all my requests. I am most grateful for the advice and support of Bill Walmsley, secretary of Bishop's Waltham in Bloom, and of Tony Hunt, managing editor of St Peter's parish magazine.

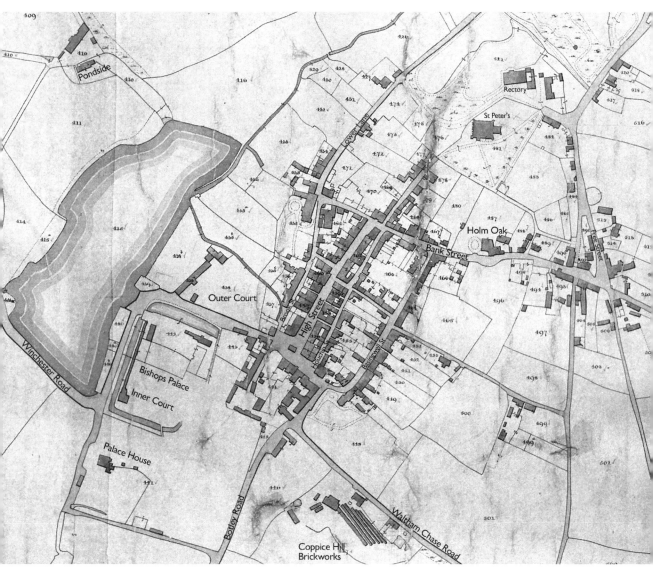

1   The tithe map of 1840 shows the medieval town huddled close to the Bishop's Palace. The turnpike from Winchester (1836) takes four right angle bends, first round the head of the pond, then past the Palace, then round the *Crown Inn* to reach the road to Wickham through Waltham Chase.

Introduction

This book describes three aspects of Waltham in Hampshire; first, the hundred or manor of Waltham which became known as Bishop's Waltham in 904 when it was exchanged by King Edward the Elder for the manor of Portchester; secondly, the ecclesiastical parish of Waltham with the church of St Peter at its centre; thirdly, the civil parish of Waltham given the responsibility of carrying out Tudor legislation, particularly the Poor Laws, begun under King Henry VIII and developed under Queen Elizabeth I.

The name 'Waltham' points to early Anglo-Saxon origin, probably of between AD 450 and 550, 'walt' meaning an area of forest, 'ham' a settlement. R.M. Huggins[1] has suggested that places with the name 'Waltham', settled near Roman roads with fertile soil which could produce a surplus of food, were early royal estates; certainly Waltham belonged to the King until 904.

The manor or hundred of Waltham stretched from the high ground of two spurs of the South Downs along the whole Hamble valley to the estuary at Fairthorn. The chief settlement was Waltham but there were others at Durley, Upham, Bursledon. This manor, consisting of 38 hides[2] (4,560 acres) of land, was exchanged by King Edward the Elder for the 40 hides (4,800 acres) of Portchester manor, previously held by the bishop of Winchester. From 904, therefore, it became known as Bishop's Waltham, or Waltham Woolpit or South Waltham, to distinguish it from North Waltham, one of the episcopal manors in north Hampshire.

The parish of Bishop's Waltham lies partly in the Hamble valley, for the river rises here. It is fed with springs; some bubble up through the Moors, just south of the town, then make a stream which crosses the former hunting park of the bishops of Winchester and joins the main river near Frenchman's Bridge on the road to Curdridge and Botley. To the north and east the land rises to chalk downs.

The town of Bishop's Waltham is about 68 miles from London, ten from Winchester, 11 from Southampton. The old town lies compactly at the head of the river, part of which was dammed to make Waltham Pond. The ancient palace of the bishops which overlooks the pond, even in its destroyed state, reveals some of its former glory. The town huddled close by to provide the workforce which the

2   The Palace ruins in 1815.

3   Church Lane, now St Peter's Street, in 1913, was also known as Quality Street.

4   St Peter's Church after the south gallery had been built (1797). Inset is the piscina added by William of Wykeham. Hampshire Record Office TOP31/2/5

5 Bank Street (on the left of the picture) leads into the town past the *Mafeking Hero* (formerly *The White Hart*) with the Educational Institute on the left. The road to the right is Free Street, which passes the Methodist Mission Hall on the left and leads to Lower Lane at Northbrook crossroads.

palace required. Near the palace lies St George's Square from which a grid pattern of planned streets reaches out. Four of these – Brook Street, High Street, Houchin Street, Basingwell Street – run north and south; three remain, for Houchin Street has become a car park. Three streets – Cross Street, Middle (Red Lion) Street, Bank Street – run east and west. To the north, off Bank Street, lies St Peter's Street, which leads to the church of St Peter. Bank Street to the east runs past the former Gunner's bank to Free Street, where the *Mafeking Hero* formerly *The White Hart* (now an Indian restaurant) and the *Wheatsheaf Inn* (now houses) marked one entry into the town. Bank Street to the west runs down to Lower Lane, now a by-pass which leads to Northbrook crossroads, thence to Corhampton and Winchester. There are no grand houses here but some elegant town houses, for it is a pleasing collection of buildings from different centuries; some, originally timber-framed, have been refronted in Georgian or Victorian times.

Beyond the palace across the pond Newtown developed in the 19th century, along a new road leading to Winchester. Here houses were built for the workers at the Clay and Tile Works, in production until the 1950s. Waltham Chase, once

6   View of the *Wheatsheaf Inn*, now houses, which marked the entrance to Free Street from Swanmore.

part of the ancient hunting ground of the bishops, lies to the south-east along the road to Portsmouth. The Rareridge estate with modern schools and old people's bungalows was developed in the 20th century; it lies on the east along the road to Swanmore. Further east lay the former tithing of Hoe, where some of the old cottages remain.

Country roads lead to the extremities of the parish. Dean is a small hamlet along Dean Lane which follows the bottom of the Downs until it peters out to become a footpath to the beautiful manor of Preshaw, where King George VI spent his honeymoon. The road to Ashton leads north-west up the chalk of Vernon Hill, then through deep-set lanes to this once populous settlement. The lane to Dundridge, often flooded, runs to the east. It lies at the bottom of a wooded hanger and leads to an unexpected cluster of houses with an inn, then on to Swanmere and Droxford.

I

The Hundred or Manor of Waltham

The hundred or manor of Waltham contained not only the town of Waltham, but also settlements at Durley, Upham and Bursledon. It was part of the Kingdom of Wessex and conformed to the laws of King Ine (688-726) and his successors, the most notable being the great King Alfred (871-99). Administratively Wessex was divided into shires which were sub-divided into hundreds, each in theory consisting of one hundred hides of land which would support one hundred peasant families. All the freemen of the hundred met monthly in the open air at a hundred court, where disputes were settled by customary law. Waltham belonged to the King who granted land in return for military services, or other vital tasks such as the upkeep of roads or bridges. But in 904 King Edward the Elder (899-924) exchanged the manor of Waltham for the manor of Portchester to keep the coastal defences against the Vikings under his own supervision. Waltham now became Bishop's Waltham, an attractive property, described as 'fields woods meadows and fisheries'.[1]

The Vikings continued their attacks despite being paid danegeld, in an attempt to buy them off. In 1001, during the time of King Ethelred the Unready (978-1016), they invaded from their headquarters on the Isle of Wight, burning many villages and the 'residence at Waltham'.[2] This 'residence' can only be the substantial building in which the bishops lived when they visited the manor. It stood close to the pond and probably became part of the palace stable, for Anglo-Saxon remains were excavated here in 1967. The Vikings sacked the monastery here. This was never rebuilt but the town itself was: it is recorded in Domesday Book in 1086.

Domesday Book contained a valuation of all the manors which the Norman King, William I, had acquired by his conquest of England. Commissioners were sent to find the answers to a number of set questions, one of which was the extent of the manor measured in hides. They were told that the Bishop himself held the manor of Bishop's Waltham, that it consisted both in 1066 and 1086 of 20 taxable hides of land, though in fact there were 30 hides here. Part of it was farmed by the Bishop himself with six plough teams – a plough team comprised eight oxen. There were 70 bondmen and 15 villeins who owed labour services to the bishop, farming their own holdings with 26 plough teams. There were seven slaves. The manor contained three mills, meadowland of 2½ acres, a park for wild animals, and woodland (probably Waltham Chase) for ten pigs (pannage). This would reveal to the Commissioners the extent of the forested area since pannage represented a measurement for woodland. The whole manor was worth £30. Twyford, comparable with Bishop's Waltham, also held by the Bishop, was valued at £32. East Meon on the other hand, which was later to become a valuable corn growing area, was worth only 100 shillings.

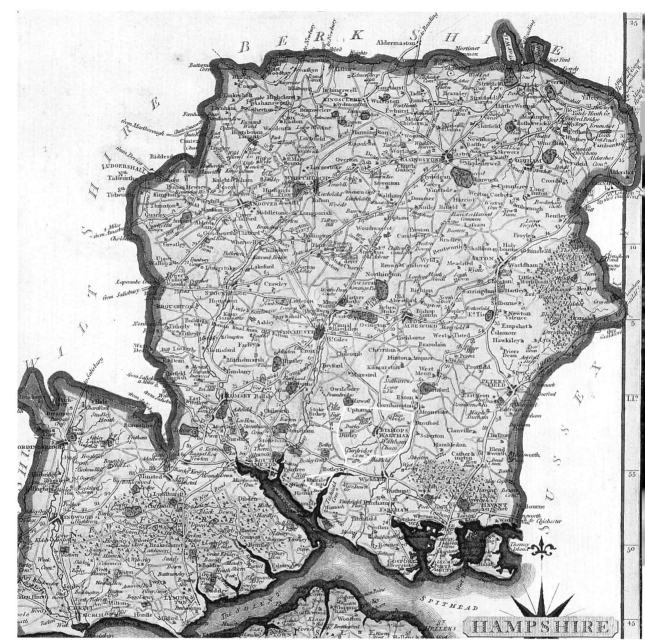

7 Cary's Map of Hampshire and the Isle of Wight, 1793. The rough area of Bishop's Waltham hundred is outlined
in white. The turnpike across Curdridge Common to Corhampton; Cobbett's road; the Bishop's Waltham to
Fisher's Pond turnpike have not yet been built. HRO, 110M89/P71.

There were three free men in Bishop's Waltham manor. One was Robert,
probably a Norman, for Domesday Book specifically notes that before 1066 the
land he farmed had belonged to the villeins. His property was valued at 30
shillings, but where he lived is not recorded. A second freeman, Ralph, was the
priest for two churches, St Peter's Bishop's Waltham and probably St Mary's

8   The Palace Mews in the 1900s. Horse-drawn vehicles could be hired here from Mr Robinson. This was part of the original palace stables which probably included the Anglo-Saxon 'residence' burnt by the Danes in 1001.

Upham. He farmed the glebe land which was worth 100 shillings, with two villeins and nine bondmen using two plough teams. Six slaves also worked for him with one plough team. He had sublet part of the glebe to a man who farmed it with one villein, three bondmen and nine oxen.[3] Only the heads of households were recorded in Domesday Book, so, allowing five people to a household, fewer than six hundred people were living in the whole manor.

The bishop of Winchester, in return for the land he held from the king, was required to finance the services of 60 fully-equipped knights,[4] a considerable expense but one which he could well afford. In 1301 the income from his estate was £5,188, while the Archbishop of Canterbury's was considerably smaller, at only £2,616.[5] Each person in turn held his land from the lord of the manor, the bishop, according to custom. When an inhabitant died his best animal became the lord's property, the heriot. Oxen, plough horses, cows and pigs were all taken as heriots. If there was no animal, a fine (a fee) of sixpence or a shilling was paid. Before a son could farm the land his father had worked he paid a fine to the bishop. A fine was required when a woman married. When her husband died his widow might pay a fine to remain in her cottage.

Bishop's Waltham was one of 29 manors in Hampshire belonging to the bishop. His land, which stretched from Somerset to Buckinghamshire, had mostly been given to the bishopric by the Anglo-Saxon kings. From 1208 accounts exist of what was produced in each manor. These were recorded on the pipe rolls which were kept in the treasury at Winchester. The Hampshire Record Office has published the pipe roll of the bishopric 1301-2, which provides an insight into the management of the manor, under its three chief officials, the treasurer, the steward and the bailiff. The treasurer, in charge of the bishop's finances, had his headquarters at Wolvesey Castle in Winchester.

The steward was responsible for all manorial administration. He rode from one manor to the next, where he presided over the hundred or manorial courts, known also as the courts leet. These were held in the palace around Michaelmas (29 September) and Hock-tide (the second Tuesday after Easter). They continued to be held as long as the bishop was lord of the manor. In 1823 the steward arrived at Bishop's Waltham for the Hock-tide court on 26 April.[6]

The manor was composed of tithings, each consisting theoretically of ten men, with mutual responsibility for good behaviour. All were involved through the ancient institution of 'frankpledge', which required all males over twelve to belong to a tithing and attend the court leet. Here tithingmen were appointed to speak for their different tithings. In 1301 tithingmen came from the tithings of 'Bishops Waltham, Hou, Ashton, Bursledon, Durley, Mensingefeld (in Durley), Upham, Wangefeld (in Curdridge), Wodekote (in Dean) and Wynteshull'.[7] Each tithingman must report petty crime, dishonesty and unneighbourly behaviour and present tithing penny, a penny tax on each male over the age of twelve.

But between the two courts leet, a lesser court, the court baron, was held, presided over by the bailiff. This too dealt with debts, trespass and disputes between tenants, but its most important function was to register the surrender and admission to land according to custom. Changes in landholding were recorded on the court rolls. Tenants could buy copies, hence the name, copyholder, known also as bondholder. This court continued to be held into the 20th century: as long as there was any copyhold land, the court had jurisdiction over it. Copyhold was finally abolished in 1926.

In 1301 the Bishop, John de Pontoise (1282-1304), kept the manor of Bishop's Waltham in 'demesne', that is, he farmed it himself. The reeve, Robert Stretthe, was his farm manager; an unfree tenant, he was appointed by the bishop or by his fellow tenants. He was responsible for everything produced or consumed. This included the care of the livestock, the cultivation of the demesne lands, the selling of produce, the upkeep of farm buildings and the repair of implements. He collected the rents from the manorial tenants and the fines imposed by the manorial courts. He, together with the bailiff, must present his accounts to the steward at Michaelmas. His position was supposed to last a year but might continue for a longer period.

The beadle was the reeve's assistant. Others were employed; a swineherd, a smith, a hayward who supervised the ploughland and pasture and woods, two shepherds, four full-time and one part-time ploughmen. There were a further nine workers together with three cottars. These held less than five acres. They must work once a week for the bishop but at harvest time they must each reap half an acre a day. Two carters doubled as reapers. There was one granary keeper. Four drovers worked the whole year, one only half the year. There was one cowherd and one dairymaid. The doorkeeper received an annual stipend of £1 10s. 5d., a penny a day, a mark of his responsible position. There were 35 manorial servants in 1301. Each was allowed a reduction in his rent; the reeve and the beadle five shillings, the others from one to three shillings.

Two bailiffs served Bishop's Waltham that year presiding over the courts baron. Roger Cosyn was bailiff from Michaelmas to Christmas, Robert de Froyle from Christmas to the following Michaelmas. Both were allowed fur for their liveries, which was a mark of their status. Roger received £1 12s. 1d. expenses, two pigs, 60 gallons of cider, wheat, a cheese, oats for his horse. Robert received £2 in expenses, wheat, a cheese, oats for his horse and for his clerk's horse.

The hayward was allowed wheat, barley and peas. The drovers, cowherd, swineherd and the keeper of the lambs were allowed only barley and peas. The manorial servant's diet was mostly carbohydrate; barley and oats provided both food and drink.[8] But the beadle, shepherd and smith received also a cheese and a lamb. In 1301 the dairymaid, suspected of embezzlement, had her allowance of barley reduced. She was ordered to give a full account of all the hens and goslings produced. Some of these servants would have been living within the curia, the area round the Bishop's Palace; indeed, the hayward dined at the Bishop's table during harvest time or when his cereal allowance ran out.

At springtime and harvest men were called in from the whole manor. In the spring 48 ploughmen must plough 52 acres. This was their labour service. Boon-work, which was over and above this customary labour service, was demanded whenever extra ploughing or reaping was necessary. Each man must plough two acres for which he received one penny, but Saturday ploughings merited 1½d. At harvest time 347 men were called on. They worked one day free, one day they received bread and three herrings (in Bitterne manor the allowance was five herrings), and one day they received bread and meat.

One wheat-growing area was Rouerigg. This is possibly Rareridge, recorded in 1840 as 11 acres, no.550 on the tithe map,[9] part of Butts Farm. More wheat was grown at la Mere and la Woth, in all 453 acres. (A 14th-century acre was smaller than a 19th-century acre). 98 acres of barley were grown at Crikelescrofte and Longehegge. (On the tithe map Longhedges is part of Dean and Metlands farm.) 405 acres of oats were sown at Langehegg, Hok (Hoe?) Legsted and Crikeles-crofte, a productive cereal-growing area. In 1860 'Crockles Croft' is described as '12 acres called Newlands late of the Demesne of the Lord … in the tithing of Waltham'.[10] In 1301, 20 acres of peas were grown at la Worth, also 59 acres of vetches at la Worth and beside Triboddestret, possibly the Roman road which passes through the manor, since 'street' frequently denotes a Roman road.

Seven people, five of them with land beside the fish pond, paid their rent in cumin, a herb which aided digestion. One person paid in pepper. These were delivered directly to Wolvesey Castle, as was the charcoal produced.

The manor contained six mills. The East mill (Waltham Chase mill) and the 'mill outside the gate' were both used for milling the tenants' grain and brought the Bishop a return of almost £8 from the sale of wheat, maslin (a mixture of wheat and rye), malt and oatmeal. Three other mills in the manor all on the Hamble river – Caldekot, Mattokeford and Frogg mill – were rented out, as was the fulling mill which depended on horse-power. This mill, which thickened cloth, was probably in Ashton tithing, built by weavers driven out from Winchester by the high taxes imposed on them in 1208.[11] These four mills brought in £2 10s.

Income came too from pannage, the money paid for the pigs feeding in the woodlands and also from pasture let out for grazing. At Martinmas (11 November) the old oxen and cows, the autumn calves, the old sheep and the feeble lambs were sold; only the stronger animals were kept through the winter.

The tanning of leather was a well established industry. Sickly animals, including the sheep which had caught murrain, a fever they were susceptible to after shearing, were killed and their skins cured. Three skins came from sheep which had rotted. In 1301 the manor produced 11 hides from oxen, cows and bullocks, 53 woolskins, 14 bare skins, 19 lamb skins. Later, certainly by 1493, there were limepits outside the gate of the palace courtyard, for the glovers' craft.[12] This tanning trade continued into the 19th century. In 1866 the Tan Yard in Lower Lane consisted of a barn, pits, sheds, 'Drying Room, Leather House, Water Bark Mill [for grinding the oak bark used in the tanning process] Stables and Water Wheel'.[13]

In 1301 the flesh of one boar which had suddenly died brought in one shilling. Five other pigs were sold at 2s. 6d. each. The manor produced wool, the clippings were sold, and the best went directly to Wolvesey. Other products included winter and summer cheeses, loppings from oak trees, peacocks' feathers. Two peacocks and three peahens were kept through the winter, probably at the palace.

But out of this manorial income came the upkeep of the mills and buildings. The great barn was falling down since the timber had rotted. It was restored and re-roofed, as was the stable outside the gate. (The great barn was demolished to make way for sheep in the 19th century,[14] the stable outside the gate for the by-pass in 1968.[15]) In 1301 the sheepcote needed re-roofing, some ploughs were repaired, new ones were made. The horses must be shod, one new cart was made, the other repaired; grease was bought to treat the sheep, with canvas to pack the wool in. Woollen and linen cloth were bought for the dairy. Bursledon tithing produced salt, presumably from the Hamble river. Pasturage in various places was let, as were the services of ploughmen which were owed to the Bishop, but had not been needed for farming the demesne.

Other income came from more than 24 people who paid fines to be released from their customary labour services. Fines came also from misdemeanours like trespass, blocking up a pathway, not looking after the sheep properly, or selling underweight bread.

The manor consisted of the cultivated fields, the park and the woods, but there were vast areas of wasteland which needed clearing of scrub and weeds to make them productive. During the 13th century the population had grown, more labour was available, so more land was taken into cultivation. One field was made in the park and another near the cowshed for the calves, with a hedge planted round it. A sluice was made for the small fish pond; a pit dug for killing foxes.

Two pieces of land, Cotehull and la Fryth, were freed from customary labour services on payment of fines. All these fines, together with the fines paid on the transfer of land holdings through death or inheritance, or for marriage outside the manor, together with the legal tax of tithing penny, brought in £38 17s. 1d. The total income amounted to £237, whereas the manor of Twyford produced £256, and the manor of East Meon with its valuable corn growing land £295.[16]

9   St George's Square in 1841 after the demolition of the Market House. The *Crown Inn* is the last building on the right. Courtesy: Bishop's Waltham Museum Trust.

The town of Bishop's Waltham was the centre of the manor. It contained the bishop's palace where the courts were held. There must have been a weekly market, for standardised weights and measures were kept here. Bishop Henri de Blois (1129-74) probably authorised this market, for he would want to capitalise on his investment in the town. Cottages were built close by, so that by 1331 they were concentrated round the market.[17] Nikolaus Pevsner suggests that the original market square stretched from Brook Street to Basingwell Street, and from the south side of St George's Square to Bank Street; that High Street and Houchin Street were built on the sites of the earlier market stalls.[18] There is some evidence for this theory. The market appears to have been built on during Parliamentary times. In 1653 Thomas Prior was granted a cottage with a curtilage ' in the Street or Markett of Waltham'.[19] Later in 1660 at a court baron, Sampson Austin was granted 'one toft and Curtilage in ye Market of Waltham … with a cottage theron built'. John Newby was granted 'the middle part of a Cottage … in ye west part to ye strete in Waltham And ye Stalls was to ye same Middle part'.[20]

The market was recorded in King Edward I's time (1239-1307).[21] It was still held every Friday when in 1810 Charles Vancouver made his survey of Hampshire.[22] Earlier it had been held so late in the day that complaints were made. The farmers and dealers agreed therefore to hold it at noon, and advertised their decision in the *Hampshire Chronicle*.[23]

In 1301 cloth-making was an important industry. The reeve kept an ell measure (45 inches) for measuring cloth, together with a weight for weighing bread, used for checking loaves on market days. Certain dwellings carried with them the rights to market stalls. This continued into the 19th century. The tanyard (423 on the tithe map) owned five stalls, probably all used since medieval times for the sale of leather goods. In 1825 they belonged to George Bond, tanner. One cottage on the east part of the High Street brought with it three market stalls.[24]

10 St George's House about 1800 with open market stalls in front. It has now become Barclay's Bank.

In 1301 masses were probably said daily in the chapel. The reeve was responsible for vestments, altar frontal, chalice and paten, missal, a book of anthems and two books of saints. All these were kept at Bishop's Waltham, but a second set of vestments and service books was sent on to the next manor, Bitterne. Churchscot, a tax for the support of the priests, provided 172 hens; 154 were sold. The priests were also given in tithe six bushels of wheat, two calves, 16 lambs, one piglet, 16 summer cheeses and wool from 53 fleeces. There were by 1301 six churches in the manor; at Bishop's Waltham, Bursledon, Durley, Upham, Ashton together with the bishop's chapel in the palace. This and St Clement's chapel at Ashton no longer exist.

The reeve was responsible for the lord's money as it accumulated in a chest. He also had charge of an inventory which listed three brass pots, a pitcher, a pan, a ewer and basin kept in readiness for visitors, and a lead cistern of 102 gallons, no doubt filled ready with water when the bishop came with his household. The reeve also kept an iron chain, probably used for the measurement of land, each link measuring one inch.

A further glimpse of the manor comes from the account rolls. By 1497 the 'Fulling Mill called Horsmyll' in Ashton had become derelict; it was pulled down and its site used for a new house. Now there was another fulling mill close to the palace, recorded in 1410 when a bridge was made across the water diverted for it. But by 1497 the mills at Calcot and Mattockesford, both previously let to tenants, were derelict. They had been dismantled and the sites taken back into the bishop's demesne. This left four mills: the new fulling mill, Frog mill, Durley, on the Hamble river, the East mill (Waltham Chase mill), and the mill outside the gate.

By 1497 three servants of the manor – the blacksmith, the granger and the pigman – who had all previously been allowed reduced rents in return for labour services, were instead being paid a wage. Only the reeve, the beadle and the hayward were maintained under the old system.[25]

Gates guarded the entrances into the manor. Six are recorded in the episcopate of Bishop Walter Curle (1632-47), when in 1638 the tithings were ordered to repair the gates of Marlden, Swanmore, Dodlane, and Hill (in Droxford parish); the penalty for not doing so was the heavy fine of 3s. 4d. to be paid by each tithingman. There was also a gate at Curdridge where Andrew Harlot was ordered to 'scour his ditches', while Forest gate lay between Hoe and Swanmore.[26]

2

The Palace

Bishop Henri de Blois (1129-71) gave Bishop's Waltham its prominent position and began its long association with the Crown. He was himself the grandson of William the Conqueror, the nephew of King Henry I, and the younger brother of King Stephen, whose claim to the throne he supported against the Empress Matilda. In 1129 he was appointed Bishop of Winchester by his uncle, Henry I. He was already Dean of St Martin's le Grand and St Cross at Waltham Abbey. He was to be papal legate from 1139 to 1143.[1] It was said of him that 'never … was any man more chaste or prudent, more pitiful more eager to adorn his church in structure and wealth'.[2]

He realised that his elder brother, Stephen, would need physical support to pursue his claim to the throne, so within nine years he had built three castles in Hampshire – at Wolvesey (Winchester), Merdon, Bishop's Waltham. Here, at the same time, he probably threw up the fortifications at Stephen's Castle Down, laid out the town and developed the ponds which supplied his household with fresh fish.

King Stephen died in 1153, the Empress Matilda's son Henry succeeded, so Henri de Blois fled to Cluny, the great Benedictine monastery in France where he had been educated. By 1158 he had made his peace with the King. He returned to Bishop's Waltham where he rebuilt the hall, tower and great chamber of the palace. Richard of Ilchester (1174-88) probably completed this first rebuilding.[3]

The palace now provided useful hospitality before royal expeditions to the Continent. King Henry II held a council here in 1182 to raise supplies for the Second Crusade.[4] In 1194 King Richard I ('the Lionheart') stayed in the palace before setting out on the Third Crusade when he captured Acre.

More than 150 years later, Bishop William of Wykeham (1367-1404) rebuilt the existing buildings on a grand scale; the remains of his great hall stand proudly today. Born at nearby Wickham, he began his service for King Edward III (1347-77) as surveyor of the works at Windsor Castle. By 1367 he had become Lord Chancellor. He founded Winchester College and New College, Oxford.[5]

He brought to Bishop's Waltham the craftsmen whom he was employing at his other great building works. His architects were Henry Yevele, who was involved in rebuilding the nave of Canterbury Cathedral, and William Wynford, at work on Winchester Cathedral and College. His carpenter, Hugh Herland, had charge of the massive roof of Westminster Hall. The Bishop made his private chamber in the west tower of the palace, where a new bridge was thrown across the moat to give him access from the south. Close by this tower he constructed the audience chamber with state rooms on the first floor, and to the east his chapel. He rebuilt the kitchen, bakehouse, larder and hall. Here his carpenter was Robert Brewes.

Most of the building material was local; flints were collected from the fields, and easily wrought freestone was used. By land, stone came from the quarries at Langrish near Petersfield and from Cludden. By sea, stone was shipped from Bere in South Devon and from quarries on the Isle of Wight. This must have been brought up the Hamble to 'lading Place' at Fairthorn. Other material was possibly loaded onto rafts to be carried by water to 'Raftering Place'[6] at Locks Farm. Timber came from the park, from nearby Marwell and from Farnham. The great hall was shingled and the stone tiles of the hall, the bakehouse and brewhouse, were now replaced by clay tiles, made in the Park 1372-80 in the Lord's tile house. After 1388 tiles were brought from Otterbourne and Petersfield among other places.

Wykeham resigned as Lord Chancellor in 1391. From 1401-4 Bishop William lived in a palace which he had made one of his most important residences. Here he died aged eighty. During his episcopacy he had reckoned to feed 20 poor people each day. He ordered at least one penny to be given to every poor tenant who lined his burial route from Bishop's Waltham to Winchester and four pence to those who prayed for his soul.[7]

11 Bishop William of Wykeham (1367-1404) rebuilt his audience chamber with state rooms on the first floor of the Palace. He spent the last four years of his life here. HRO, TOP PORTRAITS W/41.

12 The ivy-covered Kitchen Range about 1900.

13 The ford over the river Hamble at Locks Farm close to a Roman villa.

Bishop Henry Beaufort (1404-47), who succeeded him, was the half-brother of King Henry IV. From 1407 he began to repair the palace, mending the roofs after 'the great wind' using wooden shingles for the knights' room, and repairing the door of the lord's clerks' room; then the bridge to the inner court was made good. In 1409 preparations were put in hand for the visit of his nephew, the future King Henry V. A pentice was built next to the chapel for the Prince's accommodation; the room occupied by the treasurer of the household was re-roofed. Outside, the stable was repaired as were the sides of the moat. Four carpenters renewed the bridge at the head of the pond; the drawbridge by the fishpond was replanked.

The year 1410 saw the roofs of the outer court, which housed the stables and the great barn, restored by five roofers working for 67 days. The next year the buildings here, including the brewhouse and the chaplain's room, were re-thatched. Locks were provided for the dairy, the coal house, the poultry house and a furnace for the bakehouse.

In 1411, within the palace, the lord's room was refurnished with clothes presses, and a stool and a bench; the hall with new tables and trestles, the kitchen with dressers and ranges. From 1407 to 1411 the chapel was restored. It was of two storeys, the crypt serving as a larder. In the chapel itself the altar was repaired, the window strengthened. Then three carpenters spent 53 days making reading desks and altars for the chapel.[8] But in 1416 the Bishop began to build a new chapel which was to be glazed. This remained unfinished for more than ten years, for in 1416 and in 1421 the Bishop lent King Henry V

14 Cardinal Beaufort, half-brother to King Henry IV, enlarged the Palace, adding a further storey to the south-west tower. He rebuilt and glazed the chapel and rebuilt the Outer Gatehouse. HRO, TOP PORTRAITS B/3.

15 The marriage of King Henry VI and Margaret of Anjou. The ruby in the ring used was given to the King by Cardinal Beaufort when he crowned the boy Henry, King of France. The Cardinal bequeathed to the Queen three Arras tapestries and blue bed-hangings of gold damask cloth from the bedchamber she slept in when she stayed at the Palace. HRO, TOP PORTRAITS H/5.

(1413-22) the money to pursue his claim to the throne of France. The day before Henry V sailed on the expedition, which ended in the French defeat in 1415 at the battle of Agincourt, he stayed in the palace. The proximity of the palace to Southampton and France had already shown its use, for in 1413 the Bishop had himself been sent abroad as an ambassador.[9]

The Bishop added to his private accommodation with a further storey in the south-western tower. He also built a range of lodgings for important guests, using locally made black and white bricks for the chimney stacks. He panelled the tower and his own rooms, and paved the parlour with Flemish tiles imported through Southampton; later the hall, the cloisters and the bakehouse were tiled. In 1408 fixtures for tapestries and bed hangings had been put in.[10]

In 1431 the Bishop was in Paris, where he crowned the boy King Henry VI (1422-61), King of France. He presented him with a ruby which was later set in the wedding ring with which Henry VI married Margaret of Anjou in 1445. She often stayed in the palace. When he died in 1447 the Bishop bequeathed to her the bed-hangings which furnished the room in which she slept.[11]

In 1426 the Bishop was made a Cardinal. The following year the new chapel was finally completed, and that same year the Bishop led a crusade against the Protestant Hussites. His last major building was after 1438 when the old gatehouse was taken down. A grand one was made, looking into the town, with a chamber on either side and a hall. The tile house in the Park may again have supplied the tiles in 1441 for this rebuilding, but after 1439 most came from Marwell.[12]

In 1446, the year before he died, the Bishop assigned this newly built gate-house to John Thornebury, the Keeper of the Manor. He was 'to have for his dwelling the outer gate called le Yathows which is facing the town and all the dwellings, rooms, casements and other buildings on both sides of the gate and adjoining rooms above, which extend from the gate to the paling of the episcopal park'. He was also allowed 'two small gardens and two crofts which are next to the pasture lying between the ... buildings and the paling, a stable and shed for hay and a room on the north side of the gate.[13] Outside this gatehouse stood 'the mill outside the gate' and the lord's pound (the hundred pound) of two acres.[14]

During Bishop William of Waynflete's time (1447-86) the Palace was visited by King Henry VI in 1450, and by King Edward IV (1461-83) in 1476. It was on this visit that the Bishop gave up his own accommodation to the King, while he himself lived in 'the Lord's House formerly Thornebury's'. Ten years earlier the palace had stood neglected, the courtyard full of weeds, the kitchen well putrid. All had to be put in order for the King so, two years before the visit, Bishop William Waynflete began his improvements. He made a new bridge for the garden and a drawbridge, 'leading to the Garden door beyond the Little Lake as far as the East Park'. This lake had been created by damming the stream which now runs beneath the palace house. The following year Thornebury's orchard became a field.[15]

It was probably Bishop Thomas Langton (1493-1501) who used the by then fashionable bricks, made locally, to build the wall which we see from the road. It

16 One of the towers built into the Palace wall, probably by Bishop Langton.

probably had three corner turrets; two now remain. Bishop Langton also faced in brick the existing timber buildings. King Henry VIII (1509-47) often stayed here with his godfather, Bishop Richard Fox (1500-28), who went blind in 1516. In 1522 King Henry VIII and the Emperor Charles V, excluded from Winchester because of the plague, came to the palace to conclude their alliance against France, the Treaty of Waltham. The town was then described as 'a village containing but six or seven houses'. In September 1535, the King made a progress from Bishop's Waltham to Winchester.[16]

There were few later alterations to the palace which was now a great complex of buildings. The inner court and garden were surrounded by Bishop Thomas Langton's brilliant orange brick wall; on the north was the outer court, the Gate House court, with barns and the great stable; to the east lay the town.[17]

For a very short time the palace returned to royal ownership. In 1551 the Protestant Bishop, John Ponet (1551-3), surrendered the palace and the manor to the Crown, in return for an annual payment. It was granted to William Paulet, the King's treasurer, and the boy King, Edward VI (1547-53), stayed here in 1552, describing it as a 'faire great old house'. When he died Queen Mary Tudor (1553-8), a Roman Catholic, restored their lands to the bishops. She herself stayed in the palace while she awaited the arrival of King Philip II of Spain, before their marriage in 1554 in Winchester Cathedral.

Later bishops enjoyed the palace as a place of residence. Robert Horne (1560-80), the first married Bishop of Winchester, lived here with his wife and their family. She was buried in St Peter's, he in Winchester Cathedral. The palace was a favourite residence of Bishop Lancelot Andrewes (1619-26).

The first Civil War (1642-6) finally brought the palace to an end as an episcopal dwelling. Held for the King by Colonel Bennett, it was under siege by Parliamentary troops led by Colonel Whitehead. In February 1644 an attempt was probably made to capture it; a Captain Slatford and three soldiers were buried at St Peter's[18] but the palace was not taken. On 29 March other Royalist forces were defeated at the Battle of Cheriton: Winchester surrendered. Major General Browne's London brigade marching home from Southampton, were informed of the situation at Bishop's Waltham.

Bringing up their ordnance they joined the siege on 6 April. Cannons, set up probably on Battery Hill, bombarded the Royalist garrison. It capitulated on 9 April and was allowed to retire. The palace was plundered and fired. From that moment the whole character of the town changed. It was no longer the home of the powerful and wealthy bishops of Winchester, entertaining a succession of royal visitors. It was reduced to a small market town which retained the smouldering ruin of a magnificent episcopal residence.

3

The Fish Ponds

Fish ponds were an important source of food for the medieval bishop. Enjoined to fast in Lent and on special days, and to eat only fish on Fridays, freshwater fish was a necessity for the life of a cleric. Bishop Henri de Blois probably enlarged the original fisheries which are recorded in the 904 Anglo-Saxon charter. He probably also diverted a leet off the river to run through Brook Street into the moat, and through the palace garden. The pond was controlled by this ingenious system of by-pass channels and sluices built possibly after 1158, when Bishop Henri de Blois returned from his exile at Cluny; for most of the bishops' fish ponds in Hampshire were constructed from 1150 to 1208.

By 1220 the fish ponds were thriving. Close-by was probably a boat-house and boat-building yard, for two boats were built here and another mended. Three times in 1257 a boat was carried 12 miles from Bishop's Waltham for use on the Alresford Pond.[1] (In 1785 this boat-building area consisted of a boat-house and a garden, built on part of the waste where the fishermen had formerly dried their nets. In 1806 it was encroached on by Mr Compton who then claimed it as a freehold.[2])

17   Boating on the palace pond in 1784.

Fish were caught with a seine net; one end was attached to the shore, the other gradually let out from the boat. This was rowed back and the net with its fish was hauled on to the shore by several fishermen. Most fishing was done in winter since fish was especially needed at Christmas, in Lent and at Easter.

From 1244-62 Master Nicholas, the fisherman, was in charge of the bishops' fish ponds in Hampshire. He was paid 3½d a day, £5 2s. 6d. a year,[3] together with free forage for his horse, altogether a substantial sum and a reflection of his expertise. By contrast in 1301 the doorkeeper at the palace, also a position of responsibility, received only 1d. a day, £1 10s. 5d. a year.[4] In 1245 Master Nicholas was restocking several ponds. He employed Bishop's Waltham men to carry fish to Bishop's Sutton, probably in canvas lined barrels. Earlier, live bream were brought from the Bishop's pond at Taunton to Winchester, where 30 men were then hired to carry them on to Bishop's Waltham.

The fish caught were specifically for the consumption of the Bishop and his visitors. Pike, considered a royal fish, was particularly sought after. On his first visit to the diocese seven pike and 300 roach were taken from Bishop's Waltham pond to Bitterne, to welcome Bishop William de Ralegh (1244-9) from the Continent, where he had taken presents to the Pope who then confirmed his appointment to the bishopric.[5] At the enthronement of Bishop John de Sandale (1316-19) the pond supplied fish for a feast at Wolvesey. Fish were needed also for royal visitors; four pike were carried to King Henry III (1216-72) at Winchester in 1268, and in 1289 fish were carried to King Edward I (1272-1307) at Bedhampton. They were eaten fresh; transported alive and wrapped in wet grass they lasted a day: Bishop's Waltham was within a day's journey of Winchester. In 1393 when Bishop William of Wykeham (1366-1404) entertained King Richard II (1377-99) at Wolvesey, fishermen were sent to the pond for pike and bream and perch. From 1230-90 fish from Bishop's Waltham were carried to Bitterne, Merdon, Wolvesey, Bishop's Sutton, Selborne, Hambledon and Bedhampton.

Master Nicholas the fisherman also constructed traps for eels in 1257 at Bishop's Waltham.[6] In 1877 when the Lighting Committee were considering where to place street lamps in the town, one of the sites they chose was 'opposite the old Eel House near the railway station',[7] probably the original medieval eel house. Swans too were bred on the pond for times of feasting. They nested on the small islands where they still come today; in 1251 foxes ate five of them.

When the bishopric was vacant, the royalty of fishing returned to the king. In 1240, after the death of Bishop Peter de la Roche (1205-38), King Henry III made good use of a six-year vacancy. He ordered the ponds at Bishop's Waltham, at Alresford, Marwell, East Meon to be well fished, the pike caught to be salted, the other fish put into paste and all to be delivered to Westminster before Christmas. In 1244-5, 19 pike and 800 roach were caught at Bishop's Waltham, whereas in the 60-acre Alresford pond 79 pike and 57 perch were caught.

Fishponds were drained periodically and allowed to dry out; this was done in 1257 when salted eels were carried to Bishop Aylmer de Valence (1250-61), the half-brother of King Henry III (1216-72), who had been appointed to the bishopric despite being in junior orders and unable to speak English. After the

18 The Palace ruins are shown in the distance, the Abbey Mill is in the centre, and on the right is the site of the lower pond which became Flowces and Penstock meadows.

pond dried out that year it was dug with spades to remove the accumulated mud and silt, and then planted with barley.[8] Under Master Nicholas the pond was drained every five years; left exposed to the air it became more fertile.

At this time there were two fish ponds which lay together; the large pond and the little pond, to the south-west. (By 1777 the little pond had been drained. It is described in the lease registers as 'two little meadows one of which is now divided, four acres now called Flowces and Penstock Meadows'; penstock meaning a sluice.) There was a third fish pond, the New Pond, probably further down the river.[9] In 1301-2 the expenses of the manor included a carpenter making a sluice for the small fishpond. Men were hired each day to dig the foundations of the sluice, to carry earth and turfs, as well as making and nailing stakes into place.[10] The stakes would act as a barrier. Probably wattle hurdles were placed in front of them, as had been done in 1224, to prevent the fish escaping.

By 1409 a drawbridge crossed the great pond; close by was a stew pond of an acre where possibly the 'Tronke',[11] complete with lock and key, conserved fish ready for the table. This pond was in the palace garden.[12] In the Park there may have been yet another fish pond, possibly constructed by Bishop Henry Woodlock (1310-11). It may have been this pond (810 on the tithe map) which was noted by William Houghton, a 19th-century resident. He recalled a meadow called 'Fish Pond Field' where he had found traces of a pond.[13]

In 1660, the advantage of the fertile soil, which the fish pond brought when it overflowed, was recognised and specifically noted in a lease to James Russell granted by Bishop Duppa. The ponds themselves were let for £8 a year to 'Walter Underhill, fishmonger, of Old Fish Street, London, with liberty to stock the pond and the Moate thereto adjoining ... to take out fish at his will' to supply the

Bishop when he demanded with 'six well grown Breames and six well grown Carpes and like quantity of other good fish'. He was 'to make and sett all the Grates necessary about the pond' and was granted the use of the 'Stew Pond in the Garden of Waltham House'.[14] An additional advantage after 1664 for those who leased the ponds was that, being within the bounds of the park, they were tithe free. This meant that the lessee did not have to hand over a tenth of his catch to the rector, for Bishop George Morley gave 100 acres of the Park, roughly a tenth, to the living. He thus abolished the payment of tithe within the park lands.

By 1777 the pond was silting up and its value had decreased. It was now leased by Bishop John Thomas (1761-81) to John Clewer of Botley Hill, timber merchant, for 20 shillings a year. He was to cleanse it of weeds and sedge and flags, to make it as large as formerly, to stock it with 'more and better sorts of fish as he shall … think will increase and grow in the pond and are proper sorts of fish to stock there'. He was to serve the Bishop with the best fish 'which the Pond shall produce or John Clewer can catch'. He was allowed timber to keep the grates and hatches in repair.[15] In 1797 he renewed this lease with Bishop the Hon. Brownlow North (1781-1820). Again Clewer was to improve the pond; 'making it larger than it now is' and stocking it with more fish 'of the better sorts'. He was to serve the Bishop with the best fish when demanded by letter, but he was no longer allowed wood for repairs. Timber had become a scarce commodity, much in demand for ship-building in the wars against France.

John Clewer continued to rent the pond until 1826 when James Warner the Younger, yeoman, of Botley took it. Warner renewed his lease with the following Bishop, Charles Sumner (1827-69), but protested that this new fee for renewal was far more than he had paid to the previous Bishop, George Tomline (1820-7).[16]

James Warner had married as his third wife, William Cobbett's sister-in-law, Eleanor. They lived at Manor Farm, Botley. He rented the pond on exactly the same terms as John Clewer. When he died in 1857 the pond formed part of a trust for his widow and sons. They assigned the remainder of their lease to Arthur Helps, who in 1862 founded the Bishop's Waltham Clay and Tile Company. Two years later Arthur Helps secured the lease of the Great Pond for a fine of £22 10s. 0d. He took the opportunity of buying out the copyhold and creating a freehold.[17]

The Great Pond must have been much larger in medieval times than it is today. The fact that the rent went down from £8 a year in 1664, to only £1 a year in 1770 shows how much its value had decreased. The constant references to clearing the pond of sedge and flags and weed reveal that it was silting up. But even in 1804 the area of the pond was 13 acres. In a survey of 1826 the Little Pond, which had been a meadow for the last 200 years, was described as three acres of inferior ground south-west of the pond; it carried the added expense of 'watering and keeping up the hatches which are now out of repair',[18] suggesting that the land was liable to flooding.

There are elegant engravings of the pond being used for boating in the 18th century, and it continued to provide both fish and eels for the townspeople and for those who passed through. Certainly, when the steward of the manor came to hold a manorial court here in 1828, he carried away with him a large pike which cost him ninepence.[19]

4

The Park and the Chase

The deer park, alongside the palace, provided a source of fresh meat during the winter months for the Bishop and his guests. It also provided recreation, for hunting was restricted to the nobility. The Park was probably part of the original 38 hides of land given by King Edward the Elder in 904 to the Bishop of Winchester, in exchange for the manor of Portchester, as hedgerow counts reveal that the boundary of the Park is mostly Anglo-Saxon.[1]

This 'park for wild animals' in Bishop's Waltham is one of only 35 parks recorded in Domesday Book. It was about 1,000 acres of grassland and wood surrounded by a ditch and a massive bank, on top of which an oak fence or pale prevented the animals from escaping. The ditch was one lug, 16½ feet, wide. It 'lay on the western side of the road from Winchester to Wickham … in part [it follows] the boundaries of Upham, Durley and Bishop's Waltham'.[2] It lies beside the bishop's palace and encloses the fish ponds. The Hamble river where otters were hunted runs through it. In 1248 Jordan the Hunter took two otters here.[3]

The park pale, the fence on top of the park lug, kept the deer confined within the park; but for sporting purposes they might be released through one of four gates – Laune, Shedfield, Breach and Hampton – into the unfenced Waltham Chase or Forest, which was also known as Horder's Wood. Forest was not originally a term for an area of trees but in Anglo-Saxon times was used for land with woody glades. Waltham Chase adjoined the Park to the south and east, and almost formed part of the Forest of Bere.[4]

It was probably Bishop Henri de Blois (1129-71) who altered the original Anglo-Saxon Park, for as a Norman he would enjoy hunting fallow deer, of which there were none in England before the Norman Conquest. The magnificent red deer were native and the two species were incompatible; the fallow deer required food and shelter during the winter months. Bishop Henri de Blois must therefore have created the Little Park for the management of the fallow deer. This would account for the incidence of medieval hedges planted to enclose the Little Park within the original Anglo-Saxon Park, which then became known as the Great Park.

There were two methods of hunting: either pursuit on horseback with hounds, called the chase; or the stable, when beaters drove the deer on, to be shot by marksmen from butts. Perhaps this latter system was used in the Little Park for it was a contrived landscape of 43 acres. It was divided by hedges and ditches with rails; there were also enclosures which allowed the deer to be marshalled as the huntsmen required. The nature of the terrain is revealed in a lease of the Little Park in 1664 to Richard Trod, yeoman. He was required not only to keep up the 'hedges, ditches, rails and enclosures', but also the buildings which provided

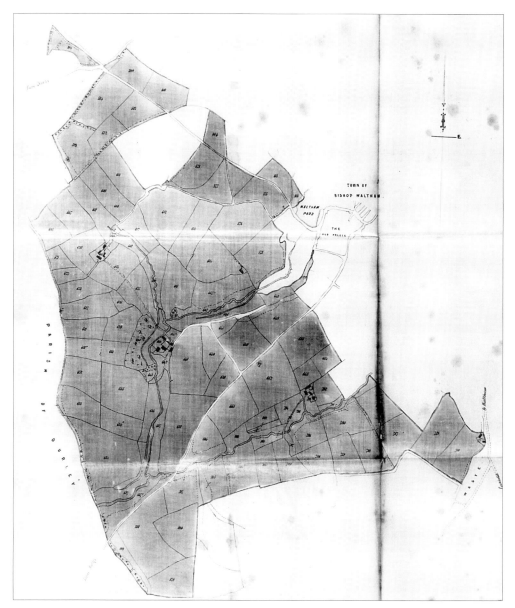

19 Map of the area bought by Arthur Helps in 1862. It includes almost the whole of the former parks, except for the 100 acres given to the living in 1663 by Bishop Morley. HRO, 11M59/E2/155514.

shelter for the deer in the winter, and the barns where the hay was stored. He was to keep up 'the bridges stiles gates pales and mounds'.[5] The mounds were created for spectators to view the sport. Nearby, but outside the park, was 'La Laune', a name which denotes land where the deer might graze. Should the huntsmen require a larger field, Shedfield and Laune gates allowed the deer into the unfenced Waltham Chase and beyond. As late as 1810 Charles Vancouver wrote of this part of Hampshire as 10,600 acres [which] lies open to the range and feed of the king's deer'.[6] He might also have added 'and of the bishops' deer' for this had always been a source of conflict: as early as 1224 King Henry III had summoned Bishop Peter de Roche for encroaching on his forest rights in Hampshire.[7] In the Great Park, Tower Close along the Botley Road, as its name implies, probably contained a tower from which the hunt could be viewed. Here again there were 'hedges, ditches, fences, gates, rails and enclosures'.[8]

Within the Park itself one area was quite intensively farmed, as is shown in the 1660 leases. The use of these fields must go back to earlier times, for cultivation was a slow process; 'pasture, meadow and watered ground' was as much a necessity in 1301 as it was in 1660. In 1660 this home farm was divided into smaller meadows; the Lower Horse Mead with water for stock, and the Upper Horse Mead which lay below the water trench (probably an artificial water-course). These two made nine acres. The Barley Close was 13½ acres. Another area of arable, 14½ acres called The Thicketts, lay above the water trench; a further 29½-acre meadow, also called The Thicketts, lay below the water trench. Colthouse Close, where the young horses must have been kept, was 27 acres. There were also two acres for growing flax for linen, and ten acres for turnips;[9] these began to be cultivated as a field crop in the 17th century.[10]

20   The park lug in the 20th century. A pale or fence on the top of this bank would have kept the deer confined within the Park.

In 1208-9 King John or his huntsman was hunting at Bishop's Waltham where the huntsmen, grooms and hounds lived for most of the year. A hundred years later one huntsman, three grooms, eight greyhounds (like today's Irish wolfhound) and 24 brachet hounds, which hunted by scent, lived at Bishop's Waltham for more than nine months of the year, at a cost of £26 6s. 8d., probably at Lodge Farm (now Brooklands), a very ancient farm near the Hamble. This hunting lodge, close to Southampton Gate, included gardens, barns, stables, outhouses, the old hall and the pigeon house.[11]

21 Brooklands Farm, off the Botley road, originally called Lodge Farm. Here the Bishop's chief huntsman lived with deerhounds and brachet hounds in 1309. This important hunting lodge had gardens, the old hall and the pigeon house.

In 1231 Stephen the Hunter, the professional huntsman in charge of all the bishop's deer parks, probably lived here. In 1251 he took deer in carts from Bishop's Waltham to the new park which Bishop Aylmer de Valence (1250-61) had ordered to be made at Hambledon. He was probably also in charge when Sir Walter de Ralegh hunted red deer at Bishop's Waltham in 1249.

When there was a vacancy in the bishopric, the royalty of hunting returned to the king. King Henry III, after the death of Bishop Peter de la Roche, made good use of this: in 1242 he sent huntsmen to take ten bucks from the Park, for bucks were the best eating. While William Edington (1346-66) was Bishop, in 1363 two men and six horses carried venison to Highclere in Hampshire, and to Farnham in Surrey, to Wargrave in Berkshire, and to Witney in Oxfordshire.[12]

The management of the Park in 1301 is revealed in the Pipe Roll of Bishop John de Pontoise (1282-1304). £5 3s. 2d. came from letting the pannage, allowing pigs to feed on the beech mast. (Later in 1352 there was so much beech mast that pigs were driven over from East Meon to feed on it.[13]) Some of the pasture, let for livestock, brought in £5 15s. 6d. Fifty yearlings, which were grazed in the park and then sold, brought in £19 7s. 7d., but had cost £17 18s. 2¼d. to buy and keep. Two dead trees, felled in Waltham Chase for the honey stored in them by wild bees, brought 2s. 2d. Five shillings came from cablish (trees or branches blown down by the wind), 6s. 8d. was received from the sale of heath but nothing came from nuts.

Two changes were made in the extent of the Park at this time: land near the mill which had previously been rented out was taken into the Park, a loss to the manor of 6s. 5d. in rent: another meadow was added, being drained by a ditch for

10 shillings. It was enclosed and hedged, which cost 3s. 8d. A stream was dammed to provide water for livestock, which cost 3s. 6d.

In 1301 the pale on the park lug needed renewing and mending, costing £1 8s. 10d., but loppings sold from the trees felled brought in 10s. 6d. However £1 3s. 8d. was the cost of felling the oaks and digging a ditch to catch predatory foxes. These, valued for their skins, were probably starved to death in pits: in 1208, 71 fox skins had been sold to a dealer from Winchester.[14] Two of the park keepers, Richard le Wyte and John Boefs, had been illegally selling wood. They were each fined £1.[15] Timber was a very valuable commodity which the Park provided; in 1335-6 some was sent to the palace at Wolvesey in Winchester for building work, and the Park was a source of timber for Bishop's Waltham palace in the re-buildings here. During Bishop William of Wykeham's alterations, tiles were made in the 'Lord's tile house' in the park from 1372-80, and this tile house was probably again in operation in 1441, during Bishop Henry Beaufort's rebuilding. Gravel was dug in the park in 1400,[16] probably at Northbrook, where gravel was still being dug in 1802 for building a new turnpike road.[17]

The Park must have varied in size at different times as some meadows were taken into it. After the Black Death in 1348, when 65 per cent of the inhabitants of Bishop's Waltham died,[18] with much less labour available, parts returned to the wild.

In 1431 Thomas Uvedale Esquire was master of the Bishop of Winchester's hunt, and keeper of all the parks and chases and woods of the bishopric.[19] In Hampshire he was in charge of 12 deer parks, 11 created in the 12th and 13th centuries: all the bishops' residences except Wolvesey possessed deer parks. William of Wykeham (1367-1404) enlarged some of the existing parks including Highclere, but, although Highclere with 3,000 acres was larger, Bishop's Waltham was central and remained the headquarters of the Bishop's hunt.[20]

Certain meadows were assigned to provide hay for the deer in the winter, if necessary. In 1630 they were Calcott, just outside the Park (923,924 on the tithe map), Horsemead, Balsmead (394), Les Moores (Mill Moors 669) and Long Mead. These last two had generally been rented out, but in 1630 no rent was received 'because it was mowed for the keep of the Lord's game stock during the winter'. In 1645 none of these meadows was let, 'but all the crops were mowed and stored for the Lord for the use of his Game Animals in the winter'.[21] But who was then lord of the manor? In April 1644 Bishop Walter Curle had fled. It was not until 1647 that Robert Reynolds bought the manor for £7,999 14s. 10¼d. It included the Park, a useful source of income.

5

Robert Reynolds, a Parliamentary Lawyer

A great change came to the manor with the Civil Wars and the establishment of the Commonwealth. In 1643 the House of Commons voted down episcopacy. Bishops' lands were confiscated. At first some of the income from them was used to pay the army. But in 1646 Parliament needed more money; that November the sale of episcopal lands was authorised.

On 27 September 1647 Robert Reynolds bought from the Trustees for the Sale of Bishops Lands the manor of Bishop's Waltham for £7,999 14s. 10¼d.,[1] a purchase he came to regret. This was not its real worth but a written down valuation which would make such land attractive to potential purchasers. It was extremely important to the Parliamentarians to maintain the ancient manorial customs to prevent the country lapsing into anarchy, and to raise cash.

Robert Reynolds was a lawyer; in 1644 Parliament had made him a member of the Middle Temple 'without paying any fee'.[2] They allotted to him Sir Edward Hyde's chamber and his books and his manuscripts. Sir Edward Hyde, 1st Earl Clarendon, was meanwhile with the King at the court he had established at Oxford. Robert Reynolds was the second son of Sir James Reynolds with land in Chesterford, Cambridgeshire. His elder brother, John, a keen Parliamentarian, was Commissary-General of the Horse in Ireland.[3]

Reynolds represented Hindon in Wiltshire: in 1644 he was made a member of the Westminster Assembly, established by Parliament in June 1643. This was composed of clergy and laity with Scots representation. Its purpose was to plan church reform. In 1645 it produced the Directory of Worship which was to replace the Prayer Book; in 1646 it produced the Westminster Confession which abolished episcopacy, replacing the clergy with presbyters.

Robert Reynolds refused to act as one of the 135 Commissioners appointed to sit in judgement on the King. But in 1648, after King Charles I's execution, he again sat in the Long Parliament which voted him Abingdon Hall, and lands to the value of £400 per annum, and £2,000 in money.[4] In 1650 he was appointed Solicitor-General.

How much time did Robert Reynolds spend in Bishop's Waltham? He may well have been living in the town in 1649 when the parish register records that Thomas Walker, specifically described as 'servant to Mr Reynolds' was buried. Robert Reynolds certainly was here in 1650 when the registers record the baptism of his daughter Priscilla.[5] The following year he was again in Hampshire, for he was asked 'to stir up' his fellow Commissioners,[6] to get the Parliamentary forces into a state of readiness. But when in 1653 Oliver Cromwell expelled the Long Parliament and became Lord Protector, Reynolds left London; possibly again he stayed in Bishop's Waltham. The following year, 1654, saw him again in Hampshire, appointed by the justices at Winchester as one of the treasurers of the county, with the duty of paying out money to invalid soldiers. He spent £36 14s. 6d. on them.[7]

These 13 years during which Robert Reynolds held the manor appear to have passed relatively quietly. The *Parliament Scout*, a Royalist tract, had stated in 1644 that 'Walton the Bishop of Winchester's house is in … ashes'.[8] Since 1647 Robert Reynolds had probably allowed parts of the ruins to be used as a quarry for stone; indeed the south aisle of the church was rebuilt from this stone.

Robert Reynolds as lord of the manor made no changes; the manorial courts were held as usual, the difference being that it was not the bishop's steward but Robert Reynolds' steward who was in charge. The lease registers reveal that, when the Parliamentarians destroyed the palace, they left the building where the courts were held intact. Manorial business continued without interruption: here the tithing men brought their 'Lawday money' (their recognition of the lord's right to hold his court). Among its concerns in 1658 was clean water. The court reprimanded the 'person who had washed and cleansed gutts and other noisome things in the River above the Lord's bridge whereby the water is corrupted to the great distress of people living there'. A penalty of 2s. 6d. was ordered; Andrew Colpas was 'to take care a like offence was not committed'.[9]

Some of the Park, however, was already divided up. Two copyholds had been stolen. William Dunce had completely ignored the court in 1656 when he had passed copyhold land, called Parkyard, and a cottage and field called Versey Crofts in Curdridge, to John Pierce, gentleman. These copyholds did not belong to Dunce; legally they belonged to Thomas Lee 'in the time of peace … of King Charles late King of England'. John Pierce had kept them illegally. But in 1659 Susan Pierce, probably John's daughter, was to marry Reuben Cleverley and the property was to be her dowry for 'the heirs of their two bodies (in case the sayd marriage take effect)'. The tenancy of the land therefore needed confirming. This came before the steward, Richard Dennett, and the bailiff, Thomas White, gentleman. Dunce was 'solemnly called' to appear before 2 o'clock. He did not come 'but departed in contempt', so Thomas Lee's prior claim was confirmed 'according to the Custom of the Manor'. He therefore legally passed on these two copyholds to Reuben and Susan.[10]

There are other hints of illegal proceedings. In 1653, carefully concealed among the lists of parish officers, come the words 'Richard Hockley bad deeds and John deane found it out'.[11] There were encroachments on the commons.[12] But the courts were held as before. The tithingmen from all the tithings in the manor – 'Bursledon, Hoe, Woodcott, Mencingfield, Ashton, Upham, Durley, Wintershill, Curdridge, Waltham' – came to the court and presented their customary dues as a matter of course.

Oliver Cromwell died in 1658 and was succeeded by his son, Richard. Parliament was recalled, so in 1659 Robert Reynolds returned as M.P., this time for Whitchurch in Hampshire. He did not support Richard in his attempt to become Lord Protector. Reynolds was again in London in January; he was allotted Colonel Sydenham's lodgings in Whitehall.[13] That year Parliament, making the most of what they probably realised would be a last opportunity, granted a deer to each Member.

Richard Cromwell abdicated on 24 May 1659. The army was now in charge; in October it dissolved the 'Rump Parliament'. By the end of 1659 order was collapsing; in London the apprentices were rioting, the goldsmiths were moving their valuables out of town. Associations of tax-payers were refusing to pay taxes.[14] All this is reflected in the manorial court at Bishop's Waltham.

In March 1659 the tithingmen came to present their 'hundred shilling', recognition of the lord's right to hold the courts. Edward Barfoot, tithingman of Curdridge, presented 16s. 10d., Robert Kerby, tithingman of Ashton, 15 shillings, Thomas Woodman, tithingman of Hoe, five shillings, but the tithingman of Waltham, William Golding, 'appeared not by reason he was in the service of the Commonwealth, therefore he is excused Hundred silver this day'. This seems strange. Why had not another member of the tithing brought the money? At the following court in 1659, 'work silver', which represented the ancient labour services owed to the lord of the manor, must be brought. The tithingman from Curdridge, Henry Baker, brought the enormous sum of £3 6s. 5d., the tithingman from Ashton brought 15s. 1d., the tithingman from Hoe, Robert Prowting, brought 19s. 6d. But the tithingman from Waltham, Robert Penford, arrived 'with his whole tithing sworn', to declare that 'they give to the Lord, worksilver, att this day, nothing',[15] a total refusal to pay the customary dues by which they held their tenancies. However, the rebellion was a brief one. At the next court leet normality returned. All the tithingmen, including Robert Penford, brought both 'pannage' and 'law day money'.

General George Monck was now in command of the country. Robert Reynolds joined him. He became attorney-general, treated with the army officers, with the admiralty and with the navy. He was a member of the Convention Parliament summoned in March. It met on 25 April to negotiate Charles II's return to England. In May 1660 Charles II was proclaimed King, the bishops' estates were restored and a general amnesty was declared.

Robert Reynolds was now called to account. He was examined by Sir Geoffrey Palmer, Charles II's attorney-general, about his purchase of episcopal land. He replied that he had paid the whole purchase price for the manor, had received the income from it as had others who had bought episcopal property. He said he had done nothing wrong, for the Act of Indemnity and Oblivion, which required the restoration of episcopal land to the bishops, also decreed that those who had bought this land were not to be prosecuted.[16] Reynolds had in fact bought the manor of Cheriton as well as the manor of Bishop's Waltham.

That same year Robert Reynolds asked the King's permission to retire to the country. In his petition Reynolds said that he had 'never meddled with Crown lands but was overpersuaded in 1647 to contract for Bishops lands' and not allowed to give up the contract 'though he offered £500 … he offers His Majesty the disposal of the[se] lands, on enriching which he spent thousands of pounds'. He also said that he had 'opposed … the trial of the late king … the setting up of an usurper and [had] absented himself from the House detesting the force put upon it'.[17] King Charles II granted his petition. He even conferred a knighthood on him.

6

The Park Leases after the Commonwealth

From 1650 to 1660 Robert Reynolds had been paying £4 10s.[1] in poor rates for his land in the Park. In 1660 this money is entered in the rate books as being paid from 'The Parkes'. Within five years 20 tenants were paying poor rate from the 'Parkes' which remained a separate unit for rating purposes for more than fifty years.[2] It was not a tithing, since it had no tithingman or churchwarden or overseer.

Robert Reynolds, in his petition to King Charles II, declared that he had spent thousands of pounds on enriching the lands he had bought; certainly during this time two new barns and stables and houses had been built in the Park.[3]

At the Restoration in 1660 Brian Duppa, Lord High Almoner, was appointed Bishop of Winchester (1660-2). Ecclesiastical land was returned to the church; the Park once more belonged to the Bishop. He acted swiftly in re-establishing his position as the legal landlord, giving leases probably to some who had been farming the Park in Parliamentary times. The new tenants were men of substance, mostly yeoman farmers, one a gentleman, another a butcher. Peter Browne, gentleman, leased Tower Close. He was responsible for keeping the hedges, fences, gates, rails and enclosures in order, as well as scouring the ditches. In 1664 the succeeding Bishop, George Morley, allowed him also two loads of firewood yearly 'he … having been a long time servant to the Bishop [and] the hedges … and enclosures so well kept'.[4] This clause continued to be written into this lease; even in 1862 when Tower Close, now described as 19 acres of arable land divided into four fields, was leased by James Clark, these two loads of firewood were still assigned to him.[5]

During the Civil Wars and the Commonwealth trees had been cut down, coppices grubbed up.[6] The Restoration lease registers show that about 150 acres of the Park had been ploughed up, but other large areas of parkland remained. Huge undivided 'closes' are described. Peter Cooke, yeoman, leased Godwins Close, 108 acres with newly built houses and barns and stables. These were probably erected by Robert Reynolds for Richard Bassett, the previous occupier. Peter Cooke also leased 49 acres of pasture, called the upper part of Godwin's Close, which he was already occupying. Godwin himself, a butcher, leased Shedfield Hill, which was 20 acres of pasture, and Shedfield Gate Close, another 24 acres near Waltham Chase. Henry Dipnell, yeoman, leased the 28 acres of Corner Close: David Prowting of Ashton, yeoman, leased 70 acres of arable and pasture with a barn. He could request timber from the woodward for repairs.[7]

James Hampton leased 48 acres, but this was being farmed by Christopher Hawkesworth. Anne Kelsey, widow, leased 32 acres, part of Shedfield Close adjoining Waltham Chase. Richard Moringe, blacksmith, leased Mill Close, which was 32 acres of meadow and pasture. It included a newly built barn with access through Laune Gate. By 1660 the Laune (numbers 1112,1118 on the tithe map[8]) was no longer grazing land but described as arable land and premises outside Waltham Great Park bounded on the east by the Waltham Chase road. It was leased to William Colnett, gentleman, but farmed by Andrew Deane.

James Russell leased 111 acres where he was probably already farming. This was the land around the Palace and fish pond which must always have been the home farm. He also leased the dwelling house and brew house and all the ground within the moat, but not the moat itself. He was allowed wood for repairs to gates, the park pale, ploughs and carts together with 12 cords of wood for fuel which he was to cut; and the benefit brought by the overflowing of the fish pond. This flooded the water meadows for six months of the year bringing down rich silt, which made the grass flourish in the summer. He was permitted to pass through the palace gatehouse.[9] Thomas White leased part of this land near the Palace together with the gatehouse, the gatehouse yard, barns and stables. He also leased the lodge house with its gardens and pigeon house and old hall together with land between Durley Lake and Ashurst.

The Bishop leased Pope Stile Close which was 85 acres of arable, and Middle Close, a further 24 acres of arable to John Woodman, yeoman, for £50 per annum. Before 1645 these 109 acres must have been pasture. The Bishop imposed the condition that within four years Woodman must build a barn. The Bishop had leased his land for an annual rent of £354. From these transactions the steward's fee was £5 2s. 3d., specifically for the entertainment of the officers at the manorial courts.[10]

In 1662 Bishop Brian Duppa died. During his episcopate he had spent very little of his vast income on the restoration of the episcopal palaces, less than £700 on Wolvesey Palace (this included £80 on ropes for the stairs) and only £2,400 on Farnham Castle. His surviving executor, Sir Richard Charworth, was therefore sued by the succeeding bishop. It was reckoned that 'Bishop's Waltham [palace] with Barnes Stables and Edifices belonging, could not be … putt into the same condition that formerly they were under £30,000'. Brian Duppa was Bishop for only 18 months: during this time he received £5,857 19s. 9d. from his estates and another £17,904 1s. 8d. from fees for the granting and renewal of leases, in all £23,762 1s. 5d.[11] of which he had spent just over £3,200 on repairing his palaces.

George Morley (1662-84), a loyal supporter of King Charles I, succeeded Brian Duppa as Bishop. He devised a completely different policy for the park and his land in Bishop's Waltham. He obtained an Act of Parliament which allowed him to lease out the demesne (the land the bishops had previously farmed themselves) and dispark the Park.[12] One condition of the Act was that by 1668 he should have raised £7,000: £4,000 of this was to be used to buy a house in London for future bishops of Winchester; the rest was to be spent on repairs to Farnham Castle. There we can still admire the substantial oak staircase with its Grinling Gibbons carving and his other improvements. He built a ceiling for the great hall and added a minstrel's gallery and a grand fireplace. He also repaired the medieval palace of Wolvesey in Winchester, using material from Bishop's Waltham Palace:

he then replaced the old palace with a new baroque
residence, in part of which the bishops of Winchester
still reside.[13]

In 1664 Bishop Morley reduced the number of
tenants holding land in the Park. Waltham Little
Park, with access through Hampton and Breach
gates, was leased for £3 15s. 3d. a year to Richard
Trod who was already farming there. The Bishop now
abolished the piecemeal tenancy of the Great Park by
giving leases to two people only. One was Francis
Morrison of Lincoln's Inn. Morrison leased two
farms. Moorings Farm, 169 acres, had previously
been farmed by five different tenants; Prowtings
Farm, 147 acres, by six. The Bishop stipulated that
these two farms were to be rented by two farmers
only, who were allowed wood for building new barns
and stables. He reserved the eight acres of wood with
free right of way through Hampton and Breach gates
for himself and his servants, together with the
royalties of hunting and hawking and fishing. The
rent was £27 18s. yearly.[14]

22 Bishop George Morley disparked the Parks in
1663 and founded the Free Grammar School in
1679. HRO, TOP PORTRAITS M/11.

Three other farms, in all 761 acres, were leased to Lord Henry Powlett for £66
8s. 4d. a year. These were Cookes Farm of 229 acres which had formerly been let
to four tenants; Lodge Farm, 333 acres, formerly let to eight tenants, Russell Farm,
199 acres, formerly let to three tenants – 15 people in all. Each farm was now to
be occupied by one tenant only. The Bishop again allowed wood for repairs and
for building new barns and stables and outhouses.

In 1665 an Act was passed to make the Hamble navigable from Botley to
Bishop's Waltham. The Bishop, therefore, reserved the right to cut waterways and
trenches through this land and bring boats to the town from the sea near Botley.
He had leased the 43 acres of the Little Park to Richard Trod, 316 acres of
Moorings and Prowtings farms to Francis Morrison, 761 acres to Lord Henry
Powlett all at 1s. 9d. an acre; in all 1,120 acres. The annual income was reduced
from £354, which Bishop Duppa received, to £99 1s. 7d. However, like Bishop
Duppa, he had another source of income from the fees which were paid to renew
these leases. These were generally made for 21 years, but might be renewed earlier.

The Bishop was engrossing his land. Today it would be called rationalising. It
was much easier for his steward to receive the rent from three substantial tenants
instead of 27 small farmers. But despite Bishop Morley's stipulation that there
must be one farmer to each farm, it seems that the land was still sublet. The
evidence for this comes from the poor rates. The ratepayers from the 'Parkes' –
Peter Cooke, John Woodman, Peter Browne, Henry Dipnell, Richard Moringe,
Richard Godwin, David Prowting – were all leasing land from Bishop Duppa in
1660. Five years later these eight were still farming there and they had been joined
by 11 others.[15]

The rector had by custom enjoyed the right to pasture 12 cows and one bull on the 'two disparked Parkes' from 1 May to 14 September. In order to free the land from this obligation, the Bishop gave 100 acres (a tenth, a tithe) of the Great Park to the living. The Bishop would divide off this 100 acres with a hawthorn hedge which the rector must maintain. This would 'much augment the Revenue of the Rectory ... and be much more beneficial'.[16] By this gift the Bishop made the land in the park tithe free; those farming there were not required to give a tenth of their produce to the rector. The park lands became very desirable. This 100 acres of glebe, given to the living with its little tithe barn, paid a rent of £15 per annum if leased out,[17] as it was in 1840 when Thomas Nation farmed it. (In 1794 the cover of a tithe rental book lists '30 Barley, 30 Wheat, 14 Barley, 15 tons hay, 60 lambs, 14 Fleeces, 2 Cows', probably the produce which the Rector, Edward Poulter, had received that year in tithe.[18]) This 109 acres of glebe remained attached to the rectory until 1909. It was then sold to William Gough for £2,150.[19]

The tenants in the park continued to increase; by 1683, 38 people held land there. Four years later the tithing of Curdridge complained that 'the Parkes' being tithe free were paying less than their rightful share in local taxes. Curdridge demanded a diminution in its poor rate. 'The Parkes' continued to be shown as a separate unit until 1717 when 17 people were renting land there, one of whom was the wealthy Robert Kerby who endowed the grammar school. But by 1722 the ratepayers in the 'Parkes' had been absorbed into the tithings of Ashton, Curdridge and Waltham.[20]

The boundaries of the park farms were redrawn yet again by Bishop the Honourable Brownlow North (1781-1820) in 1797. Cookes Farm of 229 acres, Lodge Farm of 333 acres and Russell Farm of 199 acres, with Balls mead, a meadow which lay adjacent to but outside the Great Park, and also the 43 acres of the Little Park, were now divided into four farms with names which we know today. Lodge Farm was to be occupied by George Whale, Pondside Farm, which included the Little Park, by Richard Prowting, Pope Stile Farm by Henry Flower, Tangier Farm by James Callear.[21] This land had formerly been rented by nine tenants. Bishop Brownlow North too was rationalising his property, which had increased in value since the outbreak of war with France.

Charles Sumner became Bishop of Winchester in 1827. The following year a valuation was made of the park farms which were now all being leased to William and Thomas Houghton. Farming had passed through the Napoleonic wars when there had been a premium on land and high prices for corn, to the aftermath of the wars when corn could again be imported. Land therefore fell drastically in price. Pondside, 146 acres, was typical; valued in 1810 at £184, but in 1820 at only £126, Clewer who had been farming there 'had lost his all'. The land had 'lain uncultivated one whole year'. It was 'full of springs and so very poor a great portion will not pay for cultivating'. The best of the park farms was Lodge Farm, described as 275 acres 'divided by good live hedges and lying in a ring fence'. But Pope Stile and Locks, 183 acres rented by Edward Privett, was 'in a very bad state ... the tenant is now farming without capital'. Tangier Farm, a name which had become fashionable after the marriage of Charles II and Catherine of Braganza in

1662, when Tangier was part of her dowry, was in hand, but 'had been used as arable until it would grow no Corn and then allowed to … produce what Grass it would'.[22]

In 1847 Arthur Helps, author and later Privy Councillor and private secretary to Queen Victoria, came to live at Vernon Hill House. The vast land-holdings of the Church, including those of the bishops, were under review. It was thought that the income from this land, instead of rewarding the bishops, should be used to pay the incumbents of poor parishes. The land therefore was made the responsibility of the Ecclesiastical Commissioners. In 1859[23] Arthur Helps began to buy up the leases of the park farms with the right to the freehold. He bought part of Prowtings Farm, 157 acres, for £3,087 16s. 2d. in 1859. In 1862 he bought the reversionary interest in the freehold of the park farms, 835 acres, for £10,143 (with a charge on them of £25 a year for a perpetual curate at St John's Winchester).[24] After more than 700 years of episcopal ownership the Park had become private property.

7

The Park and the Chase after 1663

Although the Park had been disparked in 1663, it continued to be managed by the manorial officers who were appointed by letters patent, documents which were authenticated by the bishop's official seal. Such offices were obtained by paying the Pipe Office, the bishop's treasury in Winchester, and might be handed on. They brought with them valuable incomes, for, as well as a salary, various fees were chargeable. When he died in 1721 Robert Kerby left his offices of bailiff and clerk of the manor to his cousin, John Binsted.[1]

In 1685 the copyhold tenants of the parishes of Droxford and Bishop's Waltham with common rights in Waltham Chase, known also as Horder's Wood, complained that Bishop Peter Mews (1684-1706) was feeding deer in the Chase. But the Bishop that year had other matters on his mind, for he led the royal artillery at the battle of Sedgemoor, in Somerset, against the Duke of Monmouth, King Charles II's illegitimate son. The Bishop was wounded, but the Duke of Monmouth was defeated, captured and executed.

To the south-east of Waltham Chase lay the royal forest of Bere, through which the royal deer roamed at will. There had always been rivalry between the Keeper of the Royal Forest responsible for the king's deer and the Keeper of Waltham Chase responsible for the bishop's deer. This was resolved when in 1693 John Lewkenor was appointed to both offices. When he died, the Warden of South Bere forest, Richard Norton, suggested that Queen Anne should create a new patent office, which would make the Warden of South Bere forest the Ranger also of Waltham Chase, for 'otherwise', Norton wrote, 'he places an Enemy … near our Frontiers' because it is 'wholly in ye power of ye Bps ranger, by laying in wait for them to cut off great numbers of her Mjties Deer passing over (as they constantly doe) to feed in ye … Chase and Grounds adjoining'.[2] But Norton's suggestion was not acted on.

After the death of Bishop Peter Mews, Sir Jonathan Trelawney (1707-21), Cornishman, the son of a Royalist, whose property had been sequestered during the Civil Wars, was appointed Bishop. He had been priested in 1676 and succeeded to the title when his brother had died in 1680. He had himself called out the Cornish militia against the Duke of Monmouth in 1685. He was ardently Protestant. When James II in 1688 issued his second declaration of indulgence to Roman Catholics, Trelawney was one of the Seven Bishops who drew up a petition against it. They were imprisoned in the Tower, charged with seditious libel, tried, and declared not guilty.

In 1707 he came to Winchester. He was determined to restore his family's wealth, so appointed a Dr Heron as his steward, ordering him to examine the customs of the manor, and 'zealously to restore lost Rights to ye Bishopric after

23   Sir Jonathan Trelawney, Bishop of Winchester (1707-21), painted by Sir Godfrey Kneller. The Bishop was determined to restore his family's wealth, lost when his father supported King Charles I, and Trelawney inquired into his tenants' manorial rights. By courtesy of Christ Church, Oxford.

so many Years Neglect and Discontinuance'.[3] This caused great resentment, for by the time his predecessor, Bishop Peter Mews, died at the age of 89, the tenants had become used to organising themselves without interference.

The very same year, 1707, that Trelawney became Bishop, Robert Kerby, attorney, bought[4] the manor and farm of Preshaw. He held six patent offices including the office of woodward, which was very profitable for he licensed the felling of trees, and was entitled to all the wood above the second branch of the trees felled. He took his fees in bark and lops and tops. Waltham Park was part of his responsibility.

Dr Heron, as he had been ordered, began a thorough investigation of the customary rights, examining each in turn. Why should timber always be allowed free for the repair of bridges and pounds? Why should all the officers including the underkeeper of the Chase, a woman, have their horses shod twice a year at Bishop's Waltham for nothing?

Dr Heron and Robert Kerby soon clashed. Eventually Kerby sent a long list of complaints to the Bishop. Heron had seized 'Heriots on your Ldps Tennants Deathes where none were due'. He had taken a fee of £5 for every lease he had granted, though it cost less than ten shillings to write. He had ignored the 'Advice of the Ancient officers … which know the Customes'. He had bullied the tenants.

He had refused to pay 'for the Game brought to your Lordship According as has been paid for 50 years'.[5]

But the real disagreement came over the woodward's licence to take a proportion of the timber allowed in the leases of the bishopric farms. Dr Heron decided to prevent this by permitting the tenants themselves to cut timber on their farms without reference to the Woodward. Moreover, Dr Heron inserted a new clause into these leases. It said that, if all the wood on the tenants' farms was exhausted, then the bishop would allow them timber from the chases. But, Heron told the Bishop, this clause could safely be ignored. He triumphantly informed him that Kerby was now only responsible for the woods and chases and those few farms on which there was a substantial amount of timber. But Dr Heron's stewardship came to an end in 1712 when he was found 'delirious'.[6] He was replaced by an equally demanding steward, Edward Forbes. However Robert Kerby was still bailiff of the manor, able to take the tenants' part against this steward too. In 1721 Kerby died. He left some of his land to create a trust for the education of poor children and for the relief of the poor.[7] Robert Kerby had probably acted as a restraining influence between a demanding bishop and his manorial tenants.

That year, 1721, Bishop Sir Jonathan Trelawny also died. He was succeeded by Bishop Charles Trimnell (1721-3) who in 1722 appointed John Cleverly, gentleman, of Bishop's Waltham, Gamekeeper within Waltham manor. He was to preserve game 'with Gunns, Doggs, Netts … to hunt, shoot, course fish … to carry away all or any sort of game & fish for my use as he shall think fit'.[8]

The very year that John Cleverly was appointed to preserve the Bishop's deer, the Waltham Blacks appeared in the Chase, 'determined not to leave a Deer on the Chase, being well assured it was originally design'd to feed Cattle, and not to fatten Deer for the Clergy'.[9]

The Waltham Blacks were masked men led by 'King John'; with black faces and black gloves, with fur caps and deerskin coats, they seized the Bishop's deer. They dominated the area. One farmer near Waltham Chase who informed on them had his fences destroyed, and his cattle driven into the standing corn. When a Mrs Beverley refused to give up her pew in the church at Wickham, they cut down her avenue of trees, spoilt her garden, and, in revenge on the parson, flung his beehives into the road. They sent out 'Circular letters' and 'threatened with burning' the houses of those who opposed 'their Search after further Supplies of Venison'.

It began to be rumoured that the Waltham Blacks were Jacobites intent on restoring James Stuart, the Old Pretender, to the throne. When he heard this, 'King John' distributed notices – these had been printed in London – stating that 'he and his were faithful … Subjects to their Leige Lord and Sovereign King George'.

'King John' announced that he would appear at the Inn on Waltham Chase in March 1723. A crowd of 300 arrived to see him. Once again 'King John' with 15 of his followers made a great show of declaring allegiance to the Hanoverian King, George I (1714-27). He then publicly disbanded the Waltham Blacks but also took nine fat deer while the crowd, including the keepers, looked on.

Was 'King John's' vehement declaration of loyalty to George I cover for a Jacobite plot? E.P. Thompson in his book *Whigs and Hunters* has given some credence to this suggestion. In 1722 Francis Atterbury, the Bishop of Rochester, plotted to seize the Bank of England, and, with the help of France, to restore James Stuart (the Old Pretender) to the throne. Sir Henry Goring, a fellow conspirator, wrote to Atterbury with the promise of five troops of dragoons commanded by five Hampshire gentlemen. These troops, Goring wrote, were none other than the Waltham Blacks, who, as he pointed out, were already well mounted and armed.[10] On 17 April the Atterbury plot was revealed to Prime Minister Sir Robert Walpole.[11] By 9 May he had made the connection with the Waltham Blacks. On that day the King's Council, assembled at St James Palace, wrote to the Duke of Bolton, custos rotulorum and lord lieutenant of Hampshire, stating that 'several [of the King's] subjects … have entered into a wicked Conspiracy in Connection with Tyrants abroad for rayseing a Rebellion in this Kingdom in Favour of a popish Pretender with … design to overthrow our Excellent Constitution in church and state'. All the justices were summoned to an extraordinary meeting in the *George Inn*, Winchester. They must 'suppress Ryotts Tumults & unlawful assemblies'. They must immediately confiscate horses and arms from any recusants and confine them to their homes and, most important of all, report back to the Council.[12] Habeas Corpus was suspended for a year. This was a provision not against deer stealing but against a Jacobite rising. But the following year, in great haste, Parliament passed the Waltham Black Act, not against the Jacobites but against deer stealing.

There must have been an over-riding reason to make the penalties for deer stealing suddenly so much harsher. Was it that the Prime Minister used this opportunity to protect property, or was this Act passed ostensibly against deer stealers, but perhaps actually to put in force measures which would make enormous difficulties for any future Jacobite conspiracy? After all, the Atterbury plot in 1722 was the third attempt in George I's short reign (1714-27) to restore the Stuarts. The plot failed; Atterbury himself was arraigned and sent into exile in Europe where he joined James Stuart, the Old Pretender.

Before the Waltham Black Act of 1723, the penalty for deer stealers was to stand in the pillory for one hour, be confined in prison for a year and a day, and pay a fine of £20.[13] But in 1723, after the passage of the Waltham Black Act, deer stealing when armed became a capital offence. This was the penalty also for any person who stole or hunted venison, hares or rabbits, who blacked his face and carried arms, appeared in any chase or enclosed land, took rabbits or hares, cut down trees in avenues, gardens or plantations, set fire to stacks of corn, hay or wood, took fish from fish ponds, maimed cattle, or demanded money or venison by letter. Seven Hampshire Blacks paid this penalty, though none from Bishop's Waltham. They were tried in London and hanged at Tyburn.[14] Indeed, one man from Bishop's Waltham, Earwaker, was shot fighting the Blacks in Alice Holt. His brother was awarded £50 in compensation.

Richard Willis (1723-34) became Bishop in 1723, appointing John Cleverly gamekeeper for both Bishop's Waltham and Droxford. Cleverly was now ordered to seize unlawful hunters of game, to reserve the 'Fallow Deer in Waltham Chase

... to take them for the Bishop only when he received directions in writing, to prohibit all persons from ... destroying ... deer ... to seize all engines that may be brought for that purpose'.[15]

'King John's' reign of tyranny in Waltham Chase had made the tenants fearful for their common rights. The first presentment at the manorial courts had always referred to the whole manor: it categorically declared that 'all our Tymber growing on our Copyholds ... bee our own as part of our Inheritance to be disposed of as we please and have been so time out of mind'. After September 1724, at each court leet, a new presentment appeared. It declared 'the Erbridge and Bushes of Waltham Chase to be in the right of ye Tennants and have been so time out of Mind'.[16] The courts kept a close watch on invaders. Benjamin Machis junior had encroached on the bishop's elms. He was ordered to restore them within three months. In 1737 Richard Frankham must remove the enclosures he had made in the lord's waste near Waltham Chase. In 1749 James Tomalin must remove a fence he had erected round land there; he must also restore the flow of water from Pile's well which he had diverted,[17] cutting off supplies to several cottages.

The Waltham Black Act had restored some order to the Chase. When the parish officers realised that the spread of smallpox could be prevented by isolation, the Chase was the obvious solution. Here in 1723 in her own house Mary Bassett successfully nursed parishioners suffering from the disease.[18] When smallpox again devastated the town about 1740, the Chase was proposed as the site for an isolation hospital, a Pest House. The parish officers petitioned Bishop Benjamin Hoadley (1734-61).[19] He granted them half an acre of the waste, and 20 tons of timber for building. The Chase was now no longer thronged with deer. When in 1742 the Bishop was urged to restock it, he refused, saying it had made mischief enough.[20]

Waltham Chase, though no longer the haunt of the Waltham Blacks, remained a magnet for vagrants who lived there illegally. Claims made by some of them to belong to the parish were examined at Fareham in 1758, and were dismissed.[21] Later, in 1786, when nine intruders were examined, each was allowed one shilling relief. There were frequent complaints of wood stealing; in 1763 Richard Trod of Ashton was fined three guineas 'for having cutt bushes in Horders Wood having no right of common there'.[22]

The importance of Waltham Chase for the supply of timber is shown in a letter in 1800 from Mr Serle, steward, to Bishop the Honourable Brownlow North. Timber was needed not only for building houses and barns, but was in great demand for the navy. Mr Serle calculated the amount needed for a farm leased at £300 per annum. His aim was to make it self-sufficient. He wrote, if 'Tenants were obliged ... to plant Quick Fences' (hawthorn), which they could procure from the Chase 'they would fence themselves in 7 years' for the old hedges on their farms would supply fuel for the oven and fire: then instead of two tons of butt (the thicker) timber, a ton and a half would be sufficient, with half a ton of cheaper wood from the woodward, since ploughs, drags and harrows required only small stuff. He also suggested that if the labouring poor were given 'half a hundred of Faggotts [worth] 7 shillings, [this would] lead more than any other thing to the preservation of Timber'.[23]

The relevance of this proposal is shown in the report of Charles Vancouver who was surveying Hampshire for the Board of Agriculture. He wrote in 1810 that even the young trees on Waltham Chase had been cut down. He describes 'the hovels on the wastes and commons usually built of mud; the roof and other materials commonly purloined from the adjacent woods'.[24]

The bishops and their stewards battled continuously to maintain their rights over Waltham Chase. In March 1800 a notice was fixed to the church door. It said that existing illegal encroachments would be thrown up. But families had been cultivating this land for some time, so it also said that the Bishop 'has taken this step at this early season that no Crops might be Sown and as little Inconvenience suffered as possible … if any Person shall … persist (in his incroachment) the Crop will be dug up and the Person prosecuted',[25] which was a hard policy towards those who had suffered during the famine years 1795-1800.

In 1800 the Bishop himself made an enclosure (still noted on the ordnance survey map as the 'bishop's inclosure') to preserve a nursery of young trees which would otherwise be trampled down and barked by wandering cattle: with a ditch and railing it cost £83 8s. 9d. The bondland tenants immediately threatened to prosecute the Bishop; they would pull down this enclosure unless it was removed within three months.[26]

Legally the Bishop was in the right: he could enclose this land to protect his timber, but only for 20 years. William Cobbett saw this enclosure soon after it was made, 'the ground was bare except for a few bushes and branches of heath'. He saw it again 20 years later in 1826 when it was 'covered with fine young Oaks twenty feet high'.[27] That same year, no doubt in the light of this success, Bishop George Tomline (1820-27) petitioned Parliament for an Act to enclose Waltham Chase. The Bill was passed by the Commons but thrown out by the Lords. Cobbett declared that, had it become law, 'more than 1,000 poor people would be driven from the skirts of the forest as would '572 horses, cows, heifers and pigs and probably 1,000 geese' which he had counted as he rode across it.[28]

In 1813 Cobbett had written of Waltham Chase as 'this great tract of land which is called waste … the borders studded with cottages … the greater part of these are (illegal) encroachments, but the … Steward has never been harsh and the tenants have had too much compassion … to pull them down'.[29] When in 1816 he saw the agricultural distress caused after the Napoleonic Wars, he thought of Waltham Chase as a local solution. If the poor had land to cultivate they could feed themselves. He therefore proposed to Bishop's Waltham vestry that those who had made enclosures illegally in the Chase should be given the right to hold them legally, provided they were parishioners, that the Bishop be asked to permit this, and further, that other land there should be enclosed for allotments. None of the vestrymen agreed with him. His proposition was defeated. Worse than that, in 1818 the bondland tenants, jealously protecting their common rights, met at the turnpike gate to throw up these illegal enclosures.[30]

Cobbett had given his reasons for enclosing some of the land in the Chase; a bondland tenant gave his for enclosing all of it, in an anonymous pamphlet printed in 1826. He wrote that there were about 1,300 statute acres (a local

24 Waltham Chase in the 1930s.

measurement) of common in the Chase.[31] He himself would be entitled, on an allotment of one acre of common to each acre he held, to 200 statute acres should it be enclosed. None of the 20 families living there received poor relief at present, but if the Chase were enclosed they would need it. On the other hand, the actual enclosure would provide work for the poor for several years, so there would be no unemployment and no increase in poor rate. The cottages already there must be allowed to remain. But if the Chase were not enclosed 'we shall shortly have (no ground) to claim. One takes a slice here and claims a right to dig soil or clay or turf … and many acres have … been spoiled'. The timber there was negligible, consisting only of 'naked and mutilated stumps' nicknamed 'Bishop's timber'. The Bishop himself would probably receive about 100 enclosed statute acres, much better than the unenclosed Chase which was now 'exposed to the bite of every man's cow and … mutilated by every man's axe'. And the value of this enclosed land would rise from £13 for 20 acres to 30s. per acre.[32]

The 1820s were times of great hardship for the agricultural labourer. Population had increased and food could be imported, but the Corn Laws kept the price of bread artificially high. Agricultural machinery, particularly the threshing machine, had decreased the demand for manual labour. Finally, the labourers, despairing of their situation, banded together, attacked barns and threshing machines and demanded higher wages, in an uprising which became known as the Swing Riots.

Bishop Charles Sumner (1827-69), as Cobbett had done earlier, produced a solution for this distress. The Bishop wrote on 30 December 1830 from Farnham

Castle to the parishes of Bishop's Waltham, Droxford and Upham, offering the parish officers land in Waltham Chase for allotments to the poor … provided sufficiency of Herbary and Turbary (pasturing their animals on the commons and digging turves for fuel), remained for the commoners. The Bishop's Waltham officers enclosed 12 acres. Within two years the bondland tenants threw down the fences. They were rebuilt.[33]

In 1862 the bondland tenants listed their rights in the Chase. The timber belonged to them. They could turn out one cow to each acre they farmed of arable land, two cows to each acre of pasture, but no pigs, geese or asses were to be kept on the Chase. They could dig clay but not put dung there. They had the right to herbage, bushes and underwood but must not cut between 1 April and 1 November. No soil or turf was to be removed.[34]

As soon as Bishop Charles Sumner retired in 1869 the Ecclesiastical Commissioners, a body set up in 1834 to manage church lands, took over the bishopric estates. Waltham Chase was enclosed; 65 people were allotted land, according to the amount they were already leasing as copyholders with common rights. Mostly the awards were small: George Apps, having five acres of copyhold, was awarded just over two roods. Arthur Helps with 26 acres received two acres: William Knapp Jonas and his sister Mary, with 84 acres, received seven: Edward Wyatt with 98 acres was awarded eleven. Twenty-three acres were sold for £1,442 to fund this enclosure.

The old roads through the former park (some leading to the *Fountain Inn*) through the Great field, Long Meadow, Coppice Close, Barn Close and other ways were stopped up. The Swanmore road was widened to 30 feet. Two public drift-ways for the passage of animals, together with private ways for the copyholders, were created. A public pond and dipping place for sheep was to be be maintained by the churchwardens and overseers. Four acres were reserved for recreation, with a rent charge of £5 per annum on two holdings of 11 acres for upkeep.[35] The Waltham Chase over which bishops and kings had hunted now receded into history.

8

The Demesne

The Act of 1663 which granted the disparking of the Park, allowed the demesne, the land formerly farmed by the bishop, to be leased. Hazleholt lay in both Bishop's Waltham and Droxford parishes. It had formerly been woodland. When in 1665 it was leased to Richard Hancock it consisted of 50 acres of 'arable land late wood with two little Barns lately built'.[1] Another part of the demesne, Calcott (tithe map 945, 928), was an 11-acre meadow just outside the park in Curdridge tithing. Cleverly Wood in Dean in 1790 consisted of 40 acres, which was rented to Thomas Bulbick. He was allowed to cut three acres of underwood each year, but the oaks there 'are small unkind trees and should be cut, for they will not grow more'; they had 'suffered a great abuse by cutting the boughs or lops from the young oaks'.[2] These had been taken by the cottagers for fuel.

The East mill (Waltham Chase mill) had been an integral part of the demesne. During Parliamentary times it had been occupied illegally. But in 1661 it was restored to William Colnett whose grandfather had been the rightful copyholder, the Bishop appointing Peter Browne and William Andrews his attorneys to take possession and deliver the property to Colnett.[3] By 1788 'the building and Mill Tackle [was] much out of repair … there is nothing of any sort except the Mills and a Roof over … and Mill pond'. They were leased to Daniel Jonas, miller, who was allowed clay, sand and gravel to repair the banks. By 1799 they were declared a very valuable property since now 'very few if any Mills … do more business', for

25   Waltham Chase mill (the East mill), probably on the same site as the Anglo-Saxon mill. It is worked by water from the Moors.

26 The Mill Pond which powered Waltham Chase mill.

since 1793 England had been at war with France so more corn was produced at home. The building itself was shaped like a letter T; the perpendicular belonged to the Bishop. It contained four pairs of stones. One pair was kept for grinding malt but only two pairs of stones could be worked at a time.

The Moores where springs feed the Hamble, part of the demesne east of the mill, were leased in 1788 to William Lacy. The surveyor reported, 'A great part of it is quite a Quagmire, it's so bad ... there is no walking over it ... the water in the Mill pond as drives Waltham Mill is higher than the land ... There is 8 oak trees on it almost dead and want to be'. In 1806 the Moores, 30 acres in extent, was sold to Daniel Jonas.[4]

In 1699 Bishop Peter Mews (1684-1706) leased the 17-acre site of the palace to the Rector, Francis Morley, and the Trustees of the Poor, for 18 shillings a year, on condition that £8 was raised from it annually, and distributed among the poor as the trustees thought fit.[5] The lease was granted for 21 years. It was renewable every seven years when a fine was paid, half by the tenant, half by the trustees. Should these fail to renew the lease, the tenant might himself apply for it, paying £80 to the trustees. In 1792 James Munvill, the tenant, paid this £80 and secured the lease.[6] It was a bargain. Over the years it had produced far more than the £8 stipulated for the poor: the extra money had been invested in stocks and shares; the interest on these was paid to the poor on St Thomas' Day (26 December), at either the market house or the poor house by the rector or bailiff.[7]

There were still habitable buildings on the palace site for although in 1777 the 'Mansion House [was] now demolished' a lease to John Clewer of Botley Hill records 'the manor house of Waltham' held by Thomas White and Catherine Russell.[8] A survey of the palace in 1785 by George Cobbett shows that it consisted

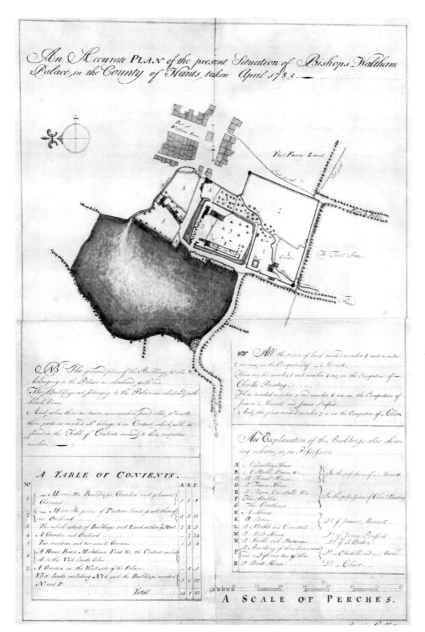

27 Plan of Bishop's Waltham Palace made in 1785 by George Cobbett, possibly William Cobbett's father. HRO, 5M87/61.

of a house (the present Palace House) with other buildings, a garden, orchard, pleasure ground and pasture, in all 5½ acres worth £35 17s. 6d. Within the moat was the area leased by Charles Prowting. This included the farmhouse, yard, barn, stables, cowstalls, carthouse and other buildings, a 2½-acre garden and orchard, with six acres of pasture for feeding cattle. Outside the moat at the east corner he leased another garden and orchard of one acre. James Munvill leased a house, yard, barn, stable, cowhouse, two meadows and two small gardens, in all one and three-quarter acres. John Cluer (probably John Clewer) held a quarter-acre garden

28   The Palace ruins in 1784. HRO, TOP 31/2/6.

on the west side of the palace. James Penford rented a malthouse; James Baker and others a stable and store house; Mr Ubsdell and Incers a building with three lower rooms, two of them with lofts over. The lease of the whole site produced £70 19s.[9]

Over the years the curtilage of the palace was encroached on. There had been the gate house facing the town, part of Cardinal Beaufort's rebuilding. By 1787 nothing was left except the site. Robert Baynes' lease records 'one cottage with curtilage ... late of the waste soil of the Lord before the Door wheron a porch is built'.[10] In 1891 this became a freehold with the payment of a fee to the bishop.[11] Austin & Wyatt's estate agents marks the site of this cottage.

When in 1805 John Penny leased the palace, he discovered that instead of 17 acres he had only nine. He wrote to Bishop Brownlow North (1781-1820) querying John Clewer's occupation of the 'hermitage Garden etc'. He considered that this reduction in acreage had been caused by slackness on the part of the trustees of the poor. After they 'had got all the void grounds ... [they] gave up their lease to one of their number Mr Horner. He being a party concerned contented himself with the reduced property'.[12]

John Penny was right. The palace land had certainly been encroached on, first by a boat house with a garden, built on the waste which had been part of the original 17 acres, then by a stable and store also built on a vacant area, its roof resting on the palace wall. This too was claimed as freehold.

A further change came in 1842 when William Houghton leased the Palace House. He built the flint wall along the moat, thus effectively separating the house from the palace grounds which were now rented by John Crouch and James Lampard.[13]

29   The Princesses Helena and Louisa and Prince Arthur in 1865 attended a concert after opening the Royal Albert
Infirmary. It was held in the former Palace refectory. The royal party are seated in front of one of the fireplaces. By
courtesy of the National Portrait Gallery, London.

By 1863 the Palace House was in poor condition; unoccupied for several years,
it was dilapidated, the grounds were ruinous owing to the financial problems of
Arthur Helps, the lessee. He was in the process of developing the Bishop's
Waltham Clay Company, and the Bishop's Waltham Railway Company, and
raising funds for the Bishop's Waltham Infirmary being built in Newtown. He had
insufficient capital for his ventures, so the Palace House had suffered. The old
farmhouse was being used as two tenements. A new cartshed replaced one which
had burnt down. The large thatched barn remained, with lean-to sheds and
stable.[14] In 1865 the ancient refectory was used for a grand amateur concert to
entertain Queen Victoria's children, the Princesses Helena and Louisa and Prince
Arthur, when they came to open the unfinished Infirmary. Afterwards Arthur
Helps allowed the buildings to deteriorate; later the barn was pulled down to
make room for sheep.[15] But the occasion was recorded by an oil painting of
Arthur Helps with the royal visitors.

When in 1869 the Ecclesiastical Commissioners took up the management of
the episcopal land, they sold the palace to the Jenner family. Its most famous
owner, Viscount Cunningham of Hyndehope, the brilliant Admiral of the Second
World War, handed the care of the palace ruins in 1952 to the Ministry of Works.
This site is now in the care of English Heritage.[16]

9

Enclosure

The official enclosure of the Park began when Bishop George Morley (1662-84) donated 100 acres of the Great Park as a perpetual gift to the living of Bishop's Waltham, separating it from the rest of the Park by a hawthorn hedge (is it still there in parts?) which the rector was to maintain.[1] At the same time he disparked the remaining parkland, dividing it into farms. There was no lack of takers for this land, for here the farmer was able to cultivate his fields without having to walk from strip to strip as he must do in the common fields. Here too he could keep his animals free from the diseases which might be passed on to them from the stock of others: he could practise stockbreeding, drain and plough his land unhindered by the balks, the earthern banks, which divided his holdings in the common fields or by the opposition of his fellow tenants. Among those who were leasing this former parkland in the 1660s were Henry Dipnell, David Prowting, Peter Browne, Richard Trod.[2]

It therefore comes as no surprise to find that their descendants, Thomas Dipnal, David Prowting, Daniel Brown, Richard Trod, having proved the advantages of individual holdings, petitioned Parliament a hundred years later for the enclosure of the common arable fields of Ashton, in all 205 acres called Ashton Field, Pilard Field and Oat Field. Other petitioners included Walter Barefoot, Richard Eyles, William Horner, William Aylen, Catharine Friend.[3]

30   Beeches Hill from the Hangers in 1914. This area was originally part of the common fields of Ashton.

31 Street End Farm, probably the home of John Cleverley who illegally enclosed two of the common fields at Ashton.

32 Ashton Farm in the tithing of Ashton which once had stocks and an inn, the *Cross Keys.*

Earlier, in 1711, John Cleverley of Street End had attempted to enclose Ashton and Pilard fields illegally. His neighbours presented Cleverley at the manorial court. He was fined £10 and ordered to throw down these enclosures or pay a further penalty of £20. By September he had not thrown down the enclosures. He paid the £20. He was then ordered to pay a further fine of £10, unless the land was restored within six days. At the following court in March 1712 the jury reported that the fences had been thrown down, but not within the six days' limit set. Cleverley paid another £10.[4]

However, in 1759 not only was the enclosure of Ashton and Pilard and Oat Fields sought but also the enclosure of Stephen's Castle Down, another 120 acres. This was doubly complicated because the land lay within two separate manors, Bishop's Waltham and Ashton. When in 1132 Bishop Henri de Blois had founded the Hospital of St Cross in Winchester he had endowed it with the manor of Ashton, together with other manors. In 1759 the Master of St Cross was John Lynch. He was not only Lord of the Manor of Ashton but also the Dean of Canterbury.[5]

Peter Barfoot, attorney, undertook the necessary business. A man of substance, he had leased the Parsonage House from the rector, James Cutler, who was also the rector of Droxford and resided at his Droxford rectory. Peter Barfoot held four patent offices from the Bishop. He shared the office of Porter of the palace of Wolvesey and Keeper of the Prison with George Vernon; he shared the office of Bailiff and Clerk of the manor of Bishop's Waltham with James King of Upton Grey.[6]

John Lynch, Master of St Cross, objected to this enclosure: perhaps he feared that he might lose income from Ashton manor, since enclosure could result in a piece of land being awarded in lieu of tithes. Four others opposed it and nine of the almsmen of St Cross.[7] Four other copyhold tenants of the manor, John Punker, William Aylen junior, Thomas Budd, Thomas Hatch, also petitioned against this enclosure.[8] Hatch himself ran more than 200 sheep on Stephen's Castle Down.

33   Sheep on Stephen's Castle Down. These sheep runs belonged to various holdings, one of which was Dean Farm.

In the town Peter Barfoot organised a general meeting of those in favour of the Bill at *The King's Head* (Mr Coleborn's) where it was read over and signed. He then took it to the Bishop of Winchester, Benjamin Hoadley, also to Mr Thistlethwayte M.P. for the County, and to other M.P.s on whom he could rely to support the Bill through the House of Commons.[9] This took ten days; a further 17 Barfoot stayed in London, a material witness before 'a Committee on Bills' which examined the clauses.

Another witness, James Poore, who lived 30 miles from the Down, had been involved in six other enclosure appeals. He declared the soil was too poor except for feeding sheep. It was worth 2s. 6d. an acre. If it was ploughed for corn it would take 40 years to recover, for there was only two inches of topsoil, then a rubbly chalk.

Those who held this land might not be witnesses. Matthew Searle lived four miles away. He agreed with Poore that the cost of fencing would be very great since there were fourteen or fifteen proprietors (in fact there were nineteen). It was common without stint, that is, in its natural condition, had never been tilled and the common rights were attached to particular holdings. It seems that every tenant had rights in the common fields, Ashton, Pilard and Oat, but not every tenant had rights in the common land of Stephen's Castle Down. Other witnesses supported this Enclosure Bill. James Ryder who lived in the parish said there were 120 acres of bondland (land held according to the custom of the manor) worth 2s. 6d. an acre except what belonged to St Cross. Some bondholders were entitled to rights in the common fields but had no rights to the Down. Four tenants lived too far away to use the Down, but those nearby did use it. He makes clear the problems of the common-field system; 'all the owners must agree to the farming of the common fields … the fields were plowed a Year or two ago and not for twenty years before' for ' any Difference aris[ing] among ye Owners', prevents ploughing , 'but … they might be sown every third Year'. Sheep folded on the land would improve it. The soil of the Down is better than Oatfield and about a foot deep. Enclosure would give the holders an advantage of £50 a year. The expense of enclosing it with hawthorn would be two shillings a lug; allowing 18 feet to the lug, each lug would require 75 plants. Both Pilard and Oat fields had previously been downland. He had examined the cart tracks across the Down but had seen no chalk.[10]

The Bishop of Winchester left the decision to those examining the case. When the Committee met again Peter Barfoot reported that all had agreed to the passing of the Bill on condition that Stephen's Castle Down was left unenclosed. Four people only had not agreed, but their holdings were very small, being only five out of 205 acres.

Peter Barfoot was supported by the Rector, James Cutler, who twice received one guinea 'for Attendance on this Affair'. Three Commissioners, all yeomen, Henry Kennett the Elder of Hambledon, John Kersley the Elder of Sutton, and John Complin the Elder were appointed, but Complin broke his thigh so resigned in favour of George Binsted. The Commissioners were to allot the land in proportion to the existing 'shares and rights of common' of the tenants; to set out the public and private roads, the ditches, drains, bridges, gates and stiles. Public roads were to be 40 feet broad, to be repaired as the other highways were, that is, by statute labour: within 18 months of the Act the 'several parcels of land shall be inclosed, hedged ditched or fenced'. After this it was unlawful to use any other roads except the ones appointed by the Commissioners, but 'convenient openings' were to be left 'in the fences for the passage of Cattle Carts and Carriages' for a year. The former roads were taken into the enclosures. People must accept their allotments within six months; 'no one shall have the power to disturb these allotments'. But the 'Rights Royalties and Service belonging to the Lord of the Manor' would not be affected.[11] In December Peter Barfoot was able to draw up the Deed of Allotment, which being 'very long and special', cost four guineas.

He then travelled to Taunton where the Bishop must have been in residence, to explain the allotments, then back to Winchester to St Cross to explain the map. There were to be four more meetings at *The Crown* with the Commissioners before the fences were settled; even then Barfoot was 'obliged to search the old Books of Survey and Records' to discover the different tenures. After this he attended the surveyor for three days at 'My House to settle the fences, Moving Roads and Boundaries'. His bill came to £386 18s. 7d.[12]

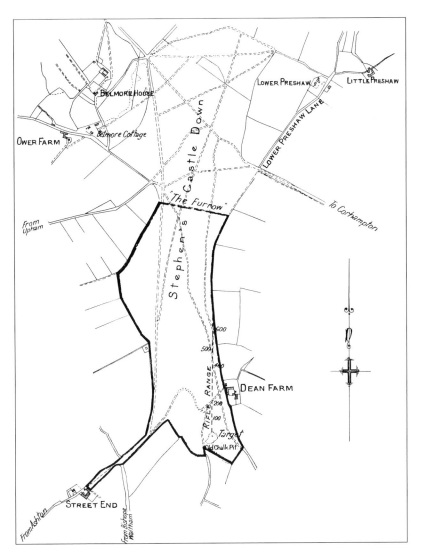

34 132 acres of Stephen's Castle Down was sold by the Church Commissioners to Sir H. Warden Chilcott in 1934. The parish was used to having access to this land. An attempt to register it as common land in 1973 failed. HRO, 107M90/196.

The boundaries were complicated. Daniel Brown was allotted 22 acres in Pilard Field; of these 21 were held from the Bishop, one from the Master of St Cross. This was therefore separated by a stone; the Master was to fence this acre when the lease of the present copyholder came up. Walter Barfoot, gentleman, was awarded two allotments in Pilard Field; of these seven acres out of one nine-acre allotment were held under the Master, the other two acres from the Bishop, defined by a boundary stone; both the Bishop and the Master were to erect the fences. He received ten acres in Pilard, four in Ashton. Thomas Hatch, gentleman, was allotted nine acres in Oat Field, one acre held from the Master was 'bounded by a stone now set up'.[13] David Prowting received 14 acres in Oat Field, Thomas Dipnell three acres in Pilard Field with two in Ashton Field, all held under the Master of St Cross. Richard Trodd received 18 acres in Pilard Field, five in Oat, four in Ashton Field. After 20 years of intermittent cultivation Pilard, Oat and

Ashton fields could all now become productive land. Fourteen years later this enclosed land was still noted as 'in the Common fields of Ashton'.[14] When in 1898 Walter Long was admitted to all the copyhold part of Dean Farm consisting of 170 acres, he acquired also the rights of commonage on Stephen's Castle Down.[15] But in 1934 the Ecclesiastical Commissioners sold 132 acres of Stephen's Castle Down to Sir H. Warden Chilcott for £300.[16]

The common fields of Bishop's Waltham are recorded in 1659 when Bridget Horner was permitted to let 10 acres 'Lying in ye common fields in ye tything of Waltham'.[17] Later these fields too must have been enclosed, probably by consent at a manorial court. Possibly the fields recorded on the tithe award of 1840, the Town Field (673) and Town Mead (668) refer to the former common fields.[18]

The enclosure of Curdridge common land

Curdridge with 322 acres of common pasture was a prosperous tithing. William Cobbett described his pleasure in coursing hares across this common in 1809 when he lived at Botley. He wrote of the importance of the commons to the copyholders for the keeping of cows and pigs and geese. He opposed the enclosure of this and other commons.[19]

35   The new church at Curdridge, built in 1888. HRO, TOP 87/2/1.

Curdridge had always felt separate from Bishop's Waltham. With the construction of a Chapel of Ease in 1835, with a priest-in-charge appointed and paid by the rector, it became more independent. By 1856 Curdridge common was enclosed, with five acres granted to the church as glebe, another five for the upkeep of the National School built close by. Four acres were granted to the churchwardens and overseers for recreation, three were to be allotments for the labouring poor with a rent charge of £3. The Bishop was compensated for his loss of rights in the soil as lord of the manor, by an annual rent charge of £10 a year on 10 acres.

The Inclosure Commissioner, George Appleby, set out the straight roads across the common in use today; one allotment was declared a quarry for stone and gravel for the upkeep of these roads. A public watercourse was made three feet deep, four feet wide at the bottom, seven at the top. The public ponds at the two inns, *The Cricketers* and *The Heart in Hand*, also the pond at Wangfield Green were to be cleansed and repaired by the allottees living near. Forty-seven people received land. They included the trustees of Robert Kerby's charity, for the 'Poor's Bargain', the land purchased under his will, for the relief of the poor and to endow free places at the grammar school, was copyhold land in Curdridge. James Warner, lord of the manor of Botley, with 372 acres of copyhold, was awarded 71 acres of common; Joseph Bernard of Rockstone Place, Southampton, with 80 acres received 16, while Henry Pullinger, tailor, who held just four acres of copyhold received one acre.[20] Curdridge common was now no more.

IO

The Courts of the Manor

Tudor legislation, particularly the Poor Law Acts, emphasised the parish as the administrative centre of government, but the manorial courts which had been in existence since medieval times continued. The courts were presided over by the steward, the bishop's officer, who notified the tenants that the court was to be held (a precept). Those unable to attend excused (essoin) themselves to the steward, paying their fee by proxy. Two juries, one for the court leet, the other for the court baron were chosen and sworn in.

The court leet was held twice a year at Michaelmas (29 September) and at Hocktide (after Easter). On these two days the court leet and the court baron were held on the same day. (The term court baron came from the King's practice of handing over a manor to a baron who was then able to hold his own court, a court baron). In between Hocktide and Michaelmas, the court baron was held probably every three weeks to regulate the business of the manor.

The court leet represented the King's Justice. Twice a year all the tithings of the manor were summoned to it; each tithing theoretically consisted of ten men who were responsible for each other's good behaviour.[1]

The steward first read out his charge to the 'Homage' (all the tenants of the manor). They must do 'a service to the Commonwealth, the Lord of the Manor and yourselves and Neighbours of this Manor by keeping a Court Leet and Court Baron'. The Court Leet 'relates to the Service of the State anciently used that the Kings and Queens … might understand how many able Men were [available] … to do them Service'.[2] The manor had fulfilled this function in 1523 when it had supplied 73 archers and 135 soldiers, armed with billhooks, to the army called up by King Henry VIII to attack France: again in 1545 when the French were planning to invade, having landed on the Isle of Wight, 200 men were summoned from the manor. Later, in 1574 under Queen Elizabeth, when England was threatened with invasion by the Catholic powers, 300 men were provided to guard the sea between Portsmouth and the Hamble ferry.[3]

The steward declared that the court leet was still responsible for 'the Administration of Justice to the Inhabitants'. On the other hand 'The Court Baron properly relates to Matters belonging to the Lord of the Manor and partly to yourselves'. Both freeholders and copyholders 'are bound to appear by your Tourne to do your Suit of Service … and [to] know the Laws and Customs of this Place and be the better enabled to performe ye duties in presenting all things that are here presentable according to the truth, not rashly or unadvisedly … without favour … hatred or malice'.

He then reminded the assembly that the four crimes of High Treason were 'Conspiracy against the State, Coining of Money, Counterfeiting of the Great

Seal, perverting to Popery'. The petty treasons were for a woman to kill her husband or, formerly, a priest his bishop. The steward then recited the felonies by statute law. They consisted of rape; 'the defacing another's face by putting out Eyes, cutting out Tongue'; servants embezzling their master's goods. There followed felonies by common law. These were stealing to the value of one shilling, robbing 'Churches, Chapells, Pigeon Houses, or other Houses or on the Highway'; for these crimes the 'Offenders shall dye or loose his lands and goods'.

Inferior offences were punishable by corporal punishment. These were 'Stealing from out of the Fields, pigs, Geese, Hens, Cloaths from Hedges, Robbing Orchards'. The steward declared that these crimes be presented at the court leet but were to be punished by the Shire courts at Quarter Sessions in Winchester.[4]

The court baron was also able to punish minor misdemeanours which included tenants not attending the court, or cases of assault. Enquiry was made into how efficient the constables and other officers had been in punishing rogues, whether anyone was harbouring vagabonds, whether all alehouses were licensed, whether there was any gaming or drunkenness, any butchers selling bad meat or craftsmen doing bad work, whether dung had been left on the highways, water courses diverted, any encroachments made on common land or watering of hemp or flax where this was forbidden. They must inquire into 'all Riots and Routs', and whether previous fines had been paid.[5]

Having dealt with these matters of civil disturbance 'the gentlemen of the Homage' (the jury) were reminded of their especial duties, for the court baron regulated the inheritance and exchange of land. The jury must reveal the names of any person who ought to be attending the court but was not present. If a tenant had died since the previous court they were to present his death, what lands he held and what heriot must therefore be paid to the lord of the manor. If a tenant held a yardland (30 acres), a half yardland (15 acres) or a farthingland (half an acre), the best beast was the heriot. If the farthingland was in the town but had a cottage on it, the heriot was still a beast. If there was no cottage then the fine of 12d. was to be paid.[6]

The next regulations dealt with the transference of land by the copyholders, so called because their holding was enrolled at the court and a copy kept by the tenant. The manorial system required that every exchange of land must be recorded in the manorial court and the fine paid. The fine confirmed the legal agreement of the conveyance of land which was held from the bishop, the lord of the manor, according to the custom of the manor. The rules were strict and were written down in a 'customary'. If a copyholder leased his land for longer than was allowed by custom he forfeited his land, as he did if he had not paid his rent or had refused to come to court to be sworn to the Homage. If he had sold any part of his estate by deed, he forfeited what he had sold. If he had allowed his house to fall down, he forfeited his estate. If a copyholder had surrendered his copyhold into the hands of two other tenants since the last court, he must pay a fine; the new tenants forfeited their copyholds. The tenant was given opportunities at three succeeding courts to pay the fine for his lands. If he did not pay or arrange for someone to pay for him, he lost his lands. If tenants transferred their lands, they must inform the next court leet, otherwise the transference was invalid. Tenants forfeited their estates if they let them without the licence of the court.[7] Other misdemeanours which must be presented included putting too many animals on the commons, and felling trees without replanting.

When a copyholder surrendered his land back to the bishop to be relet, various fines must be paid. The actual surrender of the land in court cost six-pence. Admission to a copyhold cost fivepence, enrolment of the copy in the records 1s. 5d., every new grant and copy 7s. 1d. When a death was presented in court, the cost was sixpence, a sort of registration fee. The lands of the copy-holder who had died were now available; a claim to them and a copy of the change of tenant cost four shillings. These were some of the fees due to Peter Barfoot as clerk of the court in 1762.[8] When a copyhold changed hands this was made public by the town crier in the Square after the court. In 1828 the town crier called 60 changes of copyholdings for which he received fourpence a copy. The two juries who attended the court were rewarded by the steward. That year he gave the court baron jury £1, the court leet jury 10 shillings.[9]

Custom regulated the inheritance of land. Three categories of land were in-volved: the bondland, the original holding which had owed labour services to the lord of the manor, later called copyhold. The next category, the purpresture land, was land which had been enclosed from the waste. It carried no rights of common. The third category, the demesne land, had originally been farmed by the lord of the manor himself, but was later leased by him. The purpresture land and the demesne land would be inherited by the eldest son or daughter or by the eldest grandchild. But if the purpresture and demesne land were in one holding with the bondland, the youngest son inherited all of it 'although the bondland be the least'.[10] This system of inheritance, borough English, when the youngest son inherited the land, probably went back to Anglo-Saxon times; whereas primo-geniture, the custom of inheritance by the eldest son, had been brought in by the Normans. But the court could make exceptions. In 1741 Peter, the eldest son of Richard Trod, was permitted to inherit the purpesture land, and Richard, the youngest, the bondland.[11]

Fines were the fees paid to the lord of the manor at the manorial court on the transference of a holding. A widow need not pay a fine on the death of her husband, as long as she remained chaste and single, but she could pay a fine to keep her husband's land during her lifetime. If she remarried before she paid the fine she lost the land.[12] Dr Heron, in E.P. Thompson's words, showed 'excessive zeal and rapacity 'in 1711, riding swiftly to one widow's estate to seize her five best beasts for heriots. When he next appeared at Bishop's Waltham manorial court, her son, supported by the manorial officers and several clergymen and others, publicly accused Heron of acting unjustly.[13] But Heron had been instructed by Bishop Sir Jonathan Trelawney to examine the customs of the manor and protect the Bishop's interests. Heron had soon come into direct conflict with all the manorial officers of the diocese, including those of Bishop's Waltham.

The case against Dr Heron was put by Robert Kerby, bailiff and clerk of the manor. He accused him of by-passing the manorial court by agreeing secretly with Mr Spencer, a copyholder, 'to pull down a house' for which Mr Spencer paid Dr Heron 30 shillings, thus depriving five manorial officers of their fee of 6s. 8d. each. He had also pocketed the money which had always paid the officers' expenses at court, forcing 'them to begg victualls' which must be to the Bishop's disadvantage as 'they are such officers as your Ldships Bppricke cannot be without ... Mr Heron's intent is to breake them all ... to be Sole Officer ... and at liberty to make such Accounts as he pleased, and not be detected'. He even refused the five shillings customary 'to the Jury att the Court ... to drink your Lordship's health'. In his defence Dr Heron said that these were 'Minute ... yet many Minute Expenses in a Months Progress [the visits which the steward made to the manors within the diocese] ... amount to a Sum at ye ende'.[14] But Dr Heron was no match for the Bishop's Waltham officers and in 1712 was indeed arrested for the wrongful seizure of a copyholder's heriot.[15]

The officials of the manor were appointed at the court by the bailiff and tenants. The tithingmen were chosen from amongst those holding particular lands. A document of 1727 reveals that there were 24 farthing (half an acre) lands in Waltham tithing from which these were drawn; these same lands also supplied 24 town reeves. Occasionally in the same year one person might serve both offices. In Hoe tithing there were seven bondland houses whose occupiers would be called on to serve as tithingmen. Within the whole manor 31 yardlands supplied collector reeves, 48 half-yard lands work reeves, and 48 farthing lands the office of beadle, who acted as assistant to the steward.[16] Lands which can be identified as carrying these duties are Metlands, Street End and Bishop's Down.[17]

The collector reeve served the whole manor. He was responsible for collecting all the fines imposed by the manorial courts. The work reeve must see that all labour ordered by the court was carried out. In 1608 Richard Baverstocke was collector reeve through his land at Ashton; in 1628 it was Francis Hacket for his land at Curdridge.[18] In 1722 Joanna Prowting was both collector reeve and work reeve.[19] The tenant of Kitnocks, William Wyatt, because of 'failure of Duty ... [his] refusal of the due Performance of ye Office of Collector Reeve incumbent on ye land in 1737', at the manorial court held two years later forfeited Kitnocks, which then returned to the Bishop.[20]

The bailiff and the tenants appointed the hayward. He must collect stray beasts and impound them in one of two pounds, a manorial pound of two acres near the palace, or a town pound near the rectory. If the hayward found that a tenant had more cattle on the common than he could keep on his bondland the hayward could impound those cattle. (There was a third pound in Curdridge tithing, in 1726,[21] another at Wintershill.) The hayward then 'cried' the beasts in the town; if no one came to collect them within a week they were driven to the bishop at Farnham. If the bishop considered the hayward had kept the animals longer than necessary, his expenses were not repaid. 'I found it to be the practice when I came into the See', (1811) declared Bishop the Hon. Brownlow North.[22]

The churchwardens, too, were chosen at the manorial court. In Ashton, Hoe and Curdridge there was a list of 'Farmers who took their offices by Rotation'. In Waltham one of the 'Principals in the Town [was] mercifully chosen by the

THE COURTS OF THE MANOR · 55

Rector', wrote the Reverend James Bale, curate to the rector, Henry Ford, in 1783. These names were then submitted to the justices for their formal approval. They were not entered into the 'Parish Book' which Joseph Bale is quoting from, and which has since disappeared.[23]

The common rights of the copyholders together with the labour services they owed the bishop had been commuted into money, sometimes expressed in Latinised English. In 1705 William Cleverley paid sixpence 'certain money': this money was a kind of insurance against any future penalty, threepence 'mead money' (the labour service in the fields), ninepence 'cowovis' (pasturing the cows on the commons); threepence 'hogovis' (for the pigs grazing in the park); two-pence 'Shirt rent', one penny 'little' and 20 pence 'woodloades' (the labour of carting wood for the bishop.[24] These dues were called quit rent, for when they had been paid the tenant was quit of the services he owed the bishop that year, which were part of his tenancy. When in 1733 William Horner, the tenant of Roke, omitted to pay £2 5s. 4d., his quit rent for two years, his land was forfeit to the Bishop. In 1735 Richard Brown had not paid £3 7s. 2d. quit rent for the last two years, he therefore lost the tenancies of 'Brassets, George Close and Barn, Shore Lane Purrock, Crickles and the House in High Street'.[25]

After the appearance of the Waltham Blacks in Waltham Chase, it might have been supposed that later bishops would keep a closer watch on the manor, but the presentments at the manorial court show this not to have been the case. The courts, presided over by the steward, regulated themselves as before, protecting both the bishop's interests and those of the inhabitants. The manorial pound near the palace in which straying animals were impounded was presented in 1720. It had to be presented for four years before, in 1724, it was repaired, the bishop providing the timber. Henry Kittlewell had built a stable on the waste; he must pull it down within three months. William Matthews had put up a building on land belonging to James Alexander. He must remove it within a month.

The bishop by custom had always provided timber for the repair of the many bridges. The town had only the medieval system of drainage: surface water drained naturally into the great pond, which was much larger than it is today, for the water table was high. It was to be 1940 before the Gosport Waterworks Co. was licensed to pump water from the chalk springs when it was reckoned that the site at Hoe alone could yield as much as two million gallons a day.[26] The manor was criss-crossed by many streams with bridges constantly in need of repair, the bishop providing the timber, the farmer or sometimes the surveyors of the tithings effecting them. There were bridges at Calcot, Maddoxford, and Shalford Lake on the way from Hoe to Botley. There was a lake and bridge at Northbrook; in 1747 this was ordered to be sufficiently repaired to carry corpses across, a mournful stipulation which comes after the deadly smallpox epidemic of the 1740s. There was a bridge at the Market House and at 'Holeby'. There was the Southern Bridge near the old *White Hart Inn*. In the park there was the horsebridge and the bridges through the fields on Church Ways that led to St Peter's, and bridges at Hind Mead in Horders Wood, at Gulley Mead, at Park Gate, and at Tangier. This farm was leased by the Duke of Chandos but sublet to Farmer Hinxman, who reckoned repairs were the Duke's responsibility. In 1730 the court laid a fine of 20 shillings on the Duke to repair the bridge, with a time limit of two months.

The one main bridge for which the bishop was totally responsible, which it was essential to keep in repair, was the sluice, the penstock, at the head of the pond. For more than twenty years 1723-47 the tenants presented it at the manorial court. They besought the Bishop to repair it, for crossing it was dangerous for both cattle and people. They tried laying a fine of £5 on the Bishop, to no avail. In 1732 they asked him to rail it 'as it is his right to do'. In 1738 they pointed out that a child had fallen in and would have drowned, had not a passer-by rescued him. They added, 'My lord is willing to have his dues from his Tennants, we think it a Just thing for this to be repaired'. In 1740 they ordered 'the bishop to find Timber and Workmanship … as was everly Customary … this Penstock have been often presented at our Court Leet and little notice taken of it … We therefore desire that those Gentlemen his Lordship's Servants and Actors in Such Affairs would as soon as Opportunity Permits remedy and repair the Penstock'. Finally in 1746 they took matters into their own hands, and ordered the surveyors of Waltham tithing to carry out this task by midsummer or pay a fine of £2. This, if levied, would go to the Bishop. The sluice was mended.[27]

In the 19th century the manorial services, which had been commuted into 'quit rent', continued to be added to the bondland tenants' rent. Over the years some meanings changed. In 1812 'Pannage', which in 1301 had been the 'payment made to the lord for feeding swine in a wood',[28] is defined as 'paid for the privilege of common'. 'Lawday money', an acknowledgement that the bishop was lord of the court, was paid twice a year. 'Hundred shilling' was paid in lieu of the manorial obligation of reaping at harvest time. 'Work silver' was in lieu of the ploughing duties; 'neat rent' covered the money owed to the lord for the pasturage of cows on the commons.

In 1812 the Revd Charles Walters held land in Curdridge. He paid 9s. 8d. for the two lawdays (the courts leet), 7s. 2d. neat rent (the cows' pasturage), 2d. pannage (the use of the common), 2s. 6d. hundred silver (the labour service of reaping), 9s. worksilver (the days formerly spent ploughing). William Cobbett, copyholder of Fairthorn Farm, paid 7s. for the two lawdays, 5s. neat rent, 2d. pannage. There was also a charge for three bushels of wheat levied on the tithings of Woodcot and Ashton. In 1812 it was paid by Mr Trodd and Stephen Steele, both of Ashton. The amount was said to vary with the price of wheat but 'the Sum generally collected is £4 18 shillings'.[29]

Although contemporary reports describe the palace in 1644 as completely destroyed, this was not true. The manorial courts continued to be held there. In 1660 when episcopal property was restored, Bishop Duppa gave Thomas White the tenancy of Lodge Farm and the Gate House, with the condition that he must entertain the Bishop and his retinue in the Gate House. He must also provide for the Bishop's stewards when they came to hold the courts leet. White must feed them and their horses; the Bishop would reimburse him. At the same time the lease stated that 'the Gatehouse and all those Barnes Stables and Outhouses in the said Gatehouse Yard [the outer court] [were to be] discharged from all Tythes'.[30]

36   The *Crown Inn*, early 20th century.

More than a century later the courts were still held there. In 1770, when the palace grounds were let to the Trustees of the Poor, the lease gives 'the Lord Bishop free liberty for his Officers to keep Courts at the usual places within [these] … premises'.[31] And in 1785 Daniel Jonas's lease for the East Mill still stipulated that he must deliver 'at the pantry in the House of the Lord Bishop in Waltham … one Bushell of fine wheat to be well made and baked into half penny Bread' at Michaelmas and Hocktide,[32] for distribution at the courts leet. Eventually these courts were held at *The Crown*, where they remained until copyhold tenure was abolished in 1926.

In 1829 Bishop Charles Sumner appointed his son, while still a boy, to the office of Steward and Conductor of the Tenants, a sinecure worth £100 per annum: in the same year he made him woodward, a very lucrative post, since he licensed the felling of all trees on the episcopal estates, for which he received fees. When in 1856 the Bishop gave his son the offices of clerk and bailiff of many of the episcopal manors, including the manor of Bishop's Waltham, the manorial tenants wrote a letter of protest. They said 'in former times these offices were held by different persons who resided locally'; their duties were to take the surrender of lands held by copyhold or customary tenure and assess the heriots due. These offices had now become sinecures 'to the inconvenience of the copyhold tenants who are compelled to resort to the Steward resident in London'. They suggested that all these Patent Offices which were in the Bishop's gift should be vested in the Ecclesiastical Commissioners. They added that all the churchwardens were now summoned up to town to answer 'a useless set of questions called Presentments and have to pay fees or send them by post. The whole proceeding has become farcical'.[33] The Bishop's authority was questioned, but the manorial courts remained.

II

The Church

There had been a church in Bishop's Waltham even before 720 when it is recorded that St Willibald was educated in the monastery here before he left England, sailing down the Hamble river to join his uncle, St Boniface, as a missionary to Germany. This original church was possibly sited close to the palace.[1] It was probably a priory serving the whole of the Hamble valley, with chapels at Upham and Durley and perhaps Curdridge. The only artefacts from this time are part of a preaching cross, now to be seen in Winchester City Museum, and the ancient font rescued from a garden in Basingwell Street, then restored to the church.

That first church and the rest of the town were destroyed by the Danes in 1001. However by 1086 the church had been rebuilt, for Domesday Book records Ralph as the priest. At some time after Henri de Blois became Bishop (1129), he moved the church from close by the pond to its present site. He enlarged it,[2] designing the long chancel of St Peter's for ceremonial use.[3] No part of this building now remains; the earliest dates from about 1200[4] when Godfrey de Lucy, the architect of the retro-choir in Winchester Cathedral, was Bishop (1189-1204).

37 The Saxon font found in a garden in Basingwell Street and restored to the church in 1965.

38 The four sides of the Anglo-Saxon preaching cross, probably first sited at Northbrook Cross, then in St Peter's churchyard, now in Winchester City Museum.

Bishop Henri de Blois was a man of great wealth and culture, interested in art and architecture: another church which he rebuilt in Hampshire can be seen at East Meon. In 1135 he founded the magnificent Hospital of St Cross in Winchester, to house 13 elderly men and feed one hundred poor people daily. He endowed it with the income from 20 churches in his diocese,[5] giving his Hospital the right to appoint the rector of Bishop's Waltham.[6] This later reverted to the Bishop, but rectors continued to contribute to the income of St Cross into the 20th century.[7] Another part of this endowment was the manor of Ashton. At this time there were three churches in Bishop's Waltham: the parish church of St Peter, the chapel at the palace where masses would be said daily, and the chapel at Ashton.

In 1378, when the palace was being enlarged by William of Wykeham (1367-1404), probably at the same time the chancel of St Peter's was extended and the small south door built into it. Here the Bishop installed a richly decorated piscina and sedilia, signing his work over the east window with the rose which was his badge. He also added the south porch to St Peter's.[8]

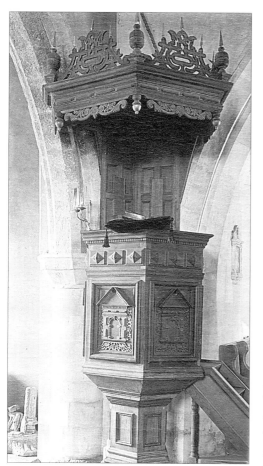

39 The pulpit presented to St Peter's in 1626 by Bishop Lancelot Andrewes.

Lancelot Andrewes, Bishop fom 1619 to 1626, gave the church its handsome pulpit in 1626, the year he died. Three years earlier he had appointed as rector his tutor, Robert Ward. He had served on the committee which produced the authorised version of the Bible.

The Ashton aisle, the north aisle, was rebuilt when Benjamin Lang was Rector in 1637; James Simes, Richard Sewat, Cuthbert Rimes, Nicholas Lambard were the churchwardens.[9] This aisle used building material from Ashton chapel which probably came to St Peter's in the following way. In 1556 John White (1556-59) had been appointed Bishop of Winchester by Mary Tudor. He was to be the last Roman Catholic bishop before the Act of Supremacy restored Protestantism to the English church in 1559. In 1557 he appointed a Robert Raynolds as Master of St Cross.

Raynolds was intent on increasing his personal fortune. He leased the bakehouse, brewhouse, gardens and orchards of St Cross to a Ralph Cleverley, in return for secret payments to himself. He went further, and sold the mansion at Ashton using the official seal of St Cross to validate the purchase.[10] This mansion can only have been the manor house with its chapel where the Masters of St Cross lived when they visited their manor. Probably the mansion was demolished and the building materials sold. The chapel was no doubt left to become derelict. Therefore in 1637 the stone and the stone tiles and the glass from it, were carried to St Peter's to rebuild the Ashton aisle.[11] The monuments were also brought. They included the memorial to Thomas Ashton who died in 1629, which can be seen built high up in this north aisle.

Despite the loss of his house and chapel, the Master of St Cross remained lord of the manor of Ashton. His steward continued to hold the manorial courts, certainly until 1785 when James Randell was steward. Ashton chapel is recalled in field names: eight acres are called 'Priest Crofts'.[12] On the tithe map 208 is chapel homestead, 210 is chapel field, 343 is coffin close.[13]

Five years after the Ashton aisle was rebuilt the Civil Wars began. Joseph Goulson became Rector of Bishop's Waltham in 1642, the year the first Civil War broke out. Parliament forebade the use of the Prayer Book and dispossessed many Anglican clergy, replacing them with presbyters. It set up committees to administer the different counties. In Hampshire 72 out of the 253 livings were sequestered.[14] In 1643 Joseph Goulson travelled to the King's court at Oxford where he was made a Doctor of Divinity.[15] In 1644 the palace was destroyed; the Bishop, Walter Curle (1632-47), fled, reputedly hidden under a pile of dung, to Soberton where he was lord of the manor. The County Committee allowed him to rent back his own property for £60 a year.[16] Here he died in 1647. What had happened to the Rector, Joseph Goulson?

In 1646 the Rector's name came before the Committee of Plundered Ministers: he was probably fined. He was luckier than others. Philip Goddard, the curate of Durley and Upham, in 1644 was imprisoned in Southampton for baptising with the sign of the cross. He was released, specifically to take the next Sunday service. His Rector, Myrth Wayferer, then ordered him to return to prison. He did not, but fled to Berkshire. Wayferer himself, the Rector of Upham, was ejected from his living. He fled to Kent, where in 1656 he became chaplain to Sir Norton Knatchbull.[17]

Joseph Goulson may well have been absent from Bishop's Waltham during 1644 and part of 1645, for three babies were then buried unbaptised, but after 1645 he was living in the town; that year he buried one of his own children. Between 1645 and 1655 nine children were born to him. In 1650 he officiated at the marriage of a relative, Elizabeth Goulson.[18] He paid a poor rate in the parish from 1650 and in 1656 he was given a receipt by the parish officers for a donation of £5 to the poor rates from James Rieley.[19]

In 1645 Parliament had ordered the Calvinist Directory of Public Worship to be substituted for the Prayer Book. However, many clergy did not use it. Joseph Goulson was probably one of these. He may even have imitated the Hampshire parson who ended the Te Deum with the verse, 'O Lord in Thee have I trusted, let me never be a Roundhead [confounded]'.

In 1648 Dr Goulson journeyed to the Isle of Wight where the King was living at Carisbrooke Castle. Here he preached a sermon before Charles I in the town of Newport[20] where there was a last attempt at reconciliation between King and Parliament. It was unsuccessful.

Dr Goulson could never have survived as the Rector without the collusion of Robert Reynolds, the Parliamentary lawyer, who bought the manor in September

40 St Peter's bells, restored in 1969. The tenor bell dates from 1597, the seventh from 1599, the sixth and fifth 1651, the fourth 1712, the third (given by Richard Norton of Southwick) in 1724, the treble and second in 1937.

1647. Reynolds himself was not a fanatic; indeed, he was in an ambivalent position, having married as his second wife, Priscilla, the daughter of the Royalist, Sir Hugh Windham, of Pillesdon, Dorset. Sir Hugh had spent £30,000 in support of the King.[21] In 1650 Robert Reynolds' daughter was baptised Priscilla at St Peter's by the Rector.[22] In 1655 Oliver Cromwell dissolved Parliament. He divided the country into military districts, each under a major-general who imposed authoritarian government. Dr Goulson's name came up before them but he was not ejected from his living, survived the Commonwealth, and in 1688 was appointed Dean of Chichester.

It is much to the Rector's credit that improvements were made to the church at this time. In 1651 when Robert Barfote, John Woodman, John Brasset and Henry Baker were the churchwardens, two bells were added to the peal. Cast by William Purdue, they were possibly made with bell metal from the palace. The following year the south aisle was rebuilt, the Rector and churchwardens seizing the opportunity which the ruined palace presented as a quarry for stone; they also salvaged the clock said to be an original 14th-century example from the palace.[23]

Attendance at church since the Reformation had entailed the Prayer Book Service with hour-long homilies or sermons, after which parish notices were given out. The church was the centre of the community, poor relief was administered from it, and the vestry made many of the decisions of importance to the town, so in the 18th century, as the town grew, more seating was required.

In 1733 William Horner, weaver, Peter Newlyn, John Nash, Richard Biggs, tanner, Harry Willis, miller, sought permission from Bishop Richard Willis (1723-34) to erect a gallery at the west end at their own cost 'to have seat room in the

Church there to sitt together to sing Psalms'.[24] Each of their houses would own a pew but there would be three pews for the singers: these are the pews in the gallery today without locks. Within a year William Horner had acquired a 'Father Smith' organ. Bernard Smith, who had been born in Germany, was a celebrated organ builder. He was also the organist of St Margaret's, Westminster. His organs were known for their lightness of tone. The organist was Ezekiel Donniger, the first of a family which was to provide three generations of organists.

By the end of the century yet more seating was required. In 1797 another petition to Bishop the Hon. Brownlow North (1781-1820) from 30 parishioners complained that they and their families could not attend 'Divine Service without entering the Pews … of other inhabitants … and infringing on their rights and Properties of sitting, standing and Kneeling … putting such inhabitants to great inconvenience'. These petitioners were a cross-section of the town: Daniel Jonas, miller, Ezekiel Donniger, organist and postmaster, Elizabeth Martin, ironmonger, James Munville, gentleman, Jemima Jones, schoolmistress, the Rev Charles Walters, curate and headmaster of

41   The Revd Henry Aubrey Veck, Curate in 1842, standing beside the Father Smith organ, reputedly brought from Southwick House in 1734 by William Horner, weaver. Ezekiel Donniger was the first organist. His father published the first Bishop's Waltham hymn book in 1812.

the Grammar School, John Purchase, maltster, William Budd, plumber and glazier, Thomas Colpas, joiner and carpenter. His pew was for the use of his house ' now in the occupation of the … Parish and used as a Workhouse'.[25]

But although the seating was being improved, the churchyard had been in a poor state. In 1770 all the inhabitants of the town had been presented before the court baron because they allowed their pigs 'to run about the … Town and … daily and hourly get into the churchyard and snuffle off the turf etc from the Graves in a most abominable … Manner notwithstanding the care … of the Clerk who makes up the Graves in a very decent and genteel Manner'.[26] The clerk was Richard Cole, schoolmaster, but the rector, James Cutler, resided at Droxford, his other living.

The musical aspect of the church services continued to be important. The organ was rebuilt in the 19th century when Henry Aubrey Veck, draper, published a book of anthems. Dedicated to the 'very Respectable Inhabitants of Bishop's Waltham', it would enable them to follow the anthems more easily.[27] It included a selection from Handel's *Messiah* and Psalm 132 set to music by the organist, Ezekiel Donniger, himself.

There was fierce opposition in 1816 to a change in the weekday services proposed by the Rector, James Ogle. He was influenced by the Evangelicals who emphasised personal conversion and salvation by faith, with a stress on the verbal inspiration of the Bible, and the importance of preaching. The Rector wished to

42   St Peter's after the 'gothicisation' of the south aisle gallery by William Brock, the Rector in 1868.

substitute a sermon on Sunday afternoons for the weekly prayers said on Wednes-days and Fridays. The vestry was outraged. Prayers on these two days had been customary since time immemorial, and 'it would be highly improper that any opportunity for prayer should be taken from the said inhabitants'. They threatened to petition the Lord Chancellor and the Bishop, but the Rector, sup-ported by a majority of the vestrymen, one of whom was William Cobbett, managed to avoid this.[28]

The 19th century saw the emphasis on the church fabric. The south gallery was never satisfactory. In 1822 it was declared unsafe and the Rector was voted £30 to prop it up with pillars. Six years later two new pews were installed; not attached to any house, they were to be the property of the parish.[29]

James Ogle died in 1832. The following year William Brock was appointed Rector at 29, a position he held until he died aged eighty-six. Within three years he was reprimanded for extravagance. He had ordered new trimmings for the pulpit at a cost of £17 13s. 6d. (£10 of which he himself had contributed), so the following January vestry decreed that the strictest economy must be shown; no considerable expense should in future be undertaken without its consent. A second-hand broom was purchased. However, water through the roof was not to be tolerated. One shilling was paid to keep this out of church and the following year rain spouts were added to the tower for £1 1s. 6d.[30]

It is easy to understand vestry's concern: by custom the nave was repaired by the parishioners who paid a compulsory church rate. They did not want any unnecessary expense. The chancel, however, was the rector's responsibility – repairs there must be paid for by him.

When the clock was brought from the palace it had no doubt been put in working order. But over the years it had obviously been neglected, for in 1836 the belfry floor was dug up to find the clock weights and then the clock was repaired

43 St Peter's in 1897 before T.J. Jackson's restoration.

by Padbury for £2 19s. 6d. In 1873 its escapement was converted by James Padbury. He gave it a pendulum of more than six cwt.,[31] the third heaviest in the world, which can still be seen in the belfry.

The Rector, William Brock, continued to make changes. In 1844 the 'Father Smith' organ was disposed of in favour of a new one. In 1873 this too was sold and another organ, made by Messrs Corps, was installed. The Rector was convinced that the best place for it would be between the second and third windows of the north aisle. Dr Arnold, the organist of Winchester Cathedral, was brought in to advise. He said the best place would be at the top of the north aisle; failing that, the best place was where the Rector wanted it to be: there it was installed. However, within two years the damp had affected it so disastrously that the bellows were falling to pieces. The Rector had made other improvements. In 1849 the west wall was found to be dangerous. It was repaired and the large window installed there above the west gallery. The following year the Rector removed the old reading desk and the clerk's pew. Parishioners were obviously furious at these changes made without their consultation. They requested a special vestry at which the Rector gave up the chair to Colonel Saunderson. Vestry then resolved that the height of the new reading desk should be raised, and the clerk's pew replaced, and the bequests and charities written up on boards for all to see.[32]

William Brock was low church. He thought that church buildings must be kept unadorned and as simple as possible. Since he himself was responsible for the chancel, in 1868, he straightway removed the elegant piscina with its carved canopy and shelf which Bishop William of Wykeham had installed.[33] This was the beginning of a major restoration. The whole body of the church was to be re-pewed to present a uniform appearance: the three windows in the south gallery were to be gothicised, for the Gothic style of architecture was thought to be more conducive to holiness: the pillars, which had been put in to support the roof of the gallery, were to be taken out. The ceiling of the nave was to be removed to display the rafters.[34] This was all put in hand just as Parliament decided that it was unfair for non-conformists, who were supporting their own chapels and schools, also to pay church rates. These were abolished. The church was now entirely dependent on voluntary contributions. But the Rector continued his reordering regardless. In 1873 he replaced the reading desk again and installed more pews. These expensive alterations did not make him popular. James Padbury, clockmaker, voiced his concerns in a letter to vestry. He said that alterations in church were made 'only to suit the whim or fancy of the moment'. Other parishioners obviously agreed, for when in 1874 the Rector nominated as his churchwarden first, J. Richardson, then James Lock, then William Renny, each in turn declined to serve.[35]

The Reverend William Brock died in 1891. He had been incumbent for 58 years. He had moved here from Highclere. In 1835 he reckoned the living was worth £940, but he wrote he had many calls on his purse: £100 to the curate of Curdridge, £220 to the poor rates, 'soups during the winter months, broth etc for the sick … help under losses, missionary bills, tracts, subscriptions to new churches in the neighbourhood'. That year he also subscribed £817 to the National School and wrote that 'the rich rector of Bishop's Waltham' would be expected to pay the newly appointed schoolmaster. During his time the Congregational Chapel was built, with its school in Newtown. William Brock saw the

44   The re-ordered interior of St Peter's in 1975.

need for improvements within the parish, for good roads, for modern drainage, but his manner was autocratic and he failed to carry the vestrymen with him.

Two years after he died the Parish Councils Act removed the civil duties from vestry, which from then on dealt with purely ecclesiastical matters. It continued to work for the good of the parishioners and its decisions were published in the parish magazine. Coal and clothing clubs continued to be subscribed to at the Rectory; the parish layette loaned to expectant mothers must be returned there. In 1900 a parish nurse, paid from charity funds, was engaged 'to attend free of charge cases of sickness in the families of the working class'.[36]

James Palmer Nash succeeded William Brock as the rector in 1892. Four years later the church was again in urgent need of restoration if the roofs were to be saved. The architect, T.J. Jackson, wrote: 'the walls [are] … built on the top of the clay soil without any footings … the ground on the inside has been actually sunk lower than the foundations to form jointed floors with an air space below … the walls have settled and cracked in several places'.[37] There were no longer church rates available so when the Bishop, Randall Davidson (1895-1903), later the noted Archbishop of Canterbury, granted a faculty, he made the proviso that no building work, even the restoration of the south arcade, be undertaken until the rector and churchwardens were sure 'that the necessary funds are provided'. The south gallery had to be entirely removed with a consequent loss of sittings. These were compensated for by putting the schoolchildren in the west gallery over the vestry, and making 34 places available for the choir in the chancel, the first time it had been used for this purpose.

The 20th century saw the east end of the south aisle screened off to create a clergy vestry, the use of the tower to spot enemy aircraft during the Second World War, the removal of the Victorian reredos from the east end of the chancel, and yet more re-ordering of the church to accommodate different forms of worship.

12

Welfare in Bishop's Waltham

We think of welfare as a 20th-century invention: in fact, welfare had been provided freely for centuries. At first it was the task of the monasteries and the great ecclesiastical households to care for the poor, but when the monasteries were swept away by King Henry VIII, the problems of the poor, the needy, the aged and the sick were made apparent, and a system of relief was devised.

The manorial courts had always fulfilled the functions of administration within the manor, but the Tudors, by Act of Parliament, created a system which imposed duties not on the manorial courts, but on the individual parishes. In 1536 a poor law was enacted which reminded parishioners during worship in church of their obligations to their poorer neighbours. They were urged to give alms, but this voluntary system produced insufficient money. A system which worked effectively was devised in Elizabeth I's reign.

In 1601 the Elizabethan Poor Law Act compelled parishioners to pay a poor rate, a local tax which was collected by voluntary overseers, who were drawn in turn at the Easter vestry from an existing list. Their appointments were certified by a magistrate and lasted for a year.

The vestry meeting, so called because it took place in the vestry room of the church, was the place where the needs of the parishioners were discussed. The money collected, the poor rate, was given in church on Sundays to those in need, generally fortnightly. Those too ill to attend were helped in their own homes. Strict account was kept of the relief given. Each of the four tithings in the parish – Waltham, Hoe, Ashton, Curdridge – had its own parish officers, a churchwarden and an overseer. From 1633 to 1720 a list of churchwardens, overseers and, intermittently, surveyors of the highways is recorded in the poor rate book, with the list of churchwardens and overseers continuing for another 19 years.[1]

In Bishop's Waltham it was not the dissolution of the monasteries that created the need for the poor rate, but the destruction of the bishop's palace. Here the poor had been fed. In 1259-60, when Bishop Aylmer de Valence (1250-61) was in fact on a journey to the Pope in Rome, 60 tenants in the manor received 'a farthing worth of bread for 90 days'.[2]

The town had grown round the palace to serve the bishops. They were the lords of the manor from whom the townspeople held their land, in return for customary labour services. Some shared a common surname, Veck, from 'l'eveque', meaning 'servant to the bishop'. The name is still known in Bishop's Waltham today. The palace was destroyed in 1644, the Bishop fled; the town had to manage for itself.

Within three years of the destruction of the palace, in 1647, we find a record of a poor rate of £24 9s. 3d. being collected. In 1658 the rate book shows £13 17s. 10d.

45   St George's Square in 1840 with the Market House, built possibly in 1658. The bottom storey housed the cages for prisoners; later the fire engine was also kept here. A girls school was begun in the upper floor by the Rector, James Ogle, in 1816. Courtesy: Bishop's Waltham Museum Trust.

of rate money being used to erect a building. No other money belonging to the parish was available for this purpose. It was spent on lime and sand, tiles, tile pins, slats and boards.[3] This was probably the market house (demolished in 1841) but built with outside staircase; beneath it were the cages in which petty criminals were confined, since the bishop's prison was no longer available. Nearby were the whipping post and stocks. In the next century the town required two more buildings, a workhouse and an isolation hospital, the Pest House.

In 1662 a further Poor Law Act made the parish a self-contained unit; anyone coming into a parish might be removed from it by order of the magistrate, unless he rented a property worth £10 or found someone to stand security for him. If his stay was temporary he must produce a certificate from the parish to which he actually belonged. A wife belonged to her husband's parish: a servant, to gain a settlement, must serve for a whole year; apprenticeship was a qualification. If a person fulfilled any of these conditions, then fell into poverty, his parish was legally obliged to support him. It was in the parishioners' interests to make sure that the poor rate was used wisely. Generally it was collected quarterly, but, if times were hard, it could be collected six or even eight times a year.

46   This trade token shows how prosperous Bishop's Waltham had become by 1666. Thomas Penford, grocer, produced his own half penny token which was accepted in the town. Small change was in short supply so these tokens took its place. The reverse shows the Mercers' Arms. Courtesy: Bishop's Waltham Museum Trust.

13

The Parish Officers

The churchwardens and overseers of the four tithings were drawn from many occupations but certain surnames recur; Cleverleys were overseers in 1633, 1634 and 1640. In the next century a John Cleverley was overseer in 1724, church-warden in 1726.[1] Three John Cleverleys were then living in the town, one a maltster, another an apothecary. The third John Cleverley, gentleman, had been appointed gamekeeper[2] by Bishop Charles Trimnell (1721-3) at a time when the Waltham Blacks were overrunning Waltham Chase. Joanna Cleverley, one of two women overseers, served in 1705; the other, Mary Harmsworth, overseer for Curdridge in 1726, was most competent, for she insisted on being given receipts for the relief money she paid out.[3] The overseers too came from many occupa-tions: Thomas Trod (1734) was a brickmaker; Thomas Dipnall (1736) a farmer, John Fox (1737) a tanner, Luke Kent (1738) an innkeeper, Henry Willis (1739) a miller.[4] All were tradesmen or farmers for, as the Rector, John Cooke, informed the Bishop in 1725, 'There is not any Nobleman or Gentleman of Note or Distinction that lives in the Parish'.

The overseers' accounts, kept since 1665, were regularly scrutinised by vestry. That year there had been floods so one shilling was allowed 'for drying Goody Goods grane and her mill'. In 1676 the accounts were signed by three magistrates.[5] They were complicated, because a rate collected in one tithing might frequently be spent in another; generally more was used in Bishop's Waltham tithing, where there were more people living, so the need was greater.

A further complication was that the parish officer might also be the tradesman who supplied goods to the workhouse. In May 1762 Jonas the miller supplied flour, so his poor rate of £2 6s. was set off against his bill. But the accounts were well scrutinised even in the desperate smallpox epidemic of 1774. When Christmas Hewitt, joiner, presented a bill for 'Wood Coffins & Milk' the overseer, Mr Cooke, noticed an overcharge of seven shillings, the cost of a child's coffin. He himself had already paid this bill. It was the coffin of his own apprentice, Rebecca Norris.[6] The overseers could excuse a parishioner, whom they considered too poor, from paying poor rates; in 1723 unpaid rate amounted to £1 3s. 4d.; Job Allingham, Yalden, Henry Suatt and Richard Wilkins had all been excused.[7]

The parish depended on the constables to keep the peace. Each tithing had a constable together with a deputy – a tithingman – who was appointed at the manorial court. There were stocks in Waltham and Ashton tithings.[8] Here petty criminals could be punished but serious offences required an indictment from the magistrate. The litigant then asked the constable to pursue the accused; tithing-man and passers-by might be called upon to help: the hue and cry. Anyone who captured a horse thief was excused by Parliament from serving a parish office. In

1761 Daniel Jonas was excused when he seized William Light who had stolen his brown gelding.[9]

Constables must watch out for vagrants entering the town for they might bring infection with them. When Whitear, constable in 1761, found 'a travelling Woman in Distress in Mr Jonas's barn' he was allowed 13s. 9d. for her expenses.[10] Constables took the vagrants by cart to the next parish. Mr Mears, constable in 1766, attended the petty sessions at *The Crown*, where Mary Rood's examination on bastardy charges took three days, for which he was allowed ten shillings. Her case was transferred to Fareham where he together with the parish officers attended at a cost of £1 5s. 3d. In the same year, when it was discovered that William Woodhatch had systematically been stealing from the workhouse, he was imprisoned in the Cage, the prison beneath the market house. Although he was fettered he twice escaped. In August he was tried in Winchester and imprisoned there, his keep paid from the poor rate. When he returned, William Cursell earned one shilling for watching over him that night. Later he was placed in William Aylen's charge. Aylen received eight shillings for keeping Woodhatch for four weeks 'at 2 shillings a week'.[11]

Another of the constable's duties was to carry out the sentences passed at Quarter Sessions. In 1770 Grace Sparrow, convicted of felony, was ordered to be whipped in the open market on Friday, 8 May.[12] The next day the overseers allowed her relief of £1 5s. 9d. and a pair of shoes.[13] The public flogging of females was abolished in 1817.

During the Napoleonic Wars men were needed for the navy, so the tithingmen were allowed four shillings a day to raise recruits. Daniel Baker was constable in 1801 when he took the first census in the parish for which he received £5. From 1811 to 1815, as constable, he received a monthly allowance of ten shillings from the poor rates. In 1815 he was responsible for seven prisoners-of-war, four held at *The Vine*, three at *The White Hart*.[14] The following year he was appointed High Constable. In this capacity he collected the county rates, used for the repair of county prisons and bridges, and for allowances to the families of militiamen, from Bishop's Waltham hundred. For two years he failed to pay over this money: he was arrested for a debt of more than £200, and imprisoned. He petitioned vestry to pay his debt and secure his release, but they refused.[15] They had earlier paid a doctor's bill at the birth of his daughter, and funeral expenses at the burial of his wife and son.[16] They considered they had done enough.

The constable must also deal with outbreaks of fire. He was responsible for calling out the voluntary firemen, the Watch. In 1722, 19 shillings was paid to Ben Matthews, constable, in reimbursement for money he had paid out to the Watch when they dealt with a fire at Barton,[17] possibly the site of Northbrook House. Parliament had ordered parishes to provide fire engines in 1706: 50 years later the parish had one which needed repairing.[18] In 1825 William Pink received two shillings for 'working the engine' and, as town crier, he called out the firemen; on 5 November 1828 he cried 'against fireworks' and in 1825 ordered dogs to be confined.[19] By 1868 the parish possessed two fire engines requiring £7 in repairs to the pipes, an expense which vestry allowed. But it refused to allow the installation of ten fire hydrants in the town, for the laying of pipes to them would require the road to be broken up, and incur too much expense in remaking it. In 1891 the first fire brigade was established.[20] Firemen were summoned from their occupations by bugle call; sounded across the pond it carried further round the town.

In 1864 vestry appointed seven lighting and watching inspectors who could raise a lighting rate of £100, so gas light came to the town. The assistant overseer, who in 1836 had been collecting the poor and highway rates, by 1863 was also collecting the lighting and church rates. In 1882 he was required 'to attend at his Office In Bishop's Waltham not less than two days a week'.[21]

In 1842 vestry adopted the Parish Constables Act. This allowed householders with property rated at £4 or more to be special constables, the origin of that office. Twelve were appointed at a salary to be agreed by vestry, but after 1872, when vestry still could not agree a salary,[22] these appointments lapsed. As early as 1839 the Hampshire County Police Act, providing a paid constabulary, had been passed. By 1850 the parish had a police house occupied by P.C. Wedge, and a county court, the property of the Rev. H.A. Veck.

I4

The Welfare System

The poor rate provided subsistence to those who fell on hard times, but, in order to receive this after 1662, a family must provide evidence of settlement in their parish. If they moved away in search of work it was vital to procure a certificate from the parish officers, to prove that they belonged to the parish, which then guaranteed to receive them back should they become destitute. It was only from their own parish that they were entitled to poor relief.

In an age when few could read and write, people could be unsure where their settlement was: parish officers fought vigorously against taking charge of anyone they considered belonged elsewhere. Settlement cases were resolved in the courts as Betty Brown's case was. In 1758 she must have gone to live in Alverstoke with her illegitimate child, James, who had been baptised in Bishop's Waltham.[1] A law suit was fought with the Alverstoke officers which cost £7 0s. 5d.[2] They won; Betty returned to Bishop's Waltham. Here she was allowed money, a gown, ointment and clothes, and shoes and stockings for James. She married in 1765 but before long her husband, Thomas Frankham, was living in the workhouse. He was encouraged to leave it, being given shoes and money. He immediately deserted Betty. The parish officers pursued him, brought him back and found him work digging a ditch round the Pest House garden.[3]

Society was based on the principle that those who produced children must support them – hence the parish marriage. If a single woman was pregnant, she must go to the parish officers and swear before a magistrate who the father of her child was. He was then seized and the marriage took place. This happened in 1723 with Disney Tasker.[4] This case was straightforward, others were not. The following year Thomas Saunders had to be brought back under warrant from Stubbington and was lodged and guarded in *The Dolphin* for the night, before his marriage to Sarah Barefoot, which cost the poor rates £7 19s. 6d. One way to escape a parish marriage was to volunteer as a soldier. William Weavil chose this course when prosecuted as the father of Mary Rood's child in 1767.[5]

Parson Woodforde living in Norfolk recorded his thoughts in his diary after taking such a marriage. He wrote: 'it is a cruel thing that any man should be compelled by law to marry. ... The Man was a long time before he could be prevailed on to marry ... and at the Altar behaved very unbecoming'.[6] But Parson Woodforde wrote as a well-fed bachelor, not as a destitute woman with child.

Marriage could not be the solution when the father of the bastard was already married. In these cases the father paid an allowance for the child to the parish officers. Martha Jennings and Grace Knight had each already borne one such child when again they appear in the overseers' accounts. In 1785 the father of Martha's child is unrecorded, but presumably of some standing for a jury was empannelled and messengers directed to Winchester and Southwick; both a mid-wife and a doctor attended, but the child died. However James, born to Grace Knight in 1784, survived. He was the natural son of Rear-Admiral Sir Chaloner Ogle, later Admiral of the Blue. For four years James lived in Ashton tithing with his mother, on an allowance of £4 2s. 6d. a year, paid to the overseers by his father.[7] In 1788 James was probably baptised, for certainly a James was baptised that year, the names of his parents unrecorded.[8] He then left the parish, probably to attend school as a first step towards a naval career. He is not mentioned in Sir Chaloner's will, but interestingly the Admiral's legitimate son, also James,[9] became the Rector of Bishop's Waltham in 1802.

Children who were orphaned became the parish's responsibility. Mrs Pen died in 1665, so cotton and woollen clothes were provided for her son; his wet nurse earned a shilling a week.[10] Both Goody Taylor and Goody Fisher looked after Mrs Jackson's child when she died in childbirth in 1722. Seven shillings a month was allowed Mary Bassett in 1726, when she took in her orphan sister, Mary Colpas. The overseers supplied the child with clothing, shoes and stockings and a coat and aprons and a cap and handkerchiefs.[11]

If the child was old enough he would be sent to earn his living either as a servant or as an apprentice. When the Widow Fisher died in 1722, her daughter Ann was ten. She went to live with Mr Hollis the miller, who was given one shilling a week as child allowance. When she was 12 she was apprenticed to Robert Wateridge.[12] The indentures signed at apprenticeship were critical, for, if wrongly drawn, the master could be released from his bargain. This happened when Hannah Heath, aged ten, was apprenticed in 1766 to Thomas Cook. The parish officers had supplied her with clothes and shoes, a buckle and a ribbon.[13] Thomas Cook appealed against this imposition at Quarter Sessions.[14] He won his case, so at 16 Hannah was apprenticed to Captain Burdon, who was then responsible for her until she was twenty-one or married.

William Heatrell could prove his settlement in Bishop's Waltham, having ridden back to the town from Lewes, where he was working, specifically to secure a certificate from the parish officers. He became ill and died. The Bishop's Waltham officers paid for his nursing expenses and funeral, paid his widow's rent and allowed her 2s. 6d. a week. But in 1775 the family were evidently settled at Lewes, so the Bishop's Waltham officers paid £22 19s. 1d. to the officers at Lewes, probably a one-off payment to cover their future care.[15]

Regular payments were made to those in need. In 1725 the rector, John Cooke, estimated the population at 1,400 souls; of these 27 were receiving relief. In 1723 the widow Barling had been assigned four shillings monthly for life; but the widow Beconsale was given a lump sum of 11 shillings on condition that she asked for no further help[16] from the rates. Later Ursula Edwards, an inadequate young woman, was given material for clothing with one shilling for making it up. The overseers had arranged for her spinning wheel to be mended, but despite this she was unable to maintain herself. She was in and out of the workhouse. In 1768 the overseers came to an arrangement with her father, Thomas, a grinder, allowing him £7 13s. on condition that Ursula should never again ask for help.[17]

It was not just inadequacy but continuous ill-health which the parish officers must address. Charles and Mary Lucas lived in Ashton tithing with their seven children. Charles had an attack of smallpox from which he never fully recovered. The Lucas family were intermittently supported from the rates for 38 years. Their house was repaired three times. It was rethatched. The family was supplied with money, wheat, clothing; payments were made for doctors' bills and apprenticeship fees. When Charles died in 1793 he was in receipt of 12 shillings a month; afterwards his widow received six shillings.[18]

15

The Health Service

One of the most pressing needs was help in times of illness. The details of sickness within the parish and the remedies ordered were carefully recorded in the poor rate accounts. This was no open-ended health service, for the overseers were always aware that the poor rate was finite; it came from their own and their neighbours' pockets. In 1665 Mr Newby, the doctor, was paid 12 shillings for setting Bullock's leg, and 30 shillings for his six weeks nursing care.[1] But when he and another doctor, Mr Uptiman, presented bills for £23 for their attendance on the poor, vestry considered this too much. It decided that in the future it must approve the cases which were to receive treatment. This continued to be the practice until 1716 when the poor 'fit to be treated' were to be attended exclusively by Mr William Eustace. Two years later, after the magistrates annulled this ruling, vestry decided that the poor were to be sent to Mr Robert Parkin, surgeon and apothecary.[2]

All the different ways of curing people were explored. In 1763 a quack-doctor received a guinea for curing Widow Norris's son's hare-lip. Mrs Bastard was paid to cure the ague[3] but later ague-drops were ordered; they were cheaper. Robert Pike treated the outbreak of scalp disease among the children.[4] In 1773 Harris, the lame boy, was bought a bandage and bread for a poultice,[5] and 14 years later a spring and shoes to help him to walk.

Illness made extra demands on household budgets so the overseers paid attendance allowances. In 1725 Goody Jennings received a shilling a week for looking after her sister, Mrs Yalden, but when Mr Yalden took on this task he was allowed three shillings a week. The Widow Pritchard was given six shillings to help her 'Crooked Daughter'.[6]

Childbirth was another expensive time. Although Hannah Edwards received six shillings for nursing Goody Ham during her fortnight's lying-in,[7] the standard fee was five shillings. Mrs Goodeve, attending a delivery in the workhouse, was allowed an extra two shillings for expenses. The doctor, Mr Goodwin, received more: two guineas for three deliveries.[8] Midwives must be licensed by the bishop. Hannah Skinner had already been delivering babies for 26 years when she became officially licensed in 1705 at Quarter Sessions. She continued as a midwife until her death in 1732, a career spanning more than fifty years.

The limitations of home nursing were obvious, so during the 18th century hospitals or infirmaries, as they were generally called, began to be founded outside London. Winchester was among the first in 1736. The Revd James Cutler, who became the Rector of Bishop's Waltham in 1754, was one of these foundation subscribers. The founders declared that 'in obedience to the Rules of our Holy Religion ... [because] many suffer extremely and are Sometimes lost for want of Accommodation and Proper Medicines ... by Ignorance or Ill-Management' of the poor relief given them, 'desiring to find some Remedy for ... this great Misery ... [we] subscribe ... for an Infirmary [for] ... ye Poor Sick'.[9]

In 1746 James Cutler became Rector of Droxford. In 1754 he was given the living of Bishop's Waltham as well, but he preferred to reside in his rectory at Droxford. This made for difficulties for the sick of Bishop's Waltham: as admission to the Infirmary was on the recommendation of a subscriber, the overseers had to ride over for this to Droxford. Within a year a proxy had been arranged. John Jennings, schoolmaster, wrote these recommendations at sixpence a time, so the journey was saved.

Patients admitted to the hospital generally died there. In 1767 William Mitchell, given a new shirt to go to the hospital, died there. But by the 1770s the Infirmary was proving successful. In 1772 Jane Kervill, provided with stays, a hat, a cap, stockings, two aprons and a petticoat, was admitted in the spring and returned home in the autumn.[10] In 1785 Fanny Kent, after a month's stay, came back by coach.[11] Fanny had earlier been treated for lunacy in the parish.

The lunatics were kept by Dr Beech; in 1757 Fanny had been one of his patients when the overseers paid £8 1s. 0d. for her treatment.[12] In 1789 he was charging 10s. 6d. a week for keeping Ursula Whitehead.[13] But two years earlier Jo Bottom had been taken violently ill. Restrained in the workhouse by a strait-jacket and six paid attendants (who were allowed workhouse food free of charge), he was finally admitted to the Bethlehem hospital in London. His wife went up to make the arrangements and pay the admission fee of £3 5s. Jo and his wife made the journey together. Jo's lunacy cost the poor rates over £20.[14] William White, however, lived in Alresford with his deranged sister, but since he came from Bishop's Waltham, for nine years the overseers paid him 1s. 6d. a week for his sister's care.[15]

16

The Pest House

The Pest House was an isolation hospital built in 1742 when it was recognised that isolating cases of smallpox stopped the disease spreading. Isolation had been practised earlier in 1724 when two of the parish officers were Dr Cleverley and Dr Penford. They took advice from Sam Chandler, an attorney of Portsmouth. Until this time those taken ill with smallpox had stayed in their own homes, supplied with nursing care, food and beer, or fuel and malt for brewing, from the poor rates.

But when in April 1724 smallpox broke out again, those with the disease were taken by cart to Waltham Chase, where they were nursed by Mary Bassett in her own house through the summer. 'Bread Cheese Meat butter and other Necessarys' were regularly taken down for 'the Wid(ow) Sparrow and the sev'all others in the small pox'. Good nursing proved successful. In October one shilling was paid 'Mr John Reeves for going with the cart & fetching home ye small pox people'. The patients returned cured, but this illness had cost £16 out of a total rate of £249, so the parish took out insurance against further outbreaks. Three years later, in

47   The Pest House, built on Waltham Chase in 1742 as an isolation hospital for smallpox victims. Possibly the poor house which the vestry planned to build on in 1808 is the jutting out piece at the back. It became redundant after the Union Workhouse system was introduced and it was sold in 1842.

1726, fearful of another epidemic, the parish officers bribed some 'Travellers who had the small pox' with 2s. 6d. 'to pass through the town without begging'.[1]

In 1740 the disease struck again; 54 people died.[2] The parish officers, remembering Mary Bassett's successful nursing, determined to build their own isolation hospital, the Pest House. It was erected in 1742 in Waltham Chase on the land belonging to the Bishop. Benjamin Hoadley (1734-61) granted both permission and timber for it. A master and mistress were employed to nurse the smallpox cases.

Unfortunately for the parish they decided to make their own rules, refusing in 1755 to admit patients without an entry fee. This dispute was resolved by Bishop Benjamin Hoadley at the court baron when he appointed the rector, the curate and the parish officers as trustees for the Pest House.

Later, this sensible precaution of isolating smallpox cases in the Pest House was not strictly enforced. The infectious were allowed to remain in their own homes, or in the workhouse, with the result that the disease appeared in one tithing after another, with tragic results. Alcohol deadened the pain and was supplied through the poor rates.

From 1766-69 William Ledwell, who had previously been the workhouse master and 'professional' overseer, became master of the Pest House. Here he nursed Mary and Martha Bilsoe and Hannah Levelle. But in 1769 he was reappointed by the parish officers to his former position, so was no longer in immediate charge of the Pest House.[3]

The Pest House could probably not have accommodated all those who fell ill in the epidemic of 1773. The matron, Widow Light, was nursing seven patients. She was allowed extra nursing staff, another bed, borrowed from Dr Penford, her wages were raised and luxuries such as tea were sent in. There were others suffering from the disease in Hoe tithing. Food and wine were allowed them, but the poor rate went uncollected for fear of infection. Smallpox was also taking its toll in the workhouse: despite a thorough cleansing, still the inmates died. Beer, brandy and gin were given to those who buried them.[4]

In 1773, 51 people died of smallpox, in 1774, 58, but in 1775 there was a general inoculation of the parish and the death rate fell to 27.[5] Inoculation by smallpox itself was widely used before Dr Edward Jenner discovered inoculation by cowpox. By 1794 the effectiveness of the inoculation of 1775 had disappeared. Smallpox broke out again in Curdridge tithing and in Hoe. Here Richard Barter, overseer, supplied three families with gin, brandy, beer and wine. But despite this, William and Mary Blandford died as did their children, Maria and James.[6]

That year, 1794, Alexander Wyatt determined to protect his family by inoculation. He was allowed £1 11s. 6d. from the rates for this precaution. But there was no general policy of inoculation as there had been earlier, until in 1818 vestry ruled that unless parishioners receiving poor relief were inoculated, either by Dr Swann or Dr Seymour, they would forfeit this help.[7] The Pest House became obsolete when the new Poor Law Act required all the poor to be sent out of their parishes into the Union Workhouse to be built at Droxford. The Pest House was sold to the trustees of Kerby's charity and became a private house.

17

The Workhouse

An Act of 1723 allowed the parish officers to rent premises for a workhouse. Bishop's Waltham was renting one by 1729, when the first Master of the Workhouse was buried. It provided a home for the elderly, the orphans, the widows and the feckless who were placed in the charge of the workhouse master. During the smallpox epidemic in 1740, 11 burials, a fifth of all the deaths in the parish, came from the workhouse. From 1740 to 1745 three workhouse masters died in office.[1] The master's task was to put the inmates to work; what they earned contributed to their upkeep which reduced the poor rate, thus easing the burden on the other parishioners.

The workhouse was supervised by the parish officers who were responsible for all poor law administration. Serving this office was time-consuming. In 1668 the officers resolved this problem by appointing Thomas Lee and Thomas Colpas deputy collectors, with a small allowance from the poor rates. But the following year vestry annulled this arrangement.

However, in 1756 the parish officers considered this problem solved, when they appointed William Ledwell as the workhouse master.[2] He lived in Waltham Chase, leasing two copyhold houses with a hop garden. Ledwell really became a 'professional' overseer, a position which was not made legal until 1819. He both collected and paid out the poor rate; he supervised the Pest House and he sanctioned the payment of rent for the needy. He accompanied the unmarried pregnant women to court; he attended disputes over settlement cases with other parishes. He organised the workhouse, ordering food and supervising the inhabitants.

In 1757 the parish officers allowed Ledwell the whole poor rate of more than £322, reserving to themselves only £15, which was used for such things as repairing the fire engine and for repairs at the workhouse. But Ledwell's position lasted only for two years. In 1759 he was accused of fathering an illegitimate child on Eleanor Hackett, a single woman living in the workhouse. Eleanor was taken before the Justices and probably sent to the House of Correction in Winchester: the child, William, died and was buried, which cost 2s. 6d. William Ledwell was fined £2 18s. at Winchester Assizes, but bringing the action against him had cost the parish £9 2s.[3] His memory was perpetuated in the place-name 'Ludwell's Corner'[4] when Waltham Chase was enclosed in 1870.

But with Ledwell's dismissal the parish officers had to supervise the workhouse themselves, ordering in the provisions. The diet was varied and wholesome; beef, bacon and cheese, malt and hops for brewing beer. The garden was planted up and two pigs were bought in to fatten. The house was put in order, the chimneys swept, the spinning wheels repaired. The old men were shaved. The poor earned £2 13s. 6d. from spinning, so 5s. 9d. was returned to them 'as an encouragement'.[5]

However the parish officers had run up a debt of £100; the poor rates were overspent. It was cheaper to employ an agent. The overseers therefore appointed Mrs Hackett as supervisor together with John Stevens, who had supplied some of the meat. They received £10 a month, not wages, but specifically 'for the maintenance of the Poor in the House', with an extra £1 allowed 'for the Burials of such poor persons as shall happen to die … under their Care'.[6]

The town was thriving and growing but the workhouse was not large enough. The parish officers therefore leased a building in the town itself, part of the hop kilns known as 'Sweetapples' belonging to Mr William Lacy. Alterations were needed: the floor was raised, a well was sunk and the pump from the old workhouse installed, together with the furnace and the oven and the copper. The wands of office were taken down. Peat was spread in the garden, four bedsteads and a straw mat were bought, and a 'swing for a child' put up. The new workhouse was up and running; this called for a celebration and £1 13s. 6d. was spent at *The Dolphin*, 'the Majority of the Officers being present'.[7] This workhouse was probably in Basingwell Street, also called Workhouse Street. It may have been the building which is now the *Barleycorn Inn*.

Who was living in this renovated workhouse? There were the children being treated for 'scalled Heads', a type of impetigo of the scalp. Most were orphans, but one belonged to a soldier who was allowed 15s. 6d. towards clothing when he came for his child. There were the old men, shaved by Richard Skinner for 2s. 6d., and two pregnant women who were supplied with clothing and a midwife.[8]

48   The *Barleycorn Inn* in 1895, Basingwell Street, possibly originally William Lacy's hop kilns which became the workhouse in 1762. The rope walk was close by.

Mrs Hackett and John Stevens looked after the workhouse for seven years until Edward Wyatt was appointed overseer. He examined Mrs Hackett's accounts and found them incorrect. She was arrested for debt. The house itself was a disgrace; the windows were broken as was the pump. These were mended, the garden was planted, blankets and rugs were bought, together with eight dishes, platters and other equipment. Thomas Woodhatch, who had systematically been stealing from the house, was caught and imprisoned. A lock was fitted to the door.

The parish officers again ran the house, this time with Mrs Edwards and Old Colpas as supervisors, but now supplies were ordered by the overseers. They were generous; in September 1767, 149lbs of bacon and 146lbs of cheese were eaten; in October 180lbs of beef, in November and December mutton. In January, February, March and April, bacon and cheese were eaten, beef at the end of April. There is no means of knowing how many people were living in the house to eat this food. The accounts reveal the purchase of four pairs of leather breeches, £5 10s. 10d. spent on shoes, and Mary Hackett cutting out clothes for the children. The adults were occupied sifting coal and threshing, while the children picked stones from the fields under Old Edwards' supervision. Altogether they earned £3 6s. 5d. But again the parish officers had overspent, this time by £20, so William Ledwell was re-employed.[9]

He and his wife were again in charge of all poor relief, accounting for £450 annually. But within two years William Ledwell had died. His wife continued at her post until the end of her contract. The workhouse industries, as well as the usual threshing and spinning and stone picking, now included leather, for, in 1771, 40 bushels of dry tan were ordered.

The next workhouse master was unfortunate since his term of office coincided with the smallpox epidemic of 1773. There was much cleansing of the house with 'liquor to the men cleansing the Necessary House'; clean clothes and soap were supplied. The sick were given wine and veal; the old men tobacco. Despite the smallpox, the old men were shaved and the children taught to read by the Widow Barnard.[10]

Vestry next employed another 'professional' Keeper of the Poor and Master of the Workhouse, Thomas Hillary, with a 'Salary for the Maintenance of the Poor … at the Rate of £530 p[er] Ann[um]', nearly £200 more than William Ledwell had accounted for 20 years earlier. Mrs Hillary was also employed with £5 5s. allowed her for tea. In the second half of the 18th century there was a rise in population, but poor weather brought bad harvests. In 1782, 1783 and 1784 the winters were particularly severe, the spring and summers cold, so food was scarce. Vestry allowed another £60 because of 'the Extremities of the Times'.[11] By 1784 the Hillarys had left their post.

There is no doubt that the workhouse was much better run by the parish officers than by the professionals they employed. Again the officers reclothed the people with shoes, ordered 11 hats for the boys, re-equipped the house with blankets, sheeting, trenchers, wooden ware, brooms, knitting needles. They spent more than £80 on flour and began two new industries. Naval supplies were needed so the poor made ropes and also sacks. Some inmates were sent out of the house to work; Vare worked for Jonas the miller, Davis for Dr Penford, others went to Mr Clewer. The workhouse made more than £18 profit, so three shillings was given to its people to spend at Waltham Fair: at one penny each 36 people were now living in the workhouse.

But the workhouse population was not static as the paid allowances reveal. £2 was given to Hester Wareham who was probably going into service. Two men and a boy left the workhouse for London. A widow and a widower, both in need, came to live in the house. 1795 was another famine year, for the war with France had reduced imports. The poor rate was augmented by a subscription raised to buy flour for the poor. This was still insufficient; the poor rates were overdrawn by more than £41.[12] A parochial report published by the South Hampshire Agricultural Society in 1798 describes the situation in the workhouse. It says of Bishop's Waltham, 'the Poor well provided for in a poor house but not properly employed'; the same report in contrast says of the poor at Soberton, 'they are often in want of relief, and though occasionally relieved by the parish, they are suffering in the extreme'.[13]

The 19th century saw two proposed rebuildings of the house. In 1808 a committee of vestry, undeterred by the risk of infection, suggested that a poor house should be added to the Pest House in Waltham Chase. William Cobbett served on this committee. He was living in Botley but his farmlands lay mostly in Bishop's Waltham, where he paid a poor rate and attended vestry. This new poor house was to be 20 feet by 45 feet. The rent for the existing workhouse continued to be paid, by a 'Check' drawn probably on the Bishop's Waltham bank. There was now a poor house in the Chase and the workhouse in the town.

In 1810 Mr and Mrs Beckett were in charge of the workhouse in the town, Mr Beckett at £15 a year, Mrs Beckett at £8 15s. with £5 5s. extra for tea. That year Mr Beckett was able to hand over to the parish officers more than £8 which the poor had earned, so the following May they were given 16s. 6d.[14] to spend at the fair. Charles Vancouver reports that in 1810 the costs of the workhouse amounted to £567 8s. 11d.[15]

By 1816 the war with France was over. The country expected prosperity to return. It did not; the Corn Laws kept the price of bread artificially high and essential articles had been taxed to pay for the war. Moreover, corn could be imported so the farmers reduced the land under cultivation, but the discharged soldiers and sailors needed employment. Unemployment and distress were widespread. Labour-saving equipment had been invented, in particular the threshing machine. William Cobbett had one at Botley Hill, the farm he leased in Curdridge.

That year there were 13 children living in the workhouse who were considered capable of helping in a household. They were balloted out at the Easter vestry. William Cobbett was allotted a child of ten, Jane Collins. He was furious, considering that he already paid enough to the poor rates so he did not need this 'incubus'. He wrote bitterly that this child must be 'kept … clothed, fed, lodged and doctored' until she grew up.[16] But in fact the following year, fearing imprisonment after the suspension of Habeas Corpus, Cobbett fled to America. Jane was balloted out again, this time to George Bond, tanner.

In 1819 vestry again offered the orphan children in the workhouse to parishioners with a premium; £4 for the three boys as apprentices, £6 for the nine girls, or alternatively as servants with an allowance of one to two shillings weekly.[17] Poor from the house in 1822 earned £46 10s. They were employed by, among others, Messrs G. and J. Clark, merchants, and by Captain Scott, by Mr R. Woodman,[18] brick and tile maker and lime burner at Coppice Hill.

In 1823 the Select Vestry, which was a committee of vestry formed specifically to manage poor relief, 'farmed out' the workhouse. It appointed a Mr Harris who could sell the labour of the poor for his own advantage. Out of this he must clothe the poor, but was allowed 3s. 2d. a week for each inmate. Unemployed from the house were weeding in the churchyard where they were supplied with beer by the churchwardens. There were between thirty and forty people in Harris's charge. In 1828 vestry was considering whether to erect cottages on the land next to the Pest House, instead of paying the rents of large pauper families.[19] Four years later vestry realised that yet again the existing workhouse was too small. Peter Barfoot offered to loan the money to build a new one.[20]

The same year Parliament had set up a Commission of Enquiry to investigate poor law administration. The country felt threatened by the increasing poor rates, which Parson Malthus and many others considered were contributing to the growth of a population which had become dependent on poor relief. The Poor Law Amendment Act was passed in 1834 to implement a Union Workhouse system. The following year one of the Assistant Poor Law Commissioners, Colonel Charles à Court, came to address vestry on the advantages of the new Poor Law. He spoke of the economies that would result from separating the families of the poor, segregating the men from the women in a Union workhouse purpose-built for the poor of 11 parishes.

Vestry totally disagreed. It had always done its best for its own poor. It declared that it would join with Upham and Durley only, in a new workhouse which must be built in Bishop's Waltham. This would benefit the town and be a comfort to the poor who would still be close to home.[21] This was exactly what the Poor Law Commissioners wished to avoid. Colonel à Court, after making an intensive tour of inspection in Hampshire, wrote 'that the [local] workhouse holds out an encouragement to the profligate … he courts its apartments … the comforts & conveniences which he enjoys there are far beyond his wants and greatly exceed what in justice to society ought to be afforded to him'.[22] Colonel à Court totally dismissed the objections of the Bishop's Waltham vestry. The Union Workhouse for the parishes of Bishop's Waltham, Corhampton, Droxford, Durley, Exton, Hambledon, West Meon, Meonstoke, Soberton, Warnford and Upham was built in Droxford. The Poor law Amendment Act succeeded in removing its poor from Bishop's Waltham.

18

The New Poor Law

Parliament felt overwhelmed by the rising cost of the poor rates. In Bishop's Waltham in 1688 these had amounted to £65 9s. 4d.; in 1832 they were £1,954 17s. 3d. The population had grown, as had the number of rateable properties, from 222 in 1675 to 409 in 1829.[1] Households had almost doubled, but the poor rates had increased 50 times. Many Members of Parliament considered that poor relief was the cause of the increasing birth rate among the poor. In reality, other factors were at work, better food, improvements in hygiene and in the treatment of illnesses. A Poor Law Commission was set up which recommended the prohibition of all poor relief except within Union workhouses. These would house the poor of several parishes. Conditions would be made so unpleasant with families divided and strict regulation of action, dress and diet that it was felt only those really in need would go into these Union workhouses. The Poor Law Amendment Act was passed in 1834.

Assistant Poor Law Commissioners, who were generally officers on half-pay, were sent into the parishes to explain how the New Poor Law would work. Colonel Charles Ashe à Court was the Assistant Commissioner for Hampshire, paid a salary[2] of £526 12s. 6d. a year, for as an officer he also received his half-pay of £173 7s. 6d. Colonel à Court was furious at what he considered the underpayment of his salary. His full entitlement was £700 a year. Moreover he knew that Sir Edward Parry, who was a naval officer on half-pay, received the full £700 as the Assistant Poor Law Commissioner for Norfolk. (Sir Edward was later to come to live in Bishop's Waltham.) Colonel à Court wrote many letters of complaint to the three Poor Law Commissioners in London. He pointed out that he had purchased all his commissions except one. He considered his half-pay 'a reward for 34 years military service': eventually he did receive the full salary.

In January 1835 Colonel à Court explained the system to the Bishop's Waltham vestry. They were totally opposed to the new law. He wrote to Whitehall from the town, with a request for more foolscap, complaining, 'For the last two days I have been obliged to work 16 hours a day to get thro' my work. I am getting heartily tired of, thoroughly disgusted with my present life';[3] probably the Bishop's Waltham vestry did not make things easy for him. He came from Heytesbury Court, Wiltshire, the third son of Sir William à Court: his eldest brother was a professional diplomat.[4] In Hampshire he pushed on with his task. As yet no Union workhouse had been built, but that year he presided over the first meeting of the Committee of the Droxford Union, to which all 11 parishes sent representatives known as guardians. Edward Wyatt and John Hatch, both farmers, were the guardians for Bishop's Waltham.[5]

The old workhouses were still in use but were now very strictly regulated. Before long Colonel à Court wrote, 'I am perfectly astonished at the working of the Union System … The moral effect is surprising; and the pecuniary saving … varies from 30 to 60 per cent'.[6]

The pecuniary savings came as no surprise to the parish officers, for the amount of food allowed in the parish workhouses was now laid down by the Poor Law Commissioners, whose aim was to reduce the standard of living for the inmates below that of the poorest parishioner. By February 1836 the Soberton officers were complaining that the 'Diet was insufficient'. It was increased by two ounces of bread and cheese daily for all working men and boys. But these were no longer to be allowed to work out of the house, for the employers to whom they were sent complained that they were so undernourished that they were unable to do the tasks set for them. The economies made can be seen by comparing the money allowed. In March 1836 under the New Poor Law, there were 58 poor in Bishop's Waltham workhouse; costs for three months were £41 9s. 4d., about 1s. 2d. weekly for each person.[7] In 1827 under the old system, vestry had allowed 3s. 2d. weekly for each person, almost two thirds more.[8] For the time being the poor were still allowed relief in their own homes, called outdoor relief; in 1836 in Bishop's Waltham this amounted to £156 18s. 4½d.[9]

The Union workhouse was not yet built but the system was in place. People were now categorised; then families were split up and sent to different workhouses within the Union. In April 1836 the children all came to Bishop's Waltham and were to make headline news in *The Times*. The old and the idiots were sent to Droxford; the able-bodied to Hambledon workhouse; but this was not large enough for the able-bodied of 11 parishes, so 100 people were sent to the Fareham Union House at 2s. 1d. each per week. Outdoor relief was no longer allowed for illegitimate children.

Workhouse uniform was ordered: 25 suits of grey cloth for the men and boys, 100 yards of grosgraine for the women. Two yellow dresses and stockings were kept for the mothers of bastards. Fifty cast-iron bedsteads were laid in, 15 double for the women, 15 double for the boys, 20 single for the men. These proved so uncomfortable that complaints were made, so sacking was substituted for the wooden slats. The arrangement with the Fareham Union was to last a year. Meanwhile land on which to build the Union workhouse was bought in Droxford, from the Marquis of Winchester.[10]

The Commissioners expected the Droxford Union House to be completed within a year, an unrealistic target since there were not enough bricks available. This local scarcity was overcome; a handsome brick building surrounded by a flint wall was built, designed by Mr Kempthorne. The Commissioners loaned £500 towards building costs. They advised that a further £4,000 must be raised by advertising for funds in the local papers. But local people were reluctant to fund a building of which they disapproved; eventually the Royal Exchange Assurance took up the loan.

The eight parish officers of Bishop's Waltham had now been replaced by just two Guardians. There were only three relieving officers appointed, to assess cases

49   The Droxford Union workhouse with its inmates in 1891. HRO, TOP/93/3/4

of need in all the 11 parishes of the Union. That winter was severe; smallpox broke out in December 1836 and snow prevented coppice work in the woods. Some of the able-bodied workers were allowed outdoor relief. Others were in great distress. When Thomas Butler wrote to complain of the system, he was advised that the parish officers might still order relief for the needy.

Bishop's Waltham objected so strongly to the New Poor Law that in 1837 they withheld the rate money, for which the overseers were summoned before Colonel à Court and the Guardians. The parish had cause for complaint. Three children had been sent in December 1836 from Bishop's Waltham workhouse to the Fareham Union to attend school. In the following February they were returned to the town half-dead. The Rector, William Brock, drew attention to the case. The matter was raised in the House of Commons and reported in *The Times*. A Court of Inquiry was set up. Mr Lovekin, the medical officer, reported that the children had been sent to Fareham perfectly healthy. When they came back they were 'faint and exhausted, none of them could walk or stand without assistance'. But 'through the excellent nursing of the Master and Mistress whose care for the children made his visits to the house a pleasure', they were gradually recovering. They had been brought back in an open cart on a cold wet night. In the Fareham Union House they had been flogged and starved by the master and school mistress, who put them in the stocks for incontinency.

The Rector, William Brock, therefore offered to take all the workhouse children into the parish school so that such ill-treatment should never occur again. He said he knew of four families in need, who had received neither relief nor medical help. The master of the workhouse, John Harrison, complained that the diet was insufficient, with the result that the allowance of ½ lb of potatoes daily was doubled. The Curate, Thomas Scard, objected to the long journeys that the relieving officers had to make to the different parishes, which made their task impossible. He was told this was not the case. Instead of three relieving officers, now only two were appointed; the argument being that, with the abolition of statute labour on the roads by the Highway Act of 1835, the officers need no longer supervise the poor working on the roads.

The Union House at Droxford was finished by the autumn of 1837, complete with a stove and a hearse. A bone mill was ordered and erected in a separate building. Here the men pounded rotting bones into bone meal manure, but when *The Times* revealed that the inmates of the Andover Union House were so hungry that in desperation they were eating these bones, bone mills were made illegal. The former Bishop's Waltham workhouse was now empty. A last Quarter's rent was paid to Ann and Mary Colpas, and to Mrs Reading for the 'Board Room and Stabling'.[11]

The huge cost of building the Union House at Droxford depended on the poor rates, as did the repayment of the loan to build it, and also the running expenses. The Poor Law Amendment Act had ordered a revaluation of every parish with a map showing each property for a new rating assessment. This was to be three shillings in the pound on land, two shillings on houses. In 1839 the new assessment was presented to the parish by the surveyors, Messrs Lane and Appleby. Vestry objected to the valuation and complained to the Poor Law Commissioners, who referred them to the Guardians of the Droxford Union, who ignored them. Vestry therefore appealed to the magistrates but without success. The parish was no longer in charge of its poor rates, though it still had its poor. But officially the duty of providing for the poor of Bishop's Waltham was now the responsibility of the Guardians of the Droxford Union.

Vestry realised that the needs of the poor had been increased, not decreased, by the Union Workhouse system, for people preferred to starve rather than enter the House. In 1839 vestry relieved this distress by raising a subscription to distribute food and fuel to the poor; soup was to be made weekly, a gallon allowed to each family, coal was to be sold at sixpence a cwt and clothing distributed; the idle and disorderly were to be excluded from such benefits.[12]

19

Employment and Rates

The parish economy depended on full employment. There was no place for idle hands. The overseers would assist parishioners by supplying what was needed for their work. In 1760 Francis Bassett received 10 shillings 'to assist him in his trade'; Davis was given a grub axe, old Kervill five shillings-worth of rushes, and in 1794 John Green hedging gloves.[1] In 1785 the overseers re-established Freemantle in his trade as a blacksmith, after his imprisonment. They rebuilt his forge, sent for his bellows, paid for beans and seeds for his new garden. When Henry Heatrell, a cobbler, left the parish to find work, he was allowed a guinea; when he returned three years later in 1787, the officers bought him new lasts and a seat.[2]

From 1812 the overseers began to find cases of more permanent unemployment. In 1814 Thomas Monday could find no work after the harvest season, so was allowed his rent.[3] The end of the Napoleonic Wars in 1815 revealed the extent of the agricultural distress, which depended for alleviation on the poor rates.

In 1815 Parliament ordered a reassessment of the poor rate. Magistrates imposed a rate of one shilling in the pound on both land and houses. Vestry protested, declaring that for the last 20 years the rate had been one shilling in the pound on land, but only eightpence in the pound on houses. It took legal advice, but the consulted barristers assured vestry that it must pay the authorised rate.

Within two years the poor rate had risen to two shillings in the pound. There were now 20 men out of work. Many parishes were using the Speenhamland system by which the unemployed were sent to the farms; half their wages were then paid by the farmer, the rest from the poor rate. However Bishop's Waltham was different. That year vestry decided that it would be far better to pay the men directly an agricultural labourer's wage of nine shillings a week. At present the 20 unemployed men were totally dependent on the poor rate, which it was reckoned would rise from two shillings to 2s. 4d. in the pound. Vestry therefore declared that any person rated at £200 a year, instead of paying poor rate, should employ and pay one of the unemployed. Ratepayers of £10 and upwards would be classed together. Each would employ a man according to the amount they were rated at. The Master of the Poor House was ordered to keep account of the system and direct the men where to go.[4] From 1822-23, 22 householders employed the poor, who between them earned £46 10s.[5] That year £2,597 16s. 11½d. was paid out in poor relief.

Vestry determined to reduce the poor rate by appointing a Select Vestry specifically for this purpose. This was a committee of vestry given its legal powers under the Vestries Act of 1819. The chairman was Admiral Edward Griffith-Colpoys, nephew of Admiral Sir John Colpoys. He had been with his uncle on board *London* at Spithead in 1795 when the crew mutinied and both were

50   Northbrook House with its elegant grounds, the home to Captain Edward Griffith Colpoys and Sir Edward
Parry, arctic explorer and hydrographer, among others.

imprisoned. Admiral Edward Griffith-Colpoys had later come to live at
Northbrook House, whose grounds lay alongside those of the Rectory.

The first act of the Select Vestry was to offer the parish children living in the
workhouse to any householder, with a payment of 1s. 6d. a week for a year. It
halved the salary of the assistant overseer, James Perrin, and contracted out the
maintenance of the poor in the workhouse at 3s. 2d. per head. It sent out
reminders to those who had not paid their poor rate. It sued Thomas Perrin, the
previous assistant overseer, for £109 16s. 6d. rate money he owed. It declared that
every agricultural worker should receive eight shillings a week. It appointed Fox
and Company, the Bishop's Waltham bankers, as treasurers. There were now two
bodies in charge of the poor rates, the vestry and the Select Vestry. The rates
became increasingly difficult to collect: two which had been partially collected in
1828 were declared illegal. Finally, in that year vestry decided to make a reassessment of the rates in order to correct and equalise them. But when these new
valuations were presented to the parish in 1829, so many objections were made
that vestry abandoned the task. However they did discover 179 people who paid
rents of £4 or less, whom they considered too poor to pay. These were struck off
the list of ratepayers.

In 1830 there were still so many unemployed poor that they were sent out as
roundsmen to the householders of the different tithings. Each ratepayer was to pay
'not less than 18d per day and as much more wages as their services seem to entitle
them to'. But, if land was available, the poor could feed themselves. Bishop Charles
Sumner offered land in Waltham Chase for this purpose; meanwhile vestry rented
40 acres of cultivated land for immediate use. In 1833 it adopted the Labourers
Allotment Act which provided land free of charge to heads of families with more
than four children. Nineteen families applied, having between them 95 children.
After the first year's harvest the families were not expected to apply for poor relief.[6]

20

The Highways

In medieval times the roads through the town to Winchester, Southampton and Portsmouth, which witnessed the passage of kings and bishops, were maintained by manorial labour. The road to Winchester carried supplies from the manor of Bishop's Waltham; in 1301 wool, charcoal, cumin, pepper were transported by packhorse, together with the money raised from the proceeds of the manor.[1] This was the road travelled by the steward and his clerk when he presided over the manorial courts. He returned over Stephen's Castle Down, then by Morestead through Twyford to Winchester.

In 1555, by Act of Parliament, the upkeep of the roads became a parochial responsibility. Each parish must appoint two surveyors of the highways to oversee their repair within the parish. Parishioners, according to their abilities, must supply horses, carts, implements and labour for four days a year (in 1562 increased to six days). This statute labour remained a legal liability until 1835; after 1773 it might be commuted for money. The surveyors also had the power to collect a highway rate,[2] and on occasions a stone rate. The result was that, since the repair of the roads was the legal responsibility of all the parishioners, when a road was found unrepaired, the whole parish was sued for the neglect of its statutory duty.

In 1641, among other complaints, the road in Ashton was presented at the manorial court: Ashton tithing was ordered not to 'put forth there cattle along the high wayes except they follow them because it is a great annoyance for spoiling the hedges'. At a court leet in 1644 William Cowlnet, gentleman, was ordered to 'make a sufficient bridge at the old mille for the King's poore people to pass without danger'. In Curdridge the highway leading to Kirbridge was at fault; Penford had been digging out the clay, leaving potholes. He must 'scour his water course and his ditches.'[3] The same task was being enjoined more than two hundred years later; in 1864 the Droxford Highway Board requested 'all persons with land next to the highway … to scour their ditches and cut their hedges'.[4]

The increasing number of travellers coming not on horseback but by coaches with heavy wheels placed extra pressure on the roads. The postal system provided information for the government and fostered trade; by 1725 Bishop's Waltham was a post town from which letters could be sent or collected. In 1784 new light mail coaches halved the costs of the postal service. They also carried passengers, together with a guard against the robbery of the king's mails. In 1821 The Sovereign coach from Winchester called at *The Dolphin* at 5 o'clock each weekday, bound for Southampton or Gosport alternately. But the only direct conveyance to London was on Mondays by 'fly waggon' from John Woodman's in the High Street.[5]

There was no central authority to effect road improvements. These depended on the initiative of local people setting up Turnpike Trusts. Those who travelled – the gentry – were concerned to reduce journey times. Turnpike roads might be quite short stretches which linked existing roads; the average length of a turnpike road in Hampshire was only 17 miles.[6]

In the 18th century there were three turnpike roads passing through the parish, for which composition money for upkeep was paid to the Turnpike Trustees. In the 19th century there were to be three more, all created by local Acts of Parliament.

The Winchester and Bishop's Waltham Turnpike Act was passed in 1758 to repair and widen the road from Stockbridge to Winchester, to Bishop's Waltham over Stephen's Castle Down, then through Otterbourne to Southampton. But it would be 20 years after the Act was passed that in 1780 the surveyor was ordered 'to prepare a sufficient quantity of Stones for continuing the Road from Bellmore Lane to the Direction Post at the top of Stephen's Castle Down'.[7]

The next turnpike Act aimed to improve an existing road. This left the town over Stephen's Castle Down, and led through Tichborne to Alresford and to Odiham; the present road was 'ruinous narrow and dangerous'. Among its 185 trustees were the Marquis of Caernarvon, the Marquis of Winchester, the Rector of Bishop's Waltham, James Cutler and William Horner, weaver. One shilling was the charge for 'Every coach, berlin, landau, Chaise-Marine, Calash, Chair, caravan or Hearse drawn by 4 or more horses'; this was a day-return toll. No one was to pay at more than two gates between Odiham and Alresford, or more than one between Alresford and Bishop's Waltham. A penalty of 20 shillings was incurred if the toll was evaded by going through private lands or the waste.

The surveyors might dig furze, gravel, chalk, or any road-building material out of the waste, filling up the pits they made. They could cut down trees or banks. Five trustees were to decide on the line of the road. If any landowner refused to negotiate the sale of his land, a jury must decide the issue. The obsolete road could be sold. The surveyors could call on statute labour; milestones and direction posts were to be set up.[8]

In 1775 the Gosport Turnpike was created. This led from Gosport through Wickham to Bishop's Waltham to Chawton. Gates were erected at Brockhurst, Fareham, Wickham, Bishop's Waltham, Warnford and Rotherfield.[9] John Hyde was the collector for 20 years at the Bishop's Waltham Gate; his wage was £1 12s. a month with a year's allowance of £2 10s. for fire and candle. On one occasion in 1777 he was assaulted by Commander Gambier, for which he received compensation of 10s. 6d.[10]

John Compton, the parish surveyor in 1776, was allowed £5 extra by the trustees to repair this road, as well as the statute labour and composition. Waltham Chase was a good source of stone for road building. In 1779 Thomas Shepherd, the next surveyor, paid for 69 loads from the Chase at ninepence a load. The total received in tolls for the road that year amounted to £1,301 6s. 2d., while £184 covered the expenses, a good investment, which many turnpike roads were not.

War placed extra burdens on the currency. This was reflected in the accounts of the treasurer, James Bedford. The French wars reduced the import of corn and bad harvests resulted in starvation. Bishop's Waltham raised a special fund to supplement the poor rates,[11] but the highway rate was not so urgent. The other parishes through which the road passed – Alverstoke, Fareham, Wickham, Meonstoke, Corhampton, Exton, Warnford, Privett, Tisted, Newton Valence, Faringdon, Chawton – all paid up, but Bishop's Waltham was three years in arrears. However, in 1796 the parish managed to collect the money, £8 8s. a year, and even paid three years in advance.

In 1798 Bedford recorded £9 in counterfeit halfpence as well as 'Dollars and French Half-Crowns', some no doubt circulated by the French prisoners-of-war passing through the country. He was unsure whether tolls were chargeable on 'Waggons carrying Government stores' to supply the troops.

In 1811 he negotiated a contract to repair two districts of the road with Captain Robinson of Bishop's Waltham for more than £100 a quarter. But when Captain Robinson also submitted substantial bills, he lost this contract. The Trust had paid him more than £1,000 in less than two years. When Thomas Bulbeck took over the road repair in 1816, he received only £27 5s. 9d. a quarter, but how

51   Extract from the 1st edition Ordnance Survey map of 1810 showing how wooded the area was even then, useful cover for the earlier Waltham Blacks. It was updated in c.1840 to show the newly built London and South Western and Gosport Junction railways. The turnpike road (1801) from Bishop's Waltham across Curdridge Common is clearly shown as is Botley station. HRO, Sheet 58 6" OS 1968.

much of the road was his responsibility is not recorded. In 1821 the town gate was taking about £8 a month.[12]

The next turnpike was created in 1801 specifically to join the Botley Turnpike via Curdridge Road with the Gosport Turnpike Road in West Meon, 'with a branch on Corhampton Down to Corhampton village'.[13] Again the Trustees were the local gentry. The chairman, Thomas Lewin, was the owner of Ridgeway Castle near Southampton. Others were James Ogle, the Rector of Bishop's Waltham, Jo Wallace, the Rector of Botley, and Richard Baker, his successor. The road must be 30 feet wide but over Corhampton Down it might be reduced to 20-24 feet to preserve the adjoining land,[14] an economy which was to prove a mistake. £2,000 was borrowed on the credit of the tolls, money which was probably never repaid. Richard Veal undertook the construction of this road for £840, at £1 1s. a rod. Through the town the cost was reduced to 15s. a rod, but £1 1s. was allowed through the watery meadows at Northbrook. Two toll gates were to be erected, one at Harfields Lane next to Curdridge Common, another at Withycut End.

This road from Botley through Curdridge was the first major alteration to the park since it had been divided into farms after the Commonwealth. The main problem for the road-maker was the crossing of a tributary of the Hamble river, and the watery nature of the ground, supplied as it was by springs from the Moors. A bridge was therefore to be built in 'Hind meadow' and a culvert in 'Park valley'. Roads were mostly built on a foundation of bavins (bundles of brushwood) and faggots; this wood was placed horizontally on the road's surface, then covered with a layer of gravel. The Trustees of this road considered gravel the most important material for road-building. They stipulated that it should be 'gravelled two feet thick on the crown'. Within a year it was in poor condition, so Shephard was ordered to 'new gravel' it. Road-building material was to be obtained from the palace being rented by Mr John Penny. Richard Lomer was to place the stones and gravel on the sides of the road between the Great Bridge in the park and Curdridge Turnpike gate, for the road was slipping away at the sides. More road-material was needed, so in December that year Captain Charles Robinson was asked by the Trust to bring stones every morning from Hazleholt, and to cart gravel from Northbrook with his teams of horses, until he had used the £50 in cash he had promised to subscribe. But the gravel disappeared only too quickly. In 1803 Farmer Mears' team was engaged by the surveyor to cart gravel on Curdridge Common with two carts and four horses and one man, to work for eight days at 13s. per day. Ezekiel Donniger was especially thanked for his very liberal statute labour with his horses, but later had to be compensated, having been injured digging gravel at Northbrook. Ralph Shephard, the surveyor, demanded statute labour from all the parishioners where no composition money had been agreed.

£400 was borrowed on the security of the tolls. Parishioners might pay a lump sum to be excused toll. Thomas Bulbeck did so in 1804 for the Northbrook gate. John Clewer, in 1805, paid five guineas 'in lieu of all Tolls on horses and carriages through the Curdridge gate'.

Shephard now lowered Harfields Hill at Curdridge, moving 300 cubic yards of earth from the top to the bottom for £12. (Forty years later this hill was again lowered, to make an easier approach to Botley station.) The result was that the road became raised well above the level of the adjoining ground, so for safety it had to be fenced. The water from the springs in the Moors continued to be a problem; in 1812 more culverts were built between the bridge and the gully in the park. The hollows in the road were to be filled with stones, which were to be covered with 'screened gravel ready for the winter'.

The meetings of the Trustees were minimal; day-to-day management was left to the surveyor and the clerk, William Gunner. So with some surprise, in 1811 it was discovered that 14 of the original Trustees had died; new ones were elected. They included Richard Goodlad, magistrate from Droxford, Colonel James Kempt from Botley, and Thomas Fox, attorney, from Bishop's Waltham.

The drainage of water was the chief problem. In 1813 Shephard agreed to 'reform the road in the town on the convex principle' and create proper water tables for £7. The town crier was to announce that in the town no dung might be collected from the road. The convex principle, instead of draining the road, often created a surface sloping so much on both sides that the only safe way for a carriage was to drive down the middle.

The section of road from Northbrook to Corhampton was not begun until 1804, when Shephard agreed to make it and repair it for two years for £105. Turnpike trustees were legally entitled to stop up by-ways, thus forcing people to

52   Chalky Lane leads through the trees to the Dundridge road past several chalk pits. The open gate looks towards the Hangers and Corhampton Down.

use their new road, so Chalky Lane, Windmill Lane, Watery Lane, the end of Limekiln Lane which led to Dean, were all stopped up, as was the lane which by-passed the road by cutting over Galley Down. But from the beginning parishioners avoided paying the Northbrook toll by using these ancient ways.

There was an ongoing battle between the Turnpike Trust and the occupiers of adjoining land. In April 1806 the Galley Down Lane had been stopped by a high bank and a ditch dug across and wooden piles; by the autumn Captain Robinson had removed these and levelled the ground. In 1813 Thomas Bulbeck was reprimanded for allowing the passage of horses and carriages through his private grounds, which adjoined the road at the end of Galley Down, thus facilitating the evasion of the Northbrook gate, a by-pass which was still being complained of in 1833.

The narrowness and slope of the road across Corhampton Down made it hazardous. In 1809 Shephard constructed an embankment to form a fence but, despite these precautions, the following March the stage coach from Southampton left the road here. In 1818 Shephard was dismissed and George Hearle was appointed surveyor. But the following year even Crown Hill, close to the town, was in disrepair. That year and in 1820 the road was presented as out of repair at Quarter Sessions. The parish surveyors then made an agreement with the Trustees to repair their part of the road for the next seven years for £100 a year. But even then, in June 1823 a further Act was passed 'for more effectually repairing the Botley Turnpike', since 'considerable sums of money borrowed on the credit of the tolls still remain due'. The surveyor was to produce a list of persons liable for duty; the Justices would order the places and times they were to work, haytime and harvest being excluded. Another indictment was threatened in 1831. Two years later the Trustees employed a man permanently to repair the road for two or three days a week, letting off the water.

Pedestrians did not pay toll, neither did the Military, the Post, carriages during elections, church-goers on Sundays or carts used for farming operations, though those going to market must pay. There was so much avoidance of the Northbrook toll that very little money was ever collected there.

In 1824 it was discovered that the toll keeper at Curdridge had been charging as much as 3s. 6d. on four-wheeled carriages, in defiance of the tolls enacted by Parliament two years earlier, so a board with a list of charges was erected. Carriages with wide wheels were thought to have the useful effect of rolling the roads into a level surface, so in future those with wheels of six to nine inches pulled by six or more horses paid only 4d., but those with wheels up to six inches paid 6d.[15] Although the Curdridge gate continued to be profitable, a notice had to be put up in 1836 to stop people digging sand and gravel out of the road there. But the toll house at Northbrook 'erected on the road and consisting of a sitting room, small back room, bedroom and skilling [jutting out piece] the walls of single brick erected on nine inch pillars' together with its 19 rods of garden ground was sold to John Apps in 1853 for £71.[16] In 1874 the Turnpike Trust from Curdridge to Corhampton was dissolved.[17]

Cobbett's Road

When one reflects on the burden placed on the parish in terms of manual labour and money, it is not surprising that the majority of the inhabitants did not support these road-building projects. In 1809 William Cobbett, journalist and editor of the *Political Register*, was the instigator of a new road from Titchfield to Twyford, thence to Winchester. It would pass near the farms he had bought in Curdridge, thus reducing his journey-time to Winchester, but since the road would go via Fair Oak it would take trade away from Bishop's Waltham. However, once it was built, its upkeep would fall on the parishes through which it passed (Titchfield and Droxford and Bishop's Waltham). These would have to contribute both a highway rate and their labour.

Bishop's Waltham was furious. They were already severely stretched in keeping up the four turnpike roads which passed through the parish: they did not need another one. The Rector, James Ogle, called a meeting, and advertised it in the *Hampshire Chronicle*. He considered the road would be very

53   William Cobbett in 1801, engraved by Bartolozzi. Cobbett had returned from America the previous year. By courtesy of Farnham Museum.

expensive to maintain, since it was to be built chiefly on a clay soil; 'there must be an absence of road making materials close at hand'. It was moreover unnecessary; 'although it might be advantageous to Individuals it must be injurious to the

54   Seen here in 1817, William Cobbett's house in Botley, to which he moved in 1805, is no longer standing. HRO, Top37/2/2.

Hew by the face.

It is quite dark now. and so I cannot write any more.

To Mr John Morgan Cobbett God bless you.
Botley, Southampton.
For Sister Nancy
W.m Cobbett.

a land of Nancy reading the paper to Hurchet & Door & Gullingham
1 Beun — 2 Hurchett — 3 Gullingham. — 4 Nancy — 5 Aunty
6 Jenny — 7 Johnny.

55   When Cobbett was imprisoned in Newgate (1810-12) he sent instructions about the work to be done on his farms in Curdridge tithing. Anne (Nancy), his eldest daughter, reads them to the three farm workers in the doorway. Her brothers listen. Cobbett's sister-in-law, Eleanor Reid, 'Aunty' (later Mrs Warner) sits sewing. The sketch is by Cobbett's eldest son, William, aged 12, who was staying with his father and mother in Newgate gaol. Courtesy: Nuffield College, Oxford, Nuff. XXX WCjun-JMC,1.2.1811.

Public'. The tolls arising would be insufficient to repair it, the outcome would be that 'instead of having one good road [to Winchester] as at present they will have two bad ones'.[18]

Cobbett recorded some of the expenses of this road in a notebook of wages. First, in April 1809 the water was let off, then from April to August, 56 loads of gravel were dug from Cobbett's garden; in June, three loads of this gravel were laid on the hills. Where the road passed through woodland, three men cleared 277 rods in June 1810.[19] The entries stop that month. In July Cobbett was imprisoned in Newgate Gaol for seditious libel. Not surprisingly, with this lack of foundation, when he was released from Newgate in 1812 he found this road, where it went through his estate, in disrepair. He summoned the parishes for neglect, first to Quarter Sessions, then to the King's Bench. Bishop's Waltham was ordered to repair this road where it went through the parish, so the highway rate rose from 2d. to 6d. in the pound. The legal costs incurred by Cobbett's action were still being paid off by the parish two years later.[20]

Vestry itself was not in favour of road improvements. In 1817 it declared 'there is a number of Men out of employ or only employed on the Road where their labour is quite unnecessary'.[21] The Trustees of the turnpikes recognised the need for road improvements, but the majority of the parishioners, who never left the town, felt threatened by any changes. In 1821, when wooden posts were erected to fence the carriageway from the footpath, 20 parishioners including John Padbury, Joseph Veck and Charles Churcher assembled with saws and axes to cut the posts down,[22] as they did the following year, destroying 20 yards of railing. When in 1833 the Trustees of the Gosport road suggested that the unemployed poor might be used to reduce the height of Coppice Hill, vestry was unconvinced. It decided to await the surveyor's report as to the value of this work.[23] But in 1829, the year before the Swing riots, work on the roads had been a means of providing employment. In November and December 1829, 30 people – both men and women and boys and girls – were picking stones at sixpence a load[24] or working on the roads, the men being paid one shilling a day, the boys less – not a living wage. They must have been subsidised from the poor rates.

Both the Curdridge to Corhampton Turnpike and Cobbett's road had fallen into disrepair soon after they had been made. Some stone was used in their construction but the predominant gravel created an inadequate highway. In 1816 John Macadam advised that clean materials broken into small pieces must be laid on a dry subsoil, consolidated, with a similar layer placed on top and a convex surface to ensure drainage. On the other hand in 1834 Thomas Telford recommended roads should be built on stone foundations. They should be widened, drained and straightened.

The Winchester Turnpike of 1834 seems to have been built on Macadam's principle, using stone broken into small pieces. The petitioners for this road pointed out that, in the ten miles of the present road from Bishop's Waltham to Winchester, there were 'seven very steep Hills and not one mile of level road whereas the proposed new line is nearly level throughout'.[25] This road was to join the Botley and Winchester Turnpike near Fishers Pond. It was another road driven through the former park. It would 'render useless 252 yards of an ancient Highway called Park lane … which leads … towards Durley', and another 'called Old Street Lane [which leads] to Wintershill Common.[26] These were to be stopped up.

William Gunner, solicitor, undertook the negotiations. He acquired the land from the owners on the line of the road; he attended the Bill through both Houses of Parliament; he drew up the petition from the inhabitants of Bishop's Waltham and from the towns of Portsea, Gosport, Fareham, Portsmouth and Winchester. Here he attended the market on two days obtaining signatures.[27]

Two people objected to the Bill: Captain Jarvis from Fair Oak, who had formerly been a subscriber to the costs, wanted a clause exempting him and his servants from the payment of tolls. He considered the road ought to come through Stroud Wood to Fair Oak, where it would connect not only with the Winchester road but also with Southampton and Romsey.[28] James Warner, the lessee of the pond, refused to allow it to be taken for the use of road-making, so a detour was made round the head of the pond. The County Council did not have such foresight more than a century later when the by-pass, laid on brushwood in 1965, was driven straight across the pond.

In Bishop's Waltham nine owners of land were affected. Mostly the road went through the former park, then being leased by Thomas and George Houghton, grocers, drapers and tallow chandlers.[29] They were offered 25 shillings an acre for Pond Close and Balls Mead (575 and 394 on the tithe map). The road would also go through a house in the town owned by Messrs G. and T. Clark, through a garden near the pond and another at the bottom of Park Lane. Subscribers to the road included Thomas Fox, banker and solicitor, the Revd. Thomas Scard, master of the Classical Academy, George and Thomas Clark, merchants and grocers, Walter Long from Preshaw House and Alice Long from Marwell Hall.

56   The tollhouse erected in 1834 at Park Lane on the Bishop's Waltham to Fisher's Pond Turnpike was a substantial dwelling.

The Trustees of the Botley Turnpike complained that this new road would divert tolls away from their road. They threatened to erect an intermediate gate. Captain Jarvis challenged the estimated cost, declaring that a very large sum would be needed because of the nature of the soil. But Thomas Baring of The Grange, Avington, wrote that this road would be advantageous to Winchester. He took two shares adding, 'I am afraid it will be injurious to those living in the Alresford side of the country by causing the road over Stephen's Castle Down to be neglected'.[30]

Surveyors were now appointed for all four tithings. Richard Veal undertook the alterations at Wintershill Common for £93 10s. Stephen Steel, surveyor of Ashton, was paid £20 for the Wintershill road. In January, Weavell dug 17 rods of the road at 2s. 3d. a rod. Other roads must be altered, so the same month Veal broke up 52 rods of Back Street (Houchin Street). Stones picked by Weavell's boy were taken into Mr Weston's garden for the use of the surveyors. In October, five shillings was spent on beer for the men labouring in Workhouse Street (Basingwell Street). In the autumn, stone collected for the road was broken up by Hoare; gravel was dug.[31] Toll gates were built at Fishers Pond and Park Lane. Profit from these amounted to £142 in 1836 but by 1859 had dropped to £95. By November 1834, £3,459 10s. 1d. had been spent on buying land and erecting toll houses and gates, and on labour.[32]

The year 1835 brought a complete change in road-building. Statute labour was abolished. Parishes were now grouped in highway districts, the idea being that the costs could be equalised. In Bishop's Waltham the highway rate had already dropped to eightpence farthing in the pound: now there was no labour and insufficient money to keep up the roads. The composition for the whole parish came to only £184 12s. 3d.[33]

By 1838 vestry was complaining that they were unable to repair the new road to Winchester. There was a heated discussion with an amendment proposed by the Rector, William Brock. He declared that 'the Interest of the Parish and the welfare and prosperity of the town imperiously demand [the road] ... be repaired ... with the least possible delay',[34] but vestry disagreed. He was defeated by 39 to 25 votes.

While new roads might be superfluous in the eyes of the parish, it was obvious that bridges must be kept in repair. When the bridge at Curbridge needed widening in 1828, the question arose as to who was responsible for it, the county or the joint parishes of Titchfield and Bishop's Waltham. The following year timber for the repair of bridges and pounds was solicited from the Bishop, Charles Sumner (1827-69). His steward wished to refuse on the grounds that other parishes would then demand equal treatment. Bishop's Waltham threatened legal proceedings.[35] The Bishop, aware of the unsettled state of the country and anxious to make no changes in manorial custom, ordered the timber to be allowed forthwith. But the bridge at Maddocks Ford on the Hamble near Maddox Ford Farm was not a county bridge. It had been built in 1818 by private subscription, with some money allowed from the highway rate and the parish carting up to £40 of road-materials.

In 1863 the Droxford Highway Board was established. Its chairman, Bettesworth Pitt Shearer, was a shareholder in Arthur Helps' Clay Company. This considerably increased the traffic through the town. The Board complained of the dangerous state of the causeway which crossed the palace pond; Arthur Helps was informed that 'the Water-wheel at the Mill (rebuilt after the fire in 1862) ... should be hidden from view to prevent Horses taking fright'; the railway had now made the road opposite the Station Gate very dangerous.

He was not the only person to be reprimanded by this new Highway Board. In 1871 the Revd Thomas Scard had placed paving on Durley Hill, 'for the purpose of washing his carriage'; Mr Edwards had put stones and bricks on the highway near the Abbey Mill, and Joshua White had built a wall on top of a grating in the High Street. They were all asked to remove these obstructions.[36]

When Pitt Shearer retired after 14 years as chairman, he reported that the expenses of the roads were much below average. During his time Waltham Chase had been enclosed, footpaths across the park stopped, and the Swanmore road widened to a 30-foot carriageway. By an Act of Parliament in 1878 many turnpike roads became main roads, their maintenance being shared between the county and the highway district with a grant in aid from the government.

21

The Militia

The threat from France in the second half of the 18th century resulted in William Pitt's Militia Bills. The parishes were given the responsibility of providing militia-men, who were chosen by ballot. They would cover home defence, allowing the regular forces to be sent abroad to fight. Peers, clergy, parish officers, articled clerks, apprentices and seamen were exempt. Those chosen must serve for three years or pay £10 to provide a substitute.

Bounties were paid to encourage recruitment. In 1778 and 1779, during the War of American Independence, eight men joined the militia, with a bounty from the parish in 1778 of 15s. 9d. In 1780 the bounty rose to £2 10s. but Henry Pink demanded and received £4 4s. It was not until 1793, when the French Republic declared war on England, that the bounty rose to £5, which William Chip, Andrew Edney and Jessie Hellyer all received. In 1813 another six men joined, to see the final defeat of Napoleon. The families of militia men received regular allowances from the poor rates; in 1792 Francis Sandall's family received £2 11s. 4d. a month.[1]

It was more difficult to raise men to serve in the navy since discipline was harder and life expectancy lower, so larger bounties were paid and parishes grouped together to provide funds. Bishop's Waltham and Warnford together raised two men in 1795; the bounty was £40, Warnford's share being £5.[2] One-third of the bounty was immediately paid to the recruits, the rest when they were safely on board.

Bishop's Waltham, on the route to Portsmouth, had always seen soldiers and sailors passing through. In 1757, at the beginning of the Seven Years' War, Mr Jonas, the overseer, spent £1 15s. 7d. on relief to them.[3] During May 1811, 35 soldiers' wives passing through the town were each given relief of threepence.[4] When a regiment was ordered abroad, a small number of official wives was chosen by lot to accompany their husbands. (In 1800 only six women per hundred men in each regiment were allowed to embark.) In the Peninsular War these official wives could be found in the field, cooking, nursing, doing laundry and, before entering Valladolid, 'were seen stripping friend and foe alike' on the field of battle.[5] But the particular 35 wives coming through Bishop's Waltham in 1812 were the unlucky ones, who were returning from Portsmouth, having seen their husbands embark for the Peninsular War without them. Some had probably travelled miles hoping to accompany their husbands to war; as long as they were legally married they were given an allowance to return home, but common law wives were not.

22

Napoleonic Prisoners

During the wars with France prisoners were placed on parole in Bishop's Waltham. The government feared these might spread Revolutionary ideas in the town. The Marquis of Buckingham wrote to Lord Grenville in 1793, 'I have been much annoyed by the constant inundation of French prisoners who have been on the route from Portsmouth to Bristol: and my officers … report that the language of the common men [is] … very violent, particularly on the subject of monarchy … I am very anxious that you should come to an early decision respecting your parole prisoners, who are nearly doubled at Alresford and Bishop's Waltham and are hourly more exceptionable in their language … with the country people. I am persuaded that some very unpleasant consequences must arise if the practice is not checked'. Lord Grenville replied that, if that were the case, 'the prisoners on parole at Waltham ought to be ordered to a more inland quarter, for five miles from Gosport is surely too near our arsenal'.[1] There were then 160 parole prisoners at Bishop's Waltham, 200 at Alresford.

Only senior commissioned officers were sent ashore from the prison ships where, on being captured, they were first confined. They were permitted to keep their swords but not wear them; in 1812 they might sell them. They were given an allowance of one shilling and sixpence a day for themselves, with one shilling a day for their servants[2] and were limited to a walking distance of one mile from the town between sunrise and sunset; hence the name of Frenchman's Bridge on the Botley road. They must keep to the main roads: if they strayed it was assumed that they were making a bid for freedom and a guinea reward was paid for their recapture. They were often sent funds from their families, and might be sent home. It was then expected that an English officer would be sent in exchange. This rarely happened. In 1806 only three English officers had been repatriated in return for 672 French,[3] for the French reckoned that, since England was a small country, every fighting man was invaluable. Admiralty agents were appointed to take charge of the prisoners; the Bishop's Waltham agent was based at Reading.[4]

57 Frenchman's Bridge near the Hamble river, a mile from the town, was the limit on the Botley road to which French and Spanish officers, on parole here from 1793 to 1815, might walk.

58 St George's Square in the 1920s. On the right is the *Crown Hotel* where Admiral Villeneuve was quartered in 1805.

The crew and non-commissioned officers lived on the prison ships, old hulks, anchored off Portchester. Here they supplemented their rations by making models in wood, ships and chessmen from bone, plaiting straw to make hats and slippers and knitting nightcaps, all of which were sent ashore to be sold. Some attempted to escape; in 1810 so many were successful that an order was issued that, for each escape, two prisoners were to be hanged.

England was fighting the combined fleets of France and Spain, so from 1803 to 1811 630 Spanish officers were paroled in the town; mostly their stay was brief.[4] On 5 October 1805, the frigate *Fama* was captured. Among the 18 prisoners taken were seven lieutenants, one midshipman, one commissary of stores and his child servant, a surgeon, a lieutenant in the army and his servant, and the Master's mate. The following February all were on parole in the town. Most of them had returned to Spain by April. But the captain of the *Conception* was not prepared to wait. He was taken in May 1806, paroled in November that year, and the following April he made a run for it.[5] If recaptured, he would no longer be allowed parole but would be taken to the prison hulks.

Prisoners-of-war were distributed throughout the country: Bishop's Waltham was a staging post for those being returned to their native land. In August 1804,

40 French prisoners arrived here from Leek, Lichfield and Chesterfield on 15, 16 and 19 August. They went on to France via Southampton on 27 August.[6]

One celebrated prisoner who stayed in the town was Admiral Villeneuve, the commander of the combined French and Spanish fleets, defeated by Admiral Nelson at Trafalgar on 21 October 1805. Admiral Villeneuve surrendered. He was paroled at Bishop's Waltham and took up his quarters at *The Crown*. He was

59   Houchin Street in 1968. The cottages on the right were probably where some of the prisoners-of-war rented rooms.

described in a letter written by William Cobbett, then living at Botley, as 'poorly lodged, barely attended and not in good health'.[7] His correspondence was automatically forwarded for scrutiny to the Admiralty by the agent and was delayed, but the Admiral himself was allowed visitors. Amongst those who called was Admiral Stirling. Admiral Villeneuve attended Nelson's funeral and visited Lord Clanricarde at Meonstoke. In 1806 Villeneuve was exchanged for four post captains[8] but, on his return to France, overcome by the disgrace of his defeat, he committed suicide or was murdered by Napoleon's orders.

From 1803 to 1811, 630 French prisoners were on parole in Bishop's Waltham.[9] One French prisoner, Jean Louis Garneray, later wrote an account of his time on parole. He arrived in the town in January 1812. He says that at this time 1,200 prisoners were kept at Bishop's Waltham in derelict hovels;[10] perhaps he meant the former cottages in Houchin Street and in Bank Street. Some prisoners are said to have lived in the cellars of the old rectory (now Longwood). Although 1,200 prisoners seems an exaggeration, Garneray could have been counting those passing through the town, for in 1811 so many had escaped that an order was given that prisoners were to be marched 12 at a time inland, away from the coast. Some from Bishop's Waltham were sent to Oswestry.

60   Hulks moored off Portchester after a painting by Louis Garneray. In these hulks non-commissioned prisoners-of-war were quartered 1793-1815. In 1809 Garneray was imprisoned on the Hulk *Vengeance* and in 1812 he was paroled to Bishop's Waltham. By courtesy of Portsmouth Museum and Record Service.

Jean Garneray did not come immediately to Bishop's Waltham. He had been captured in May 1806, then lived aboard the prison hulk, the *Crown*, off Portchester, for he was not a senior officer but a quartermaster's mate. His English was so good that he was able to act as an interpreter. He came from a family of painters but had run away to sea when he was thirteen. After spending time on the *Crown* he was transferred to the prison hulk, *Vengeance*. On board this ship he managed to rent a cabin on the poop deck as a studio: he sold his paintings, mostly seascapes, to two Portsmouth dealers, Abraham Curtis and James Smith. Here he met and befriended a fellow painter, Colonel Lejeune. When he met Lejeune, Garneray told him, 'As soon as your rank is known you will be taken ashore. The hulks are not intended for senior officers'. Garneray was right and Lejeune was soon paroled to Odiham. He remembered Garneray's kindness and managed to have him sent ashore to Bishop's Waltham in January 1812. Here he first rented a room with five other officers for which he paid ten shillings a week; then he negotiated with an elderly widow for an attic. This must have been in Hope House, St Peter's Street, which had earlier been a girls' school. He painted scenes on the walls of red-coated English soldiers, and of the children playing leapfrog by moonlight over the tombs in the churchyard; paintings which were lost on a change of ownership of Hope House. In Bishop's Waltham Garneray continued to make a living from his painting.

In spring 1812 he with two friends was walking to a farmhouse to buy lunch. They decided to take a short cut over the fields. Thinking that they were escaping, a farmer attacked them, hurting one prisoner severely. The other French officers wished to lodge a complaint which Garneray was asked to translate into English. This resulted in a plan to arrest him. Warned by an elderly lady whose grandchild he had painted, he made his escape. He walked out of the town, then hid in a ditch until nightfall, when he procured a lift in a curricle which had room for four inside. The other three were a parson and his wife who were asleep and their daughter, who was taking a position as a governess. The curricle was stopped by some constables looking for him, but the girl assured them that Garneray was her brother, thus facilitating his escape. However, he realised that the curricle was taking him away from Portsmouth so left it, and got a coach into town. Here in 1813 with two companions he arranged to be smuggled to France, but after a fight with the smugglers who wanted not only his passage money, but also the prize money offered by the government for escaped prisoners, he was recaptured in sight of land and returned to the prison hulk, *Vengeance*. Eventually in 1814 he was freed and reached France. Jean Garneray was one of the fortunate ones to return home. Others did not; between 1790 and 1810 seven French and one Spanish prisoners-of-war on parole were buried in the churchyard.[11] But in 1815 seven others returned after living in the town where they had been guarded by Daniel Baker, constable; that August he watched over three, quartered at *The White Hart*, and was paid £6 5s. for his 'time & subsistence during the Custody of 4 Prisoners at the Vine'.[12]

23

The Last Private Country Bank in England

Gunner's Bank, the last surviving country bank in England, with premises in Bank Street, was founded in 1809. It was not called Messieurs Gunner & Co until 1851; originally it was Fox, Steele, Seymour & Gunner. It opened at a unique time in the history of banking. England had been at war with France since 1793, which created an enormous drain on our currency. Gold was needed to pay our allies and supply the army. As early as 1797 the Bank of England suspended payments in coin but authorised payments in notes. During the war national expenditure rose from £19,000,000 to nearly £100,000,000. The Bank of England and the country banks met this need by printing notes. Indeed they printed too many, especially after 1808. By this time our ports were blockaded by the Continental System, and imports and exports were severely restricted. This over-supply of money led to inflation, the depreciation of the currency and increased agricultural distress.[1]

The Bank of England notes did not circulate beyond the London area, so country banks sprang up to finance expansion in other parts. The Bishop's Waltham Bank was one of these. When loans had been needed in the 18th century James Alexander, attorney, had supplied money to the townspeople. He lent John Earwaker, innkeeper, five guineas in 1738; in 1749 he made 34 loans, including three guineas to Dr Beech who kept the lunatic asylum.[2] It was an obvious progression for an attorney to found a private bank and William Gunner was an attorney. The other founders were Thomas Fox, wine merchant, Stephen Steele of Ashton, farmer, John Seymour, surgeon. They aimed 'to increase their respective fortunes'.

The articles of partnership stated that each partner must provide capital of £1,000. No partner was to deal in government securities on his own account. Should he place bets on horses or on any game of chance and lose £100, he would forfeit £2,000 to the other partners; his name could be struck out. No partner was to sign a bankrupt's release certificate. Each was to have his own account book; each had the right to peruse or copy from the others' books. Rooms were rented in William Gunner's house in Bank Street where clerks were appointed. Here each partner in turn must attend daily from noon until 3 p.m.[3] On the first day, 11 October 1809, the Bank issued £1,200 in £1 notes and £650 in £5 notes; in November £100 in £10 notes.[4]

Agreements were made with existing banks: at Portsmouth (Godwin, Grant and Brodidge), at Gosport (Jukes), at Southampton (Sadler, Harrison, Hunt), at Winchester (Knapp, Waller, Wickham), at Petersfield (Patrick), at Alton (Vincent and Grey), at Romsey (Warner), for the exchange of notes. Each Monday Mr Grant brought up 'all the Waltham notes' from Portsmouth to Wickham receiving his own in return.[5]

61   Bank note printed in the 1820s by Bishop's Waltham & Hampshire Bank (Gunner's Bank) unused – it is neither numbered nor signed. The Bank gave up the right to issue notes in 1844. Courtesy: Bishop's Waltham Museum Trust.

The following year the Bank was complaining of receiving from Godwin of Portsmouth and Jukes of Gosport its own notes 'mutilated in a most shameful manner', with upon them 'words of a libellous tendency ... the signatures were cut ... with a Penknife' performed 'by a Person ... known here by his obnoxious Conduct'. Godwin's Bank was asked to discourage this.

At this time there was an unfortunate rift between two families in the town. William Gunner was much disliked by William Fitz-Adderley. It was probably his wife who kept the girls boarding school in Basingwell Street in 1821. The feud continued for years, culminating in a book called *Our Town* by 'Peregrene Readpen' published in 1834. In it the townspeople of Bishop's Waltham were described minutely and mostly insultingly. The Gunner family bought up and destroyed most of the copies.

But earlier, in 1810, the Bank had other troubles; that October it found a balance owing from Godwin, bankers of Portsmouth, of £1,078 18s. 4d. It reminded Godwin that they had agreed to pay balances every Thursday.[6] The Bank was itself accused of cutting banknotes in half. It justified this as 'a general practice when sending [notes] to London by a public conveyance'; adding 'we were applied to by a Western Bank to pay them the value of 4 of £5 notes which had been cut by them and the first Halves ... lost or stolen upon the Road to London', we did so 'upon production of the remaining Halves. By far the greater part of our notes which we receive back from London after payment there, have been cut [the returned halves were then matched, glued together and reissued] ... when we find it necessary to cut any Notes we always halve them with the greatest Care'.

The partners bought government stock which they deposited with Barclays Bank in London to provide a buffer should inordinate demands be made on them. One such occasion came in 1812 when they faced a demand for £3,000. Government stocks had fallen in value so they were reluctant to sell stock on a falling market. Barclays advanced the money in return for a transference to them of £4,000 of stock. Later that year two more large amounts totalling £3,570 were drawn on the Bank which was again in difficulty, as 'a considerable sum which we have advanced to a very responsible customer ... [he] has failed to repay us at the appointed time'. Barclays again provided the funds.[7]

The partners were right to be wary; money which they had sent to Faithful, the solicitor, at Winchester, they discovered had not been used to settle the designated accounts. In autumn 1812 John Clewer, living at Botley Hill, presented a 'bill' for £150 drawn on T. Guillaume which was not honoured. 'Bills' were a sort of post-dated cheque, generally paid at seven days' notice. That year William Cobbett was also in difficulties. In November 1812 he had been released from Newgate gaol, was now at Botley Hill and in need of funds. He had sent Richard Smith at Botley a 'Draft' for £176 which was 'returned to us [the Bank] as "noted for Non payment"', as was one for £52 drawn the following year on Mr Bagshaw,[8] the publisher of Cobbett's weekly newspaper, the *Political Register*. Richard Bagshaw had been most generous over the years in discounting Cobbett's 'drafts', supplying the money with which he bought the land he farmed round Fairthorn. 'Drafts' were promises to pay, generally at 30, 60 or 90 days' notice. Cobbett used this method to raise cash, even post-dating these bills of exchange for as far ahead as eighteen months. These were then sold to money-lenders for what they would fetch. This depended very much on the state of the market and the reputation of the issuer. Cobbett was using not only his present profits but also any future profits. After his imprisonment in Newgate it was much more difficult to find people willing to discount Cobbett's bills of exchange.

Although William Cobbett survived the crisis of 1814, many farmers did not. Like him they had expanded their corn-growing acreage to supply the home market since the Continental System restricted the import of corn. When this came to an end in 1814, corn prices fell rapidly; there was a financial crash. Farmers were ruined. Two hundred and forty banks stopped payment, 89 became bankrupt. The Bishop's Waltham Bank survived. It also survived the banking crisis of 1825 when the Bank of England over-supplied notes in proportion to its reserve of gold. It was, therefore, unable to supply the demands for gold by the country banks. Gunner's overcame this difficulty by the simple expedient of refusing to supply gold for any but its own notes.

By 1840, of the original partners only William Gunner was left. He took two sons, Thomas and Charles, as partners. In 1844 the Act to regulate the Issue of Bank Notes was passed. Gunners gave up their right to issue notes; instead it agreed to circulate Bank of England notes to the limit of £1,993 in return for a payment of £19 a year.

When William retired in 1851, Charles took as partners Thomas Fox, nephew of the original founder, and Thomas Ridge, part of the extended Ridge family of Kilmeston. But Charles Gunner died aged 54 in 1872, so Caroline, his wife, took her husband's place in the rare position of lady banker, promoting James Lock, the clerk, to managing partner.

James Lock retired in 1883. Caroline made two of her sons, Captain William Gunner and Charles Gunner, solicitor, partners. It was now very much a family firm. In 1918 Robin Gunner aged 31, solicitor, became a partner, in 1923 Major Frank Gunner D.S.O. followed. These two ran the Bank together until 1953 when it was absorbed into Barclays Bank, having for 32 years been the last private country bank in England.

62 The local hunt meet at the home of the Gunner family, Ridgemede House, founders of Gunner's Bank. This is now a nursing home.

The Gunner family had married into the family of Thomas Ridge, Squire of Kilmeston, founder of the Hampshire Hunt, friend of the Prince of Wales (later George IV). Ridge had 21 children, one of whom, Lucy, married William Gunner II. His son Charles married Caroline Hale of Hambledon House.[9] The Gunners built Ridgemede House where Charles and Caroline brought up seven sons and three daughters, employing nine governesses in 11 years (1862-72). Two of the boys, William and James, were articled to tea merchants, then advanced £300 to start up their own business. The Gunners took up careers in the Army, the Navy, the Church.

William Gunner, one of the original founders, had shares in both the London and Southampton Turnpike, and the Bishop's Waltham to Fisher's Pond Turnpike. The Gunners built Ridge House estate in Portsea, where they subscribed to a mission hall.[10] Gunner's Bank had created a financial resource which greatly contributed to the 19th-century expansion of Bishop's Waltham.

24

Health and Drainage

The drainage system in Bishop's Waltham was primitive, consisting of earth closets and cesspits and the town drain. The open drains in the streets ran into the Brook. Houses near the Brook used this unofficially as their drainage system. The Brook discharged into the palace fishpond, where there was plenty of water, for it was to be 1940 before Gosport Water Company was licensed to abstract supplies. It was calculated that a million gallons a day could be abstracted from one bore hole alone.[1] In 1888 there were usually some trout in Northbrook stream[2] which was used as drinking water until the mains water was put through; even as late as 1946 there were still productive water-cress beds at both Northbrook and on the Moors.[3]

In 1831 an epidemic of cholera swept the country. That June a Central Board of Health in London was set up to warn local bodies of the risk of the disease. In Bishop's Waltham ideas of hygiene were primitive: the cottagers threw their refuse and the dung from the pigs which most of them kept into the street or piled up in odd corners. This squalor was a breeding ground of infection. Vestry met immediately to take preventitive measures. The Rector, the Curate and the Parish Officers visited the houses of the poor to see that dung heaps and filth were removed, to ensure that houses were white-washed and to stress the need for good ventilation. (Charles Kingsley, Rector of Eversley, went to extremes, visiting his parishioners with an augur with which he drilled holes through the cottage walls.)

The following year vestry formed a local Board of Health to continue these measures, but, although this Board could identify nuisances, it could not take the perpetrators to court, but merely request them to deal with problems. It consisted of 21 people. It had a budget of £20 with which to enforce cleanliness. It immediately ordered the covering of drains, bringing charges against William Nelder and nine others who had illegally channelled their privies into the Brook. Fines were imposed but these made little difference. In 1833 the surveyors of the highways were authorised to cover the drain from Mr Weston's yard.[4] As the threat of cholera receded this local Board of Health was disbanded.

Sir Edwin Chadwick published his report, *The Sanitary Condition of the Labouring Classes*, in 1842. Six years later, in 1848, another cholera epidemic swept the country, killing more than 52,000 people. A General Board of Health was now established in London with Sir Edwin Chadwick as its only salaried official until 1854. This was an advisory body not an enforcing one. In Bishop's Waltham a local Board of Health was appointed as before with power to remove nuisances and cover drains;[5] once the threat of the disease was over it was again disbanded. In 1854 cholera was found to be a waterborne disease, so the purity of drinking water was now the priority.

63   Brook Cottage, Brook Street, stood beside the brook, 'the river of the lord', which ran into the pond. It was demolished in 1973. The brook was below the level of the street; it came to act as an unofficial drain.

64   Northbrook, c.1897. Here the horses were watered, the children paddled, and watercress was grown.

The Rector, William Brock, for some years had been very concerned about the lack of a proper drainage system. When, about 1851, Sir Edward Parry came to be his neighbour in Northbrook House, the two took the matter in hand. Sir Edward was a man of wide experience; not only an accomplished naval officer, hydrographer and Arctic explorer,[6] he had been an Assistant Poor Law Commissioner in Norfolk. Together they made an exhaustive survey of the town, but the proposals they presented to vestry were summarily dismissed. A drainage system was expensive; it must therefore be unnecessary. But in 1865 Parliament passed the Sanitary Act which established the Rural Sanitary Authorities.

In 1875 vestry met again to discuss a proper drainage system. Once again the Rector, William Brock, took the chair. Convinced that 'the drainage of Bishop's Waltham is not as it should be', he stressed that 'this was not only a matter of expense but of health'. In the end he compromised, 'as the meeting was evidently opposed to adopting a system of drainage … a good system of cesspools kept in order' might be sufficient. 'Many old inhabitants had certified to the healthiness of the place'.

Mr Westbrook, one of the Guardians of the Droxford Union Workhouse, said that sewage must be prevented from flowing into the river. This could easily be done by removing some cesspools and providing others. But Mr Greaves, the Medical Officer of Health, asserted that so many cesspools would have to be provided that the drinking water would be poisoned. Mr Warner said that the cesspools must be made watertight. Mr Greaves objected that this would mean more expense as they would have to be continually emptied. Mr Garnett declared that earth closets were the answer, and obviously cheap. Mr Hewitt, who had been incensed when he had been criticised for discharging his water-closet into the Brook, had written direct to the Board of Health in Whitehall. He demanded that their inspector survey the town. The Board of Health refused and suggested a local surveyor be used. Mr Edwards, brewer, said he knew that theoretically towns were healthier when they were drained, but practically they were no better.

A committee of ten under the chairmanship of Joseph Hellard, solicitor and banker, thrashed out the question. It presented its conclusions; all closets should be earth closets and cesspits should be regularly inspected. It was again pointed out that cesspits would poison the drinking water. On this point Mr Jenner asked whether any wells were known to be poisoned, but Mr Dowse said that since a public well and pump had been provided in Basingwell Street, people had neglected their own wells, so he could not say whether any wells were contaminated, but he could say that all cesspits were not watertight. Mr Renny thought the question went wider; near his house there was an open ditch into which the town drain discharged. Mr Lock said pigsties were the problem near him.

Mr Jenner suggested an independent survey be made, but Mr Matcham considered that the Rural Sanitary Authority would be cheaper, so the task devolved on Mr Cheater, the Inspector of Nuisances. Mr Hewitt declared that the Inspector of Nuisances could not discover the nuisances and survey the town on the pay he received.

65   A girl draws water from the pump in Basingwell Street. A pump was installed before 1870 so the townspeople neglected their own wells in favour of using the parish pump. A well is recorded here in 1464.

The argument had come full circle, back to the Rural Sanitary Authority in the charge of the Inspector of Nuisances, Mr Cheater, and the Medical Officer of Health, Mr Greaves. Mr Greaves said that of course Mr Cheater would do his duty. At this remark the chairman, Mr Hellard, saw red. He declared that Mr Greaves, the Medical Officer of Health, himself had a water closet that discharged into the town drain, but that Mr Cheater, the Inspector of Nuisances, had never reported it. He felt that this was a total neglect on both their parts.

The Medical Officer admitted this. He said he would be the first to make alterations once a system was prescribed. It was not his duty to report nuisances, his duty was to suppress them. Mr Wyatt alleged that Mr Greaves' drain was laid secretly in the night, but Mr Greaves denied this. The meeting broke up with a vote of thanks to the chairman, Mr Hellard.[7]

The drainage system remained unchanged, voted down by 48 to six, four of these being solicitors. The scheme proposed would have cost £15,000 but was unnecessary because 'the death rate is low, and general health very good'; the only change made was that pigsties were to be removed 50 yards from the cottages.[8] It was to be 1960 before Bishop's Waltham went on to main drainage, but in this respect it was not unlike many other country towns.

25

Arthur Helps and
Bishop's Waltham Railway Company

Arthur Helps came to live at Vernon Hill in 1847; he immmediately diverted the old road away from his house, building a new road at his own expense.[1] Later he was to buy the Park farms and lease the Palace House. He was known as the author of the *History of the Spanish Conquest in America* and *Friends in Council*. In 1839 he had been private secretary to Spring Rice, the Chancellor of the Exchequer. In 1860, after various government posts, he was appointed Clerk to the Privy Council.[2] But in Bishop's Waltham he became a developer, capitalising on the rich clay deposits he found on his land. In 1859 he bought part of Pondside Farm, with the right to the freehold when it became available, for £3,087 16s. 2d.[3] Here he discovered large amounts of clay. The following year he submitted samples for tests to Blanchard's pottery at Lambeth, and received a favourable report.[4]

66 Sir Arthur Helps, clerk to the Privy Council, knighted in 1872, developed the Clay Company and the railway but died in debt.

In 1862 he was able to buy the right to the freehold of the remaining farms of the ancient parks from the Ecclesiastical Commissioners,[5] 835 acres for £10,143. That year he founded the Bishop's Waltham Clay Company. By 1863 it was producing both bricks and tiles. He had already established the Bishop's Waltham Gas Company which he hoped would provide fuel for this enterprise; he now founded the Bishop's Waltham Railway Company to distribute his wares. The directors of the Company were Helps, his friend William Stone, M.P. for Havant, Bettesworth Pitt Shearer, living at Swanmore House, and Edward Ricketts.[6]

The line ran through the ancient parklands, much of which Arthur Helps owned and sold to the Company for £1,229. The other land required was bought from, among others, James Warner and Charles Holdaway. A junction was made at Botley to give access to the Bishopstoke (later Eastleigh) to Gosport line, which had begun to operate in 1841. Arthur Helps insisted that two sidings be made in Bishop's Waltham, one to communicate with the Bishop's Waltham Clay Works, the other at the level crossing at Lodge Farm. Anthony Rilson and Samuel Ridley agreed to construct the line; they were to receive £10,000 in cash and £6,000 in shareholders' bonds;[7] this was later to prove an unsatisfactory arrangement. Unusually the railway included eight private level crossings, which gave access to the land worked by different farmers on both sides of the line.

67   The Bishop's Waltham to Botley branch line in 1898. The first train ran in 1863, the last in 1962.

The South Western Railway Company agreed to run the line, taking 45 per cent of the profits and with an option to buy within three years for what it had cost to build. Tariffs were set: dung, grain, gravel and pig iron were carried at 2d. per mile, sugar, hides and earthenware at 2½d., but if carried in a waggon belonging to the Company an extra 1d. was charged. Other commodities which the Company obviously thought it would carry, so specified the tariff, were sheet-iron, cotton, wool and private carriages. The carriages would cost 6d. per mile to transport. First-class passengers must pay 3d. per mile and were allowed 120 lbs of luggage; second-class paid 2d. and were allowed 100 lbs of luggage; third-class paid 1½d. per mile. They were allowed only 60 lbs of luggage.[8]

The Bishop's Waltham Railway Company was in fact always underfunded; in 1863 a second Bill was put before Parliament to raise extra capital. The following August, of the £23,780 raised £23,293 had been spent; £5,000 of this had been borrowed on the personal equity of the directors. The line itself was built for £19,876, the land and compensation cost £3,483, engineering costs were £800, parliamentary and legal bills £1,280;[9] but the station and the engine shed and the goods warehouse were yet to be built.

A temporary station, put up in a fortnight for £103, opened in May 1863. Arthur Helps agreed that, to reduce the costs of building the permanent station, the line should be extended to the chalk pits; the soil thus excavated would be used for the foundations of the station. This would obviate the need to buy more land or to make another cutting. However, this foundation proved so weak and marshy that the building sank, so the walls were later made as light as possible,

68   Fine art pottery made at Bishop's Waltham in Arthur Helps Clay Works, 1866-68, with classical themes, the figures based on Flaxman designs. Helps brought Staffordshire potters and their families to the town to help in this project. A dinner service made from this brilliant red clay was presented to Queen Victoria. Courtesy: Bishop's Waltham Museum Trust.

of wood, which was later faced with slate. The goods warehouse, begun too near the pond, had to be rebuilt on 'the Knoll between the pond and the railway further from the road'.[10] In June 1863 the line opened to the ringing of the church bells. The profit in the first six months was £310 but no dividend was paid. The following year there was a dividend of 5 per cent, only because the directors later borrowed £700 from Biddulph and Co, bankers, in their own names. That year Edward Ricketts, a major shareholder in the Clay and Tile Company, sold off most of those shares and resigned as a director of the Railway Company. The profit of the Company fell from £377 for six months in 1865 to £252 in 1868.

But the railway was essential to the Bishop's Waltham Clay Company which Helps had founded in 1862. This began by producing black bricks; some of which were used in London for the building of Blackfriars Bridge.[11] Arthur Helps assured the directors that, as soon as the Clay Company was in full production, the railway would become more profitable. In 1866 he began the production of fine art pottery, but this lasted less than two years. However, he pointed out that the railway would soon have connections, either with Alton and Alresford, or with Petersfield, connections which never materialised. He also considered that the Bishop's Waltham Water Company, which Dr Williams was floating, would prove a useful customer. (The Clay Company, however, did not use the Water Company, but relied instead on a deep well which pumped water to a water tower. The Company was only connected to the Water Company for emergencies.[12])

In 1865 Helps announced that the South of England Waggon Company had not only been recently formed, but that the site chosen for its works was in Bishop's Waltham. He insisted that another siding be constructed for it, to be carried up to the station.[13] In fact, Eastleigh was later to become the venue for the great railway works which Arthur Helps envisaged.

In 1866 the Fareham and Netley Railway Company abandoned a plan to extend their line to Bishop's Waltham. The South Western Railway Company demanded an engine shed: it was also pressing for the payment of £1,060, money which it had expended on making the Botley junction. Biddulph, the bankers, were demanding the £2,700 they had earlier loaned to the Company. These debts were paid off personally, not by Arthur Helps, but by three of the other directors – William Stone, Theodore Martin and John Moore.[14]

That same year Samuel Ridley, one of the builders of the line, demanded the repayment from the B.W.R.Co. of £2,371 17s. 10d., his principal and interest in the Company. He began a law suit which went by default since the Company had no money with which to defend the case. The following year Mr Frankish, the Company Secretary, demanded the payment of the £1,938 owed to him: Mr Collister, the engineer, demanded payment of £792 owed to him: Anthony Rilson, the other builder of the line, demanded the £3,204 owed to him.

Negotiations to buy the line were begun with the S.W.R. Co. Before these could be completed Samuel Ridley sued again; the case was put in Chancery, a notoriously slow legal process. In February 1869 the directors all resigned. Twelve years later, in August 1881, the sidings and the station and the lands and the property of the B.W.R.Co. were sold to the S.W.R. Co. for the bargain price of £20,000.[15] The Clay Company was now being run by Mark Blanchard. Under him the Clay Works thrived, now the most important brickworks in Hampshire. The railway carried not only bricks and tiles, but statues and ornamental pots.

69   Bishop's Waltham station, built in 1865.

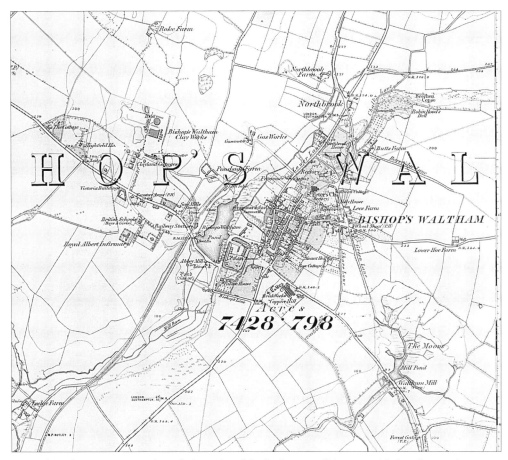

70   This ordnance survey map shows the beginning of the development of Newtown with the railway station, Clayworks, Royal Albert Infirmary, British Schools. HRO, Sheet 58 6" OS. 1868.

The railway made possible the development of Bishop's Waltham. It turned a town mostly concerned with agricultural products to one which also produced industrial material. The bricks were used to construct, among other buildings, the Victoria and Albert Museum in London and the Assembly Rooms at Edinburgh. They were shipped abroad to America and Poland.[16] The railway carried chalk from the limekilns and brought back coal for the Gas Works. The line was closed for passengers in 1933, but it continued to carry goods until 1963. Without Arthur Helps' enterprise in building the railway, industrial Newtown would never have existed in Bishop's Waltham, and the town would have remained clustered round its medieval centre. Arthur Helps continued to be fascinated by railways. In 1872, the year he was knighted, he published *The Life of Thomas Brassey*, the great railway contractor, who had died in 1870.

26

Education

In 720 Willibald, according to his biographer, was attending a monastic school at Bishop's Waltham. It is likely that the tradition of education was continued in the town by successive bishops of Winchester. They would need promising children who would later be employed on their estates. This tradition must have come to an end when Parliamentary forces destroyed the palace. After the Restoration of the monarchy, Bishop George Morley (1662-84) made good this loss. In 1679 he founded the Bishop's Waltham Grammar School, known also as the Free School. He endowed it with income from lands which had formerly belonged to Mottisfont Abbey. £10 was to be paid annually to the schoolmaster, who was to be chosen by the rector and churchwardens to teach 'the children of the poorer sort to read English and to write' free.[1]

This original foundation was added to by Robert Kerby, a remarkable man who had bought the beautiful manor and farm of Preshaw. He owned and leased barns and houses in the town, together with malthouses. (Bishop's Waltham was still known for its malting industry in 1812.) He was both clerk and bailiff of the manor and he held other manorial offices. When he died in 1721 he left all his 'Wearing Apparel of Wool to the Poor and half of my Linen … to be distributed at my Funeral'.[2] His property was sold. £400 from the proceeds were to be spent on buying land which was to be rented out; from this rent, £6 must be paid annually to teach six boys at the Grammar School without charge. If there was £7 over, both poor boys and girls, aged from five to 14, were to be chosen by the rector and churchwardens and taught in schools in the town. The boys would then fill up the places in the Grammar School as they occurred, and be called Kerby's scholars. He adjured them 'to remember to serve God and do such acts of Charity as God shall enable'.[3]

Kerby's trustees bought on the north side of Curdridge Lane 34 acres of land, marked 'Poor Bargain' on the 1866 ordnance survey map. It became known as the 'Poor's Bargain', for it was a good investment, bringing a rent of £16 per annum and periodically producing extra income from the felling of timber on the estate. (Robert Kerby had stipulated that out of this money £3 must be given to the poor at Christmas, at Easter, and at Whitsun.)

The teaching of the Christian religion was very important in the 18th century, in part to provide a robust belief against the re-introduction of Roman Catholicism, personified by James Stuart, the Old Pretender. The Society for Propagating Christian Knowledge had been founded in 1699, 'for the teaching [of] poor children … to read and write' and 'to repeat the church catechism and thus save children from Vice and Debauchery created by the gross ignorance of the Christian religion'.[4]

Mary Bone was a firm supporter of this policy. When she died she left land in the village of Lomer, deserted since the Black Death, with a charge of £20 on it for the Master of the Free School of Bishop's Waltham to teach ten poor boys, chosen by the bishop and the rector. These boys were to be kept 'constantly at school … from eight to fifteen years of age and to be instructed in reading, writing, Latin, arithmetic and the church catechism'.[5] Mary Bone also left a chalice and flagon to the church. Thirteen years later the Revd James Gibson was licensed by the Bishop to the office of schoolmaster, to teach Bishop Morley's scholars and others.[6]

At the end of the 18th century the curate, the Revd Charles Walters, was the headmaster. He was to be succeeded in 1812 by his son, also the curate, also the Revd Charles Walters (1784-1844). By then the custom was that the rector generally appointed the curate as headmaster; the curate then chose the school-master. He received a stipend of £20, the £12 remaining being retained by the headmaster, for his duties as supervisor. Under the first Charles Walters there had been one Latin scholar.[7]

In 1823 the Charity Commissioners enquired into the running of the school. The Revd Charles Walters II told them that the school was held in the room above the vestry, entered by a separate staircase in the north-west corner of the church. Thirty-two boys were being instructed in reading, writing and arithmetic. He had succeeded his father as headmaster in 1812 when he had raised the schoolmaster's salary to £25. When questioned about the teaching of Latin, he told the Com-missioners that he was prepared to teach it, but 'no one had asked for it'.[8] Both father and son supervised the Free Grammar School, but also provided an entirely classical education at their private boarding school. The Commissioners' Inquiry revealed that, although Latin had probably been taught at the Grammar School in Mary Bone's time, since Kerby's Charity did not require it, the teaching of Latin had been discontinued. Moreover, the extra £7 stipulated by Robert Kerby for the education of poor boys and girls had never been used for this purpose, but instead had been distributed to the poor.[9]

In 1822 the Revd Charles Walters continued to take private pupils in his home, one of whom, Frederick Madden, was to become the Keeper of Manuscripts at the British Museum, but that year Walters handed over his position as headmaster of the Grammar School to the Revd Thomas Scard, previously the assistant master. In 1831 Charles Walters left the parish to become Rector of Bramdean.[10]

The crisis for the Grammar School came in 1874. It was partly the result of a disagreement between the trustees of Kerby's Charity and the trustees of Bone's Charity. The rector and churchwardens were the trustees of Kerby's Charity; the rector had appointed the schoolmaster, who now combined that post with the position of curate. In 1874 William Brock, the Rector, had been unable to find a satisfactory candidate, so had high-handedly shut down the school. This caused great resentment. The trustees of Mary Bone's Charity requested an enquiry before the Charity Commissioners.

This was held in 1875 before Mr Good, one of the Commissioners. One witness was the Revd W. Allen, a former master and curate, who had served on the committee of the local Board of Health in 1848. He declared that in his time the school was very successful; 'it was a high class grammar School'. He received £15 from charitable funds and educated three boys free (considerably fewer than the foundation had stipulated). Later schoolmasters were not so conscientious; former pupils spoke of a Mr Flynn who was preparing to be a missionary, and used to 'walk up and down the room studying not attending to the boys'. Mr G. Apps, whose son was a paid scholar, said the master never gave him half an hour a morning. Asked why he had not withdrawn his son, he said there was no other school to go to.

Mr Lock declared that the people of Bishop's Waltham believed they ought to have a better school. Mr Atherley J.P. considered the 'shutting up of the school was not a proper and considerate act'. The Rector pointed out that he had paid the last schoolmaster, Mr Evans, out of his own pocket; when Mr Evans had resigned in October, the Rector had closed the school. He said that it should have been a school for boys of the poorer sort, but instead 'flourishing tradesmen have received what the poor ought to have'. Mr Atherley considered that the school was needed not so much among the poorer classes (who were in fact receiving their education at the National School in the churchyard, and the British School in Newtown) ... but by 'a class slightly above, small tradesmen, small farmers and their widows'.

The Rector considered that the conditions of entry had been abused, for at least two-thirds of the pupils were 'the children of parents who ought to have been above being indebted to these bequests ... I have always been of opinion that this school could never succeed as long as there was no house for a master's residence and no schoolroom for the boys. [It] has proved a miserable failure notwithstanding all my efforts to aid it by supplementing the miserably inadequate stipend.' He suggested that the master should be allowed to have 'an Upper Form for the boys of a superior class, whom he might train in higher subjects on their own terms'.[11]

The Charity Commissioners' plan, which was finally adopted, was to provide the money to build premises, by reducing the annual doles given to the poor by £20. This, together with the rents of the almshouses, and of the poor and recreation allotments in Waltham Chase, were to be used to provide a building. The almshouses were to be repaired and the buildings themselves sold when the trustees thought proper.[12]

These almshouses in Little Shore Lane had been founded in 1609 by Margaret Cleverley, for poor widows and other poor aged over twenty. She had appointed as trustees the rector and six tithingmen to each of whom 2s. 6d. was given on their appointment.[13]

The curriculum of the Grammar School was now to consist of English, mathematics, history, geography, book-keeping, Latin or French (two guineas extra), drawing, and vocal music. The entrance fee was ten shillings; fees were £2 to £3 a year. Twelve boys were to be instructed free, eight chosen by competition, four by nomination. The master's stipend was to be £65 per annum with £2 to £5 for each boy. The master was to live in the official house. Suitable premises were to be erected but meanwhile buildings would be rented. The meeting ended by passing a special resolution. The Royal Albert Infirmary, the hospital initiated by Arthur Helps, particularly to care for the workers of the Clay and Tile Company, which had been begun ten years earlier but was still unfinished and unused, must be acquired as a free gift for the purposes of the Grammar School.[14]

The foundation stone of the Royal Albert Infirmary had been laid in 1864 by Queen Victoria's son, Prince Leopold. It was built on high ground, so that it would be above the smoke and dirt of the brick kilns and have the benefit of sea breezes from the Isle of Wight. Fresh air was indeed the dominating principle of its construction; even the walls were made with bricks through which the air could circulate. In fact, these health-giving properties were never tested by patients.

Many people had contributed to the building fund. Queen Victoria had allowed the diaries of her Scottish holidays, *Leaves from a Highland Journal*, edited by Arthur Helps, to be sold for this purpose. The subscribers to the Infirmary considered that to use the building for the Grammar School would be fitting. They sent this proposal in writing to the Charity Commissioners. But it was only the middle of October. The Commissioners had not returned from vacation. No reply was received from them.

71 Opening of the unfinished Royal Albert Infirmary in 1865 by the Princesses Helena and Louisa and Prince Arthur; the statue to Prince Albert is unveiled. HRO, 138M84/21.

Sir Arthur Helps died in March 1875. His estate came up for auction in October. The auctioneer declared that the Infirmary, since it was built on land given by Sir Arthur, was part of his estate, more than 1,300 acres known as the Vernon Hill Estate. The Infirmary must be sold 'to clear off the expenses of the building' and pay off the creditors.

The auction held at the *Crown Inn* was a stormy affair. When bids for the Infirmary were called for, the auctioneer, Richard Austin's voice was drowned by shouts of 'You can't sell'. But despite these protests the sale did proceed. The Royal Albert Infirmary which had cost £3,000 to build, was knocked down for £1,000. The solicitor for Sir Arthur's estate offered to return a proportion of their subscriptions to the subscribers to put towards the new Grammar School, but nothing came of this.[15] Remarkably, in 1912 the Infirmary did become an educational establishment. Bought by the Roman Catholic Order, the White Fathers, it became a seminary for boys, educated to supply its mission to Africa.

The Grammar School now leased a house in Brook Street. In 1887 a last attempt was made to find a permanent site. Lee's Farm at the bottom of Free Street (now houses and a garage) was considered, but this too came to nothing.[16] In 1896 Bishop's Waltham lost its endowed Grammar School.

The Charity Commissioners combined the Grammar School endowment with the Charities for the Poor and Needy to build the Institute in Bank Street at a cost

72 Portland Square. The building on the right is the old Grammar School, shortly before its demolition in 1962 for the Lower Lane car park.

73 The Educational Institute in Bank Street opened in 1899, built with money from the Grammar School Charities and the Poor and Needy Charities. Courtesy: Bishop's Waltham Museum Trust.

of £1,800. This contained a library and reading room, and class rooms for the teaching of technical, scientific and artistic subjects. There was a public laundry room, and bathrooms for the use of parishioners, most of whose houses lacked this facility. The Institute was available on Sundays free of charge to the rector. It was open to all parishioners from Bishop's Waltham, Curdridge and that part of Swanmore which had belonged to the ancient parish of Bishop's Waltham.[17]

Private Education

Bishop's Waltham had early acquired a reputation for scholarship. A classical boarding school was conducted by the Revd James Hampton, who was described as an elegant classicist. His son became famous for a translation of the Greek historian, Polybius's *Conquest of Rome*. Thomas and Benjamin White came to this school. Born in 1724 and 1725, they were the younger brothers of Gilbert White, later the famous naturalist of Selborne,[18] who for a short while lived in Bishop's Waltham.

The town's reputation for providing a good education in the Classics (Greek and Latin), was continued by the Revd Charles Walters from 1780. William Cobbett sent his two eldest sons here in 1805, after he had come to live in Botley.[19] However Cobbett was soon disenchanted with their instruction. He removed them from the school, for he had no time for the teaching of dead languages.

In 1793 more than 120 young ladies were instructed by Miss Jemima Jones at her establishment in Church Lane, now St Peter's Street. This seems an enormous number for the existing house, but the girls would sleep two or three to a bed, although these cramped conditions meant that contagious diseases such as tuberculosis were easily passed on. They learned embroidery among other subjects. One of their worked pictures of flowers came into the possession of James

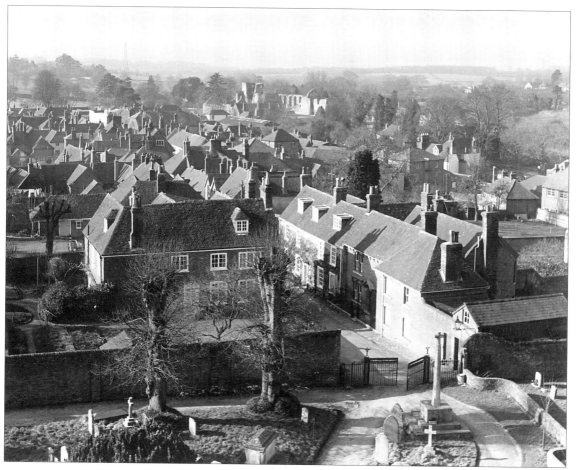

74 The town in 1962 looking towards the Palace. No demolition has yet taken place. Hope House, the boarding school for young ladies, faces the churchyard on the left.

Padbury, clockmaker.[20] In 1797 Miss Jones paid 14 guineas a year for seating in the newly erected south gallery of the church for the accommodation of some of her pupils.[21] Cobbett probably sent his eldest daughter, Anne, to this school in 1805.[22] Four years later Miss Jones retired, handing over the school to 'Mrs Hurst, a lady she can recommend'.[23] From here one of the pupils eloped with a French officer, a prisoner in the town during the Napoleonic Wars. He had been courting her with letters tossed over the school wall.

In 1835 Pigot's *Directory* lists the educational facilities available in the town. Not only was there the Free Grammar School in Basingwell Street with James Knight, the master: there were now two gentlemen's boarding schools: the Revd Thomas Scard's Classical Academy in Brook Street, the other in Northbrook Road kept by Charles Robinson. There were two ladies' boarding schools, one in Church Lane now under Maria Rosewell, while Sarah Fitz-Adderley ruled the other in Basingwell Street.

Public Education

The Revd James Ogle became Rector in 1802. He considered education necessary for all the children in the parish. As early as 1807 Samuel Whitbread M.P. had proposed a Bill to introduce public religious education throughout the country, but few people agreed with him. William Cobbett, among others, wondered whether working-class education was either advisable or desirable. It was much better for the poorer classes to learn a trade.[24]

To some extent in Bishop's Waltham the boys were already catered for by the Grammar School, but there was little opportunity for cheap education for girls, although the Rector himself contributed £2 a year for the education of six poor girls.[25] The Rector decided in 1816 to rent the room above the market hall, which William Jennings, the parish clerk, had previously used as a school room,[26] for a girls' school. It was to be run on Dr Bell's Church of England principles. Dr Bell had served in India as the superintendent of the Madras military orphanage; since there were few teachers available he had employed his pupils as monitors. The Noncomformists founded the Lancastrian Schools on the same principle, which had been publicised by Joseph Lancaster in 1798. These spread, so in 1811 the Church of England founded the National Society for the Education of the Poor, appointing Dr Bell as the superintendent.

Eleven years later, in 1822, James Ogle established a National School for Boys. Built in a corner of the churchyard, it was financed by the Rector and by the boys, who brought their school pence – a penny a week. In 1833 these schools were given a small grant from government funds but there was no compulsory state education until 1870, when the leaving age was thirteen.

Another school was built in Newtown for the children of the skilled workers who were brought from Staffordshire in 1862 by Arthur Helps for his newly established Bishop's Waltham Clay Company. The Congregational minister, the Revd W. Maunsell, was the driving force behind this project. (The Congregational chapel had been built in Lower Lane in 1862.) This school, which was built by 1865, provided places for 250 children. It cost £1,400, all raised by voluntary

75   The development of Newtown showing the *Railway Inn* and, on the right, the British and Foreign School in Victoria Road. This was built for the children of the clay workers.

contributions. Three of Queen Victoria's children, the Princesses Louisa and Helena and Prince Arthur, who had come to open the unfinished Royal Albert Infirmary, went on to view the school.

The Revd W. Maunsell addressed the company; dwelling on the necessity of education, he said 'a field left to itself would soon become barren, a garden … a ruin, a vessel a wreck. So a child left to itself would go from bad to worse till it lost all self-control, became a mere animal and a pest to society'.[27] The school was run on the principles of the noncomformist British and Foreign Bible Society. In 1870 Forster's Education Act allowed the appointment of a school board, which might raise a local rate for the school.

By 1882 the National School building in the churchyard had become obsolete; the boys were now attending the British School in New Town. The National School was therefore repaired, a classroom and a playground were added, and it became the Infants School. But 12 years later a new Infants School was built (now the library), so the old National School in the corner of the churchyard was demolished. The British School in Newtown had to be enlarged in 1894 when Ebenezer Sims was the headmaster.

The 1944 Education Act introduced selection at eleven. Pupils now went to Secondary Modern schools or to Grammar Schools so the old British School became the Junior School. In the 20th century, when the Ridgemede estate was planned, the Junior and Infant schools were both built there, with the Secondary School at Swanmore. This has now become Swanmore Technical College.

27

The White Fathers

In the 19th century enthusiasm for foreign missions was at its height. It inspired Charles Lavigerie, who was appointed Roman Catholic Archbishop of Algiers in 1867. It was the year when a cholera epidemic devastated the area; this was followed by a plague of locusts, drought, floods and finally deep snow. In the resulting famine a fifth of the population died.

The Archbishop distributed relief funds. He discovered many children left as orphans, so he established an orphanage under the Sisters of Charity. Its doors were open to all children without discrimination. They were educated as young Christians. Charles Lavigerie's plan was to use these young Arabs as Christian missionaries in Africa.

Before long other Europeans were attracted to join Charles Lavigerie. They became the founding members of 'The White Fathers' with a mission to

76   The founder of the White Fathers' Society, Cardinal Lavigerie, 1825-1892.

evangelise Africa. Seven novices were enrolled in the Order. Western dress would hinder their acceptance by the Arabs, so – like Arabs – they were clothed in white robes, with a mantle, a red cap, and with a rosary. By 1894 the Order had spread into Central Africa, Tanganyika, and Nyasaland, the missionaries coming from all over Europe except from Britain.

But in 1912 two White Fathers came to England to find suitable buildings for a school for French students. The Roman Catholic Bishop of Portsmouth suggested Bishop's Waltham, a pleasant country town within easy reach of Southampton, Winchester and London, where the school chapel would provide a place of worship for the scattered Roman Catholic congregation. They decided on the former Royal Albert Infirmary. This had been bought by a Dutchman in 1875: it had been transformed by him and the succeeding owner into a gentleman's residence with beautiful terraced gardens. It had already been called The Priory.

In 1913 a seminary was built beside the house, with room for 60 boys. Five years later it opened with 12; by 1923 there were 70 boys. The school badge was a pelican, Charles Lavigerie's own device. The boys came at 13 years of age, spent five years at Bishop's Waltham, then took the London Matriculation examination. The excitement of their vocation was instilled in them, for the house was furnished with maps of Africa and trophies; lances, poisoned arrows, the skins of wild beasts. Visiting missionaries came to describe their life.

The boys were kept hard at work, with only one hour's recreation each day and 20 minutes' manual labour, either in the gardens or at the farm kept by the Lay Brothers. They were not closely supervised, for the object of their education was to build up their character, so that as men they would act according to their convictions. There was a monthly retreat of one day and a three-day retreat each year. From Bishop's Waltham the boys went to the School of Philosophy at Autreppe in Belgium. Here they stayed two years, learnt French and received the white habit. After a holiday at home they went to their novitiate in Algeria and then to the missionary fields of Africa. There they lived a spartan existence, the offerings at Mass being their only income.

The first White Father to be educated at Bishop's Waltham was priested in 1926.[1] The White Fathers kept their school here until 1967,[2] by which time the supply of boys, who now came from the north of England, had dried up. The school was closed; the buildings were sold to become a training college for the police. The graveyard, however, remained Roman Catholic property, and the present Roman Catholic church was built nearby. The Police College in its turn became obsolete, the land was sold and is now used for houses.

28

The Accounts of James Brown Alexander

The parish poor rate book 1756-60 contains also the private accounts of James Brown Alexander, a parishioner of Bishop's Waltham. It gives an insight into a middle-class life in the town 1734-51. In it he reveals what he ate and drank and wore, the tradesmen he dealt with, his business interests, and he hints at a secret part of his life which remains secret. He has left us his name in the area known as 'Alexander Moors'.

James Brown Alexander was an attorney of moderate means. Although he knew the parish officers well, he never served as one, for attorneys, like peers and clergymen, were excused this duty by law.

Born in 1712,[1] Alexander was articled to Mr James Lacy, attorney, when he was twenty-one. His first duties were as messenger; he took instructions to Petersfield, Portsmouth and Southampton. He made a journey to London via Farnham, where he spent £1 10s. 'for Supper and Drinkables Breakfast next morning', with 11d. on 'Corn and Hay for my horse (not being well)'.

Mr Lacy acted for Admiral Vernon, so Alexander was sent to Gosport in May 1736 'to take the answer of Keble and Others Ad[vers]us Vernon'.[2] Admiral Vernon had been living in Vernon Hill House certainly since 1731, when he was churchwarden for Ashton tithing. The house was altered by Admiral Vernon but it was not built by him, for part is Elizabethan.[3] In 1739 Admiral Vernon fought against Spain in the West Indies, won the victory of Porto Bello and great popularity. He reduced drunkenness in the navy by ordering that his men drink grog, rum diluted with water. He had been M.P. for Portsmouth; later he became M.P. for Ipswich so left Bishop's Waltham to live at Nacton in Suffolk, where he gave land on which to build a workhouse.[4]

77   Edward Vernon (1684-1757), Admiral of the White, in 1745. He commanded the Channel fleet and prevented French reinforcements reaching the Jacobites. By courtesy Royal Naval Museum.

In August 1736 Alexander again went to London. Here he made special preparations before a journey; he exchanged his buckles, had one ring newly set and bought another. He then travelled to the Continent, where in Flanders he bought 'Shirts Necks and Handkerchiefs'.[5] He does not tell us the reason for this journey nor whom he was going to meet. On 10 February 1737 he completed his articles. He was sworn in as an attorney with 'Commission to take Affidavits in K[ing's] B[ench] and C[ommon] B[ench]'.

78 Vernon Hill House in 1919, originally an Elizabethan house, where Admiral Vernon was living in 1731 when he was churchwarden of Ashton tithing. It has been extended over the centuries. Later Arthur Helps lived here.

Attorneys acted as bankers, for there were few private country banks to supply credit. As Lacy's articled clerk, Alexander carried money to be put out at interest, in 1736 as much as £400 for Mrs Dansey. Ready money was tight; there was not a lot in circulation. Alexander lent money on his own account: 5s. 6d. to Christmas Hewitt's wife for a new cloak, two guineas to John Knight, shoemaker. In 1749, among 34 loans was one to John Stevens for £16.

From his mother, Anne, Alexander inherited the lease of Cleverley Wood in Dean, part of the bishop's demesne. This was cultivated as coppice with standards; in 1743 he sold one of the standing trees, 11 feet of oak, to Christmas Hewitt, carpenter, for 3s. 3d. Part of his inheritance was the patronage of the churches of Bishop's Sutton and Ropley, which he traded to Sir Berkeley Lucy for an annuity of £10 a year, but was still responsible for the upkeep of the vicarages. He re-thatched the Ropley vicarage in 1742. Today many of the cottages in Ropley are still thatched.

James Alexander kept some accounts for the Cleverley family and managed Mary Hackett's estate. Mary had been left an orphan at the age of five, her parents and grandparents having died. She inherited both houses and copyhold land.[6] Alexander obtained compensation for her when all her fields were sown with oats; a third should have been allowed to lie fallow to regain their fertility. He rented out the cellar of one of her tenements to Baynes, the innkeeper of *The Dolphin*. He repaired the middle tenement, partitioning it to make room for a lodger, and let it to Mr Franklin of Fareham for £3 a year. When one of her tenants, Brown, absconded without paying his rent, Alexander secured the goods left behind, and sold them as compensation for Mary.

From 1737 Molly, as she came to be called, boarded with Mrs Armstrong, schoolmistress, for £10 a year. Alexander paid for Molly's caps and gowns, and for a dress-hoop when she was nineteen. He allowed her money to spend on ribbons, gloves and buckles at Waltham Fair (there were four fair-days). He must have inadvertently given Molly his piece of touchgold. This gold, having been been touched by a Stuart king, was considered to have miraculous healing properties. Molly gave the touchgold back to Alexander, receiving half a guinea in exchange. Earlier he had been operated on by Mr Salmon, the surgeon, so perhaps was relying on the touchgold to complete the cure.

When she was 21 Molly was allowed to write her own receipt, for the £1 10s. which Alexander gave her to spend at Wickham Fair, still held on 20 May. In 1749 Molly, aged 23, married Ezekiel Donniger, organist, the son of the first organist of St Peter's, also called Ezekiel Donniger. Molly's husband, a mercer, died in 1755, Molly in 1764, but their son, the third Ezekiel Donniger, born in 1751, was both 'Organist of Waltham for many years' and postmaster. He lived until 1833.[7]

Alexander kept detailed house-keeping accounts until 1746. The year before, in 1745, he spent £45 18s. 3d. This included sea coal supplied by Mr Horner and wood from Thomas Earwaker. A quarter of the total was spent on alcohol. It included half a hogshead (27 gallons) of cider, eight gallons of brandy, beer and malt for brewing, and French wine, probably smuggled. He also drank chocolate, and tea at 6s. 6d. a lb. He enjoyed good food, eating oysters, whiting, duck, veal, eel (from the palace pond) and French beans. On Easter Eve he spent 3s. 6d. on a ham, a fowl and greens. In April he observed the 'Fast Day for the French war', consuming only salt-fish and eggs. He records his recipe for soup, using a small leg of beef and onions to which was added 'Sallary Leek Thyme Cabbage Spinage Watercresses purslain Endiff and you may add parsley & Marygolds'.

Four weeks in the summer were set aside for washing clothes, with extra money spent on soap, firewood and a boy to carry the water. He chiefly bought his clothes from local tradesmen. John Jones, the tailor, made his coats, Frank Penny supplied half a dozen night-caps: from Hart, who shaved him for nine shillings a year, he bought a hat and a wig. Christmas Hewitt framed his maps and pictures.

His leisure time was spent at the inns, chiefly at *The Dolphin* kept by Mr Baynes. (Today it is the greengrocery shop[8] next to the post office.) Alexander was there when the sign went up in 1736. In February that year he began to list his 'Idle Expenses' but he had abandoned this disheartening task by May. He enjoyed a game of cards, but mostly lost, and wrote himself a Memorandum 'Not to play at a publick house more', a memorandum which he did not keep. He continued to lose at cards, at quoits, at kittlepins, at cock-fighting.

James Alexander paid a poor rate, land tax, church rate, window tax. He also contributed to the briefs. These were licences given to those who had suffered disasters, mostly through fires. Their cases were read out in church and a collection was taken after the service. He contributed to the organist's salary and to the new infirmary at Winchester.

Outwardly a respectable attorney whose only vice was to forget his reminders to himself – 'mind never more to play at cards any more at Baynes nor drink by half pints'. One entry in March 1741 shows another side to his character, when he

79 The High Street, looking towards Bank Street. *The Dolphin Inn*, frequented by James Alexander in the 1730s and 1740s and by the parish officers, is the shop next to the Post Office.

paid for 'a bottle of Rum, Sugar, Lemmons pipes & Tobacco when we ate R Hackett's venison'. Venison belonged to the bishop; this venison could have been poached from the park. Had Hackett been one of the notorious Waltham Blacks, a gang who with black faces in 1723 terrorised Waltham Chase, stealing the bishop's deer? E.P. Thompson has suggested that the activities of the Waltham Blacks might have been cover for a Society of Jacobite supporters, intent on restoring the Stuarts to the throne.[9] On this occasion Alexander rewarded Bett Hackett, who had no doubt cooked the venison, with one guinea 'for her trouble', a considerable sum, indeed perhaps a bribe to secure her secrecy, for he gave his housekeeper, Hannah Knight, only three guineas for a whole year's wages. Perhaps the Waltham Blacks had not disbanded but gone underground, waiting for a future occasion to serve the Stuart cause.

There is some evidence that Jacobite supporters may possibly have reappeared in Bishop's Waltham. When Alexander made his journey to the Continent in 1736, dressed to meet someone of importance, had he been in touch with Jacobites on the Continent? Had he become a 'sleeper', ready to organise assistance when an opportunity to restore the Stuarts should occur?

From the Civil Wars onwards Bishop's Waltham, like Petersfield and Basing, had been fiercely Royalist. James II (1685-8), as he rode through from Portsmouth to Winchester, called it 'his little green town',[10] for the houses were decorated with the boughs of trees in leaf, a reminder also that the Chase was part of the parish. James II planned to restore the country to Roman Catholicism, but in 1688

William of Orange and Mary his wife became joint monarchs. James fled to France. His family became the focus for the restoration of the Stuarts. There were unsuccessful attempts in 1708, 1715, 1719, 1722. That year Francis Atterbury, the Bishop of Rochester, plotted to restore James Stuart (the Old Pretender) to the throne. Sir Henry Goring, a fellow conspirator, wrote that he could supply one thousand well armed Waltham Blacks, commanded by five Hampshire gentlemen, for this cause.[11] Alexander was then only a boy of ten. He would grow up on the stories of the Waltham Blacks and their suspected Jacobite allegiance. Were there any still living in Bishop's Waltham? Who was the 'Mountibank & Ratcatcher' whose twins James and Susanna were born at John Hacket's in 1725, their father's name unrecorded?[12]

On 10 November 1740 there is the first record of a Society which met at Alexander's house. Its purpose is never specified but its expenses are. At that first meeting 3s. 7d. was spent on 'Tobacco pipes Bread butter at ye Society'. On 1 February 1741 it met in the evening, 9s. spent on the same items together with candles and glasses, these perhaps used to toast the Old Pretender, 'the King over the water'. The next meeting in March cost £1 7s. for it included rum. On 20 May 'Wine Sugar pipes Tobacco and Rum [were bought] at the Dancing & Society'. The Society did not meet again until December 1742.

In 1742 England was fighting in the unpopular war of Austrian Succession, which many considered protected the interests of Hanover, rather than of England. Resentment of the Hanoverian King, George II, grew.

In 1743 the 'Society' met five times. That summer a French agent came over to enquire the strength of support for the Jacobite cause. In November the French began their preparations to restore the Stuarts. That December the Society met again.

The next year, in January 1744, King Louis XV of France invited Charles Edward Stuart (the Young Pretender) to Paris. He slipped in disguise out of Rome, where he had been living, to France to await an invasion force. By March this had been assembled by Louis at Gravelines. Louis gave orders that when Charles Stuart landed in England he was to issue a proclamation that he, Louis XV, was helping the English people 'to restore the rightful King and shake off the foreign yoke'. This came to nothing for a fierce storm destroyed the invasion fleet. In March, France declared war on England. The Society next met on the evening of 21 November when its expenses were 'Rum & Brandy 15.0 Cheese 5.9 Bread Tobacco … [Society] 3.1 Candles 1.7'.

The following February a very few members of the Society met, for only 1s. 4d. was spent on 'A loaf Tobacco … for Society'. It met again in May. In Belgium at Tournai British forces under the Duke of Cumberland were defeated at the battle of Fontenoy. They were then recalled to prepare for a Jacobite threat.

On 23 July 1745 Charles Stuart landed in Scotland: that same day the Society met in Bishop's Waltham. It met again in October. In November the Young Pretender crossed into England: he marched south, taking Preston in November, entering Derby in December. He then began to retreat back to Scotland. On 17 January 1746 the English forces under General Hawley were routed at Falkirk.

80   Admiral Vernon's fleet lying in Spithead in 1741. Portchester Castle is at the bottom right. By courtesy Royal
Naval Museum.

The Society met on 22 January when 4s. was spent on 'Candles Tobacco Butter
pipes'. On 16 April Charles Edward, the Young Pretender, was defeated at the
Battle of Culloden. Very few came to the next meeting of the Society on 2 July,
and only 9d. was spent. That September Alexander spent five days in London. By
29 September Charles Edward had escaped to France. On 1 October the Society
met for the last time.

Was this the record of the final meeting of a Jacobite Society centred in
Bishop's Waltham? Records of Jacobite Societies are rare for they were too
dangerous to keep; 'the custom in Jacobite days [was] to destroy all letters with
any hint of political or religious feeling in them'[13] and this must apply also to
accounts.

But the evidence is compelling. Alexander cherished a piece of touchgold
which was held to prove that the Stuarts were Kings by Divine Right. The
Hanoverians did not 'touch', regarding this as superstition.

James Lacy, attorney of Bishop's Waltham, already had a connection with the
Jacobite Caryll family through Philip Caryll who had fled to France in 1710. In
1730 James Alexander, who was to be articled to Lacy in 1733, was sent to Paris
to bring back the £300 which John Caryll of Ladyholt had loaned to his daughter-
in-law, Lady Mary Caryll, for the use of her 'particular friend', Mr Polwheel.[14]

In 1735 John Caryll, who lived at Ladyholt, South Harting in Sussex, just over the border from Hampshire, wrote to Lacy informing him of his cousin Philip's death. Lacy wrote back, 'I … am heartily sorry for the Death of my Dearest and good friend Mr Philip Caryll of Dunkirque and I in answer to you say that on the one and twentieth day of Aprill 1733 he made a Will in writing … and made me Executor'.[15] Lacy and Alexander were then both well known to the Carylls. They in turn were connected with many important Roman Catholic families among them the Gorings and the Petres.

Alexander's profession took him to London where there was much Jacobite support: from 1740 to 1750 there were eight Jacobite lord mayors: earlier, in 1733 one, John Barber, had even displayed portaits of the Stuart princes in the Guild-hall.[16] Alexander, then, was ideally placed to keep contact between Jacobite supporters in Hampshire and Jacobite mayors in London, to bring news of Bonnie Prince Charlie's successes or defeats. He had acted for John Caryll of Ladyholt, who was one of only a handful of Jacobites privy to Louis XV's invasion plan of 1744.[17] The 'Society' met in Alexander's house from 1740 to October 1746. During this time the restoration of the Stuarts was eminently possible. Charles Stuart escaped to France in September 1746. In October 1746 the Society met for the last time. The page of the account book has then been cut away.

From September 1753 to March 1755 Gilbert White lived at Bishop's Waltham Rectory while he was Curate of Durley. The old people told him of the Waltham Blacks, that to become a Waltham Black was a way of proving manliness and that some of the Waltham Blacks were not labourers but gentlemen.[18] Did they also hint that there had been a more recent Jacobite Society in Alexander's house?

But the vital page in Alexander's accounts has been cut off. However there is a postscript. In the February following the last meeting of the 'Society', Hannah Knight, Alexander's housekeeper, 'gave me warning to leave my service'. She did not, but there comes a change. Alexander no longer listed the intimate details of his household. Hannah Knight took charge of the accounts. Perhaps this was the bribe Alexander paid to secure Hannah's secrecy.

In 1749 Alexander made a garden with asparagus beds, bushes, cherry trees, raspberries, artichokes. He employed Robert Garrett as his gardener for 16 shillings a year. But Alexander had not long to enjoy the produce of his new garden, for he died in 1751. His household effects were sold; his library of books brought £12. His friends mourned his loss with six bottles of wine supplied by Mr Baynes at *The Dolphin*, where Alexander had so often been unlucky in his games of chance.[19]

29

The Growth of Bishop's Waltham

When the first census was taken in 1801, the population of Bishop's Waltham numbered 1,773; it rose steadily until 1871 when there were 2,618 inhabitants. In the following ten years it declined by 214: farming was in crisis owing to a succession of poor harvests and cheap imports from America (from 1872-1900 one third of the agricultural population of the whole country left the land). But the Clay Works were thriving, employing more than 200 men on a 20-acre site, their products being exported to Egypt, Peru, South Africa.

The composition of the parish changed. In 1838 Curdridge had separated: in 1846 part of Hoe tithing was taken into the new parish of Swanmore. Despite these losses, in 1901 Bishop's Waltham reached a peak of 3,028 inhabitants, a figure it was not to reach again until 1961. From 1911-21 it decreased by 540,[1] and arable land was converted to pasture, since milk production was more profitable but required less labour.

Farming provided employment for many who were intent on improving their skills. Technical classes were held at the old Grammar School from 1892 at one penny a lesson. They included the management of livestock, agricultural machinery, farm drainage, vegetable and fruit growing, and cultivation under glass for market gardening was profitable. (In 1899 Walter Gamblin advertised fresh vegetables grown in his own glasshouses.) Ten people passed the exam set by the travelling Dairy School. Six years later three were awarded scholarships to the County Council Farm at Basing; two were taken up, the other prize winner being a married woman. Strawberries were grown in the fields along the Botley road. School holidays in June allowed the children to help with the picking. School attendance was patchy and children were kept at home at harvest time. In 1897 parents were urged to send the children regularly, otherwise it was unfair to teachers and to ratepayers who must pay a heavier rate, for government subsidy depended on school attendance figures.

It was a time of self-improvement, with classes in wood-carving, woodwork, poultry management, cooking. Dr Charles Hemming gave a series of lectures on house drainage, cottage sanitation, water, infectious diseases, food adulteration, eyesight, sound and climate. Thirty-five attended classes in shorthand and book-keeping, English history and mensuration. Reading, writing, composition, model-ling in clay, drawing, building construction, gymnastics could all be learnt. In 1895, after a measles epidemic, 88 people attended Miss Taylor's lectures on home nursing.[2]

The Methodist chapel was built in Basingwell Street in 1909. Earlier the Methodists had met in 1805 at John Allen's house, Botley Hill. By 1817 they were meeting in William Aslett's house in Basingwell Street which was owned by

William Savage, shoemaker.[3] Later the Mission Hall was built near the *Mafeking Hero*. The Salvation Army built its second Citadel along the Winchester road; the Congregational chapel had come in 1862.

The end of the 19th century saw a movement for teetotalism. Fry's, the chemists, offered non-intoxicating ale. The *Jasper Temperance Hotel* in Bank Street sold 'good tea, coffee and cocoa at 1d per cup'. The Temperance Society met in the old Grammar School. A public meeting supported a petition to Parliament for the Sunday closing of public houses. The Cyclists Blue Cross Abstainers visited the town for a service in church, then tea in the Rectory garden. Mary Sumner, the founder of the Mothers Union, addressed the first meeting of the Bishop's Waltham group, while a branch of the Hampshire Needlework Guild sent 50 garments a year to the houses and hospitals of poor parishes in London. These included day and night shirts, flannel waistcoats, shifts, knitted stockings, knee caps, shawls and hoods.

81   The old rectory, now Longwood, in 1913 when Canon Sharpe was the incumbent. James Ogle, rector 1802-33, remodelled the rectory, building the handsome west-facing drawing-room.

The parish was self-reliant. When in 1891 the winter was severe, the First Volunteer Hampshire Regiment held a smoking concert, the proceeds spent on coal for the poor. Subscribers funded every parish event, their names published in the parish magazine. When Queen Victoria's Diamond Jubilee was celebrated there was tea and sports for 1,350 on the cricket field, the church bells were recast and a library begun at the Institute. When the Workmen's Hall, where the young men met their friends, needed refitting, an entertainment of tableaux which included 'Venus at her Toilette' was held at the old Grammar School. There was room too for private hospitality; the Revd Melville Churchill invited 200 parishioners annually to take tea at his house at Southbrook, while the choir went to Mr and Mrs Charles Gunner at Swanmore Cottage.[4]

82   Buyers crowd round to judge the animals up for auction in Bishop's Lane Field in 1909. Abbey Mill is the building in the distance.

Bishop's Waltham was thriving, the town was worth investing in. From 1870-98 Gunner's Bank profits almost doubled (£1,100-£2,100). The Capital and Counties Bank opened in the High Street in 1899: it was absorbed by Lloyds in 1918. In 1921 Barclays Bank opened opposite it.[5] The two brickworks, Claylands and Coppice Hill, were in operation, Claylands producing the strongest hand-made bricks in the country.[6] Although the weekly market was not held, regular cattle and sheep auctions took place in the Crown Field, and animals were then transported by rail. The town served a scattered agricultural community, with tradesmen supplying all requirements. There were bakers, brewers, smiths, a gunsmith, an ironmonger who was a 'Manufacturer of Steam and Hot Water Apparatus', cabinet makers, a draper (calicoes imported from Manchester), a clockmaker, cycle shop, milling. (James Duke who supplied animal feeds expanded from Abbey Mill into Lower Lane, taking over Edward's brewery in the 1920s.) There were hay and corn dealers, while threshing machines and traction engines could be hired from Pondside Farm. Farms were still part of the town; Lee's Farm occupied the corner of Free Street and a dairy farm stood next to the Institute. The old Palace stables kept horses at livery.[7] In 1921 there were 38 farms and small-holdings. The only farm of more than 150 acres was Pondside, farmed by George Doggrell. In 1939 there were 45 farms, with Sidney Trigg farming at both Pondside and Northbrook.[8]

The 19th century had seen the town expanding. Five speculative brick cottages were built at Beeches Hill, with two more at Dundridge, while close to the church a cottage and carpenter's shop adjoining Maypole Cottages was advertised.[9] In 1904, when the Butts estate belonging to the Clark family was sold, building plots were offered along the Hoe road, at Middle Hoe Farm, a mixed farm of 35 acres, and at Lower Hoe Farm, which consisted of an acre of ground suitable for poultry and fruit.[10] In and around the town larger houses had already been built: Eastways at the bottom of Coppice Hill, Mount House in Little Shore Lane, and The Thicketts along the Botley road.

83 Billhead from E.C.Miles, Bank Street, builder, contractor, undertaker. Pumping was a speciality, and he provided a windmill and engine service for dairy farmers.

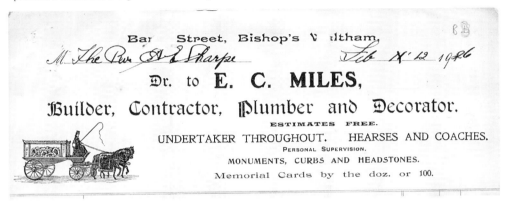

Newtown, too, was growing. Mark Blanchard, the owner of the brickworks, had built Claylands House as an advertisement for his products, while Mark's Terrace provided accommodation for his workmen. Larger detached houses were creeping along the Winchester road, smaller ones along the Avenue and Park road. Newtown was self-sufficient with its own inn, the *Railway*, butcher, baker, and post office.[11]

Motor traffic came gradually to the town in the 1930s. The South Hampshire buses began their regular services to Portsmouth, Fareham and Southampton. By 1939 John Green advertised as a motor engineer on the Winchester road as did Harry Lee on the Swanmore road, while Rookes garage in Station Road was the official repairer for the AA and RAC with garaging for 50 cars. Robert Symes in Newtown was the motor-cycle agent.[12]

In 1914 between thirty and forty men immediately volunteered to serve in the army; later Northbrook House became a hospital for wounded soldiers.[13] Bishop's Waltham's proximity to Portsmouth made it a convenient base for the armed forces. By 1939 seven army and nine naval officers had taken up residence.

84 Milk being delivered round the town in 1926 from Butts Farm, the site of the town butts off Free Street. The farm dairy shop remained until c.1965.

85 Maypole Cottages (now Old Pound) in Free Street in 1913. The Maypole stood on the green; the entry to the old rectory is on the right.

86 Mark Blanchard II, the successful owner of the Bishop's Waltham brickworks in 1900, with his family outside Claylands House, built to show off his wares.

Vice Admiral Sir Andrew Browne Cunningham KCB, DSO was living in the Palace House.[14] During the Second World War Buryfield Farm at the top of Beeches Hill was one of 30,000 listening posts for German Army radio traffic. This was passed on to Bletchley Park,[15] where the code-breaking Enigma machine was invented.

But half-way through the 20th century the town began to decline. In 1957 brick production in Newtown and at Coppice Hill came to an end. Waltham Chase mill was no longer producing feed stuffs. Duke's mill at Abbey pond was

87   The new road sweeps past the Palace and across the Pond, 1972. The central car park area has just been cleared.

being used for warehousing, although animal feeds were still manufactured in Lower Lane.[16] Farming land, which had been of such vital importance during the Second World War, was taken out of cultivation. Fewer agricultural workers were needed. The cattle auctions finished. The last train pulled out of the station in 1962.

This was of great significance to Bishop's Waltham; throughout the country road-traffic was encouraged; roads were improved, railways abandoned. Within eight years of the last train running, a roundabout had been built on the station site to speed road-traffic from Portsmouth, Southampton and Winchester.

By 1966 the government had decided that South Hampshire should become a growth area, not only to absorb a workforce which was moving to the newly established electronics and high tech industries here, but also to take in London overspill. Professor Colin Buchanan was commissioned to work out a feasibility study. He proposed the foundation of 'Solent City', a 12-mile-deep strip of coast 'bounded by the New Forest on the west, the sea on the south, the chalk hills on the north, Sussex on the east'. It would eventually accommodate 1,700,000 people. Southampton and Portsmouth, congested as they were, must be redesigned. John Arlott, writing in the *Hampshire Magazine*, described this as 'twenty-five miles by

88 Houchin Street in 1917. The first Salvation Army Citadel is the pedimented building on the right.

89 Laying brushwood across the pond for the bypass in 1965.

twelve of suburbia', 'landscaped' by green strips and clumps of woodland.[17] It would absorb not only Eastleigh but also Bishop's Waltham. It was opposed by Winchester Rural District Council.

But the effects of the increased road-traffic could already be seen in the town. In 1964 the old Grammar School and nearby properties in Portland Square were demolished to provide a car park. This was soon condemned as too far away from the centre of the town. Buildings had already been bought up by the RDC to provide space for a central car park. Old cottages in Houchin Street had been pulled down, the residents rehoused in purpose-built bungalows along the Hoe road. These were convenient, but too far for the elderly to walk into the town to shop or chat.

Bishop's Waltham was being demolished before the residents' eyes. Fortunately the planners left the inner court of the bishop's palace intact, but the outer court took the full brunt of road improvements. In 1970 the ancient palace stables were demolished, the new bypass pushed right across the palace fishpond. However the passage of the Civic Amenities Act of 1967 had contained the concept of 'conservation areas' and in 1970 the centre of the town was declared a conservation area, though this did not stop the continuing destruction of Houchin Street and the west side of Basingwell Street.

Despite all the demolition of its medieval centre, in 1971 the architectural historian, David Lloyd, wrote that Bishop's Waltham, although within one of the

90 The Millennium Clock surmounted by the Bishop of Winchester's mitre, celebrating Queen Elizabeth II's Golden Jubilee was dedicated in June 2002.

fastest growing regions of Britain, 'remained a relative backwater'.[18] A public meeting with the planners made the point that the existing inhabitants wished to welcome newcomers, not be swamped by them. A revised township plan now time-scheduled the land due for development; 22 acres 1970-75, 10 acres 1975-80, 28 acres 1980-85, 14 acres 1985-90. The planning officer in exasperation urged the inhabitants to 'accept some element of the twentieth century in Bishop's Waltham'.[19]

The sale of the allotments at Claylands allowed the development of housing there, the proceeds being used to build the Jubilee Hall. Houses began to be built around the town; Mount House, Eastways, and Pondside were pulled down to make way for them. The ground along Lower Lane was built over, the Rareridge estate developed.

The palace pond, now bisected by the Winchester road, was becoming silted up. A public meeting asked that, to improve the pond, less water be abstracted by the Portsmouth Water Company, but this was not acted on. One divisional surveyor, ignoring the fact that the pond included springs which fed the Hamble, advised filling it in completely. Mr Slater from the Portsmouth Water Board considered that it would cost £4,000,000 to restore. By 1973 so little water was flowing through that the river below the sewage works at Brooklands was totally polluted; the town had outgrown the sewage system.[20] Improvements were made.

Bishop's Waltham has become what David Lloyd foresaw, 'a dormitory for adjacent centres of employment, but still catering for local shopping and the social needs of its own population'.[21] The smiths, clockmakers, forage merchants, cattle auctioneers, animal feeds mills, the brewery – all essential to the town when it was supplying both an agricultural and industrial community – have gone.

Bishop's Waltham is thriving again. There is now a Festival in June: Bishop's Waltham in Bloom was begun in 1996. The Bishop's Waltham Society with the Parish Council keeps a watching brief over proposed development, to ensure that no more of the historic heritage is demolished. Many societies and organisations point to the varied interests of the population. The schools are well supported; Ridgemede County Junior school built its own swimming pool and now its amphitheatre.[22] The old and the new combine. Despite the increase of about a third in population from 1961 (3,171) to 1981 (5,180), to nearly 6,000 people in 1991, and then to 6,510 in 2001, the town remains a unit. It is a satisfying place in which to live, still dominated by the ruins of the bishop's palace, which point to the link between the present and the past.

Notes

Introduction
1. Huggins, R.M., 'The Significance of the place name "Wealdham"', *Medieval Archeology* XIX, p.201.
2. A hide was not strictly a measure of area, but was originally the amount of land sufficient to support a family. It has come to represent 120 acres.

1. The Hundred or Manor of Waltham
1. *Victoria County History of Hampshire and the Isle of Wight* V, p.277.
2. Whitelock, D., *Anglo-Saxon Chronicle*, p.86.
3. Munby, J., *Domesday Book*, 2,9.
4. Poole, A., *Obligations of Society in the XII and XIII Centuries*, p.40.
5. Page, M., *The Pipe Roll of the Bishopric of Winchester 1301-2*, pp.XXII, XXIV, n4.
6. HRO 21M65/G/BOX2.
7. Page, M., *op cit.*, pp.387, 388.
8. Titou, J.Z., *English Rural Society*, p.85.
9. HRO 21M65/F7/23/1-2.
10. HRO 11M59/E2/210191A.
11. *VCH* V, p.47, n9.
12. HRO 5M87/11.
13. HRO 11M59/E2/210191A.
14. Sargeant, F., *Palace, op. cit.*, p.51.
15. Lewis, E., 'Excavations in Bishop's Waltham 1967-78', *HFCAS* 41.
16. Page, M., *op. cit.*, p.XXII, n5.
17. Titou, J.Z., *op. cit.*, p.87.
18. Pevsner, N., *Hampshire*, p.107.
19. HRO 11M59/E1/123/10.
20. HRO 11M59/E1/124/11.
21. *VCH* V, p.278.
22. Vancouver, C., *General View of the Agriculture of Hampshire including the Isle of Wight*, p.429.
23. *Hampshire Chronicle*, 15.1.1810.
24. HRO 11M59/E2/210191C.
25. HRO 5M87/11.
26. HRO 11M59/E2/159643.

2. The Palace
1. *DNB*.
2. Vaughan, J., *Winchester Cathedral*, p.71.
3. Hare, J.N., 'Bishop's Waltham Palace William of Wykeham and Henry Beaufort and the Transformation of a Medieval Episcopal Palace', *Archaeological Journal* 145.
4. *VCH* V, p.277.
5. *DNB*.
6. HRO 21M65/F7/23/1-2.
7. Cassan, S.H., *Lives of the Bishops of Winchester* Vol.,1, p.238.
8. HRO 5M87/10.
9. *DNB*.
10. Hare, J.N., *op. cit.*, p.233.
11. Hare, J.N., *op. cit.*, p.24.
12. Hare, J.N., *op. cit.*, p.243.
13. Greatrex, J., *Notes from the Register of the Common Seal of St Swithin 1347-1497*, p.96.
14. HRO 11M59/E2/248950.
15. HRO 5M87/10.
16. *VCH* V, pp.323, 324.
17. Hare, J.N., *op. cit.*, p.20.
18. HRO 30M77/PR1.

3. The Fish Ponds
1. Roberts, E., 'The Bishop of Winchester's Fish Ponds In Hampshire 1150-1400', *HFCAS* 42.
2. HRO 11M59/E2/248950.
3. Roberts, E., *op. cit.*, p.131.
4. Page, M., *op. cit.*, p.255.
5. *DNB*.
6. Roberts, E., *op. cit.*, p.132.
7. HRO 30M77/PV3 9.2.1877.
8. Roberts, E., *op. cit.*, p.133.
9. *VCH* V, p.278; HRO 11M59/E2/155643, p.114.
10. Page, M., *op. cit.*, p.256.
11. HRO 5M87/10.
12. HRO 11M59/E2/155643, p.109.
13. *Hampshire Notes and Queries*, Vol. VI, p.66.
14. HRO 11M59/E2/155643, p.108.
15. HRO 11M59/E2/155498, p.133.
16. HRO 11M59/E2/248950.
17. HRO 11M59/E2/155513, p.641.
18. HRO 11M59/E2/248950.
19. HRO 21M65/G/BOX2.

4. The Park and the Chase
1. Hewlett, G. and Hassall, J., 'Bishop's Waltham Dikes', *Hampshire Field Club* 28, 1973, p.29.
2. Hewlett, G. and Hassall, J., *op. cit.*, p.29.

3. Roberts, E., 'The Bishop of Winchester's Deer Parks in Hampshire 1200-1400', *HFC* 44, p.72.
4. *VCH* V, p.278.
5. HRO 11M59/E2/155643, p.383.
6. Vancouver, C., *op. cit.*, p.429.
7. *DNB.*
8. HRO 11M59/E2/155643, p.380.
9. HRO 11M59/E2/155643, p.118.
10. Ernle, Lord, *English Farming Past and Present*, 1936, p.103.
11. HRO 11M59/E2/155643, p.114.
12. Roberts, E., *op. cit.*, p.73.
13. Roberts, E., p.74.
14. Roberts, E., p.72.
15. *WPR*, p.253.
16. Roberts, E., p.72.
17. HRO 5M54/111.
18. James, T., *The Black Death in Hampshire*, 1999, p.22.
19. Roberts, E., p.71.
20. Roberts, E., pp.81, 82.
21. HRO 5M87/18-19.

5. Robert Reynolds, a Parliamentary Lawyer
1. *VCH* V, p.277; PRO E113 BOX14.
2. *Journal of the House of Commons*, 26.10.1644.
3. *DNB.*
4. *Memoirs of the Protectoral House of Cromwell*, Vol.2, p.418.
5. HRO 30M77/PR1.
6. *Calendar of State Papers Domestic* 25/21, p.64.
7. PRO E113 Box 14.
8. Sargeant, F., *Palace*, 1958, p.19 (Thomasen Tract collection).
9. HRO 11M59/E1/124/11.
10. HRO 11M59/E1/124/11.
11. HRO 30M77/PO1.
12. HRO 11M59/E1/124/11.
13. *CalSPD*, Jan 19 1659-60, p.314.
14. Coleby, A., *Central Government and the Localities*, p.44.
15. HRO 11M59/E1/124/11.
16. PRO E113 BOX 14.
17. *CalSPD*, May and June 1660.

6. The Park Leases after the Restoration
1. HRO 30M77/PO1.
2. HRO 30M77/PO2.
3. HRO M59/E2/155643, p.118.
4. HRO M59/E2/155643, p.380.
5. HRO M59/E2/155514, p.120.
6. HRO 5M87/18/19.
7. HRO M59/E2/155643, p.125.
8. HRO 21M65/F7/23/1-2.
9. HRO M59/E2/155643, p.116.
10. HRO M59/E2/155643.
11. HRO 11M59/BP/E/B4.

12. HRO 5M87/42/1-2.
13. Biddle, M., *Wolvesey: The Old Bishop's Palace Winchester*, pp.22,23.
14. HRO 11M59/E2/155643, p.386.
15. HRO 30M77/PO1.
16. HRO 5M87/42/1-2.
17. HRO 21M65/F7/23/2.
18. HRO 5M54/78 List on the front of tithe book 1794.
19. HRO 30M77/PD14.
20. HRO 30M77/PO3.
21. HRO 11M59/E2/155502, p.281.
22. HRO 11M59/E2/248950.
23. HRO 11M59/E2/155513, p.292.
24. HRO 11M59/E2/155514, p.160.

7. The Park and the Chase after 1663
1. HRO 125M85/12.
2. HRO 11M59/BP/E/B10.
3. HRO 11M59/BP/E/B12.
4. HRO 125M85/12.
5. HRO 11M59/BP/E/B12.
6. Thompson, E., *Whigs and Hunters*, London, 1975, p.133.
7. HRO 125M85/12.
8. HRO Q1/10, p.112.
9. Anon, *History of the Blacks of Waltham in Hants*, London, 1723.
10. Thompson, E., *op. cit.*, p.305.
11. Cruickshanks, E., *Political Untouchables*, p.9.
12. HRO Q1/10, pp.49-51.
13. Anon, *The History of the Blacks of Waltham*.
14. Thompson, E., *op. cit.*, p.154.
15. HRO Q1/10, pp.224, 225.
16. HRO 11M59/E2/159642.
17. HRO 11M59/E2/159644.
18. HRO 30M77/PO3.
19. Sargeant, F., *Bishop's Waltham Ancient and Modern*, p.23.
20. *Hampshire Notes and Queries* Vol. VI, p.55.
21. HRO 30M77/PO4 29.11.1758.
22. HRO 45M69/28b.
23. HRO 11M59/BP/E/B40.
24. Vancouver, C., *Survey of Hampshire*, p.505.
25. HRO 11M59/E/BP/B40.
26. HRO 11M59/E2/159570.
27, 28. Cobbett, W., *The Woodlands*, pp.64-8.
29. Cobbett, W., *The Political Register*, 28.7.1813.
30. HRO 30M77/PV1, 30.6.1818.
31. Young, A., *General View of the Agriculture of the County of Sussex*, 1813, defined a statute acre as 160 rods, i.e. about 30 statute acres to the acre.
32. HRO 44M69/K1/18.
33. HRO 30M77/PV1 11.4.1832.
34. HRO 5M87/40.
35. HRO Q23/2/14.

8. The Demesne

1. HRO 11M59/E2/155643, p.408.
2. HRO 11M59/E2/248950 Survey No19.
3. HRO 11M59/E2/155643, p.75.
4. HRO 11M59/E2/248950, Surveys Nos.13 & 16.
5. HRO 30M77/PK3.
6. HRO 11M59/E2/155501, p.163.
7. HRO 30M77/PK3.
8. HRO 11M59/E2/155498, p.122.
9. HRO 11M59/E2/248950.
10. HRO 11M59/E2/153069.
11. HRO 11M59/E2/210191C, p.472.
12. HRO 11M59/248950, 25.11.1806.
13. HRO 11M59/155510, p.1.
14. HRO 11M59/155472.
15. Sargeant, F., *Story of Bishop's Waltham*, p.51.
16. Hare, J. N., *op. cit.*, p.28.

9. Enclosure

1. HRO 5M87/42/1-2.
2. HRO M59/E2/155643.
3. HRO 45M69/17.
4. HRO 11M59/E2/159641.
5. HLRO LP252/23.
6. HRO 7M49/3.
7. HLRO Petition against the Bill LP/252/23.
8. HLRO Petition against the Bill LP/252/22.
9. HRO 5M54/66.
10. HLRO, Committee Book, H.L. 27 April, 3 May 1759.
11. HRO 45M69/17.
12. HRO 5M54//66.
13. HRO 5M54/65.
14. HRO 111M94W/N1/17.
15. HRO 8M49/T5.
16. HRO 107M90/96.
17. HRO 11M59/E1/124/11.
18. HRO 21M65/F7/23/1-2.
19. Cobbett, W., *Political Register*, 28.7.1813.
20. HRO Q23/2/33.

10. The Courts of the Manor

1. Harvey, P.D., *Manorial Records*, p.144.
2. HRO 21M65/G/BOX2.
3. *VCH* V, pp.324-31.
4,5. HRO 21M65/G/BOX2.
6. HRO 11M59/E2/380751.
7. HRO 21M65/G/BOX2.
8. HRO 45M69/28b.
9. HRO 21M65/G/BOX2.
10. HRO 11M59/E2/380751.
11. HRO 11M59/E2/159643.
12. HRO 11M59/E2/380751.
13. Thompson, E.P., *op. cit.*, pp.128, 129.
14. HRO 11M59/BP/E/B12.
15. Thompson, E., *op. cit.*, p.133.
16. HRO 5M54/57.
17. HRO 11M59/E1/107/9.
18. HRO 5M54/64.
19. HRO 5M54/57.
20. HRO 11M59/E2/159643.
21. HRO 11M59/E2/159642.
22. HRO 21M65/G/BOX1.
23. HRO 5M54/90.
24. HRO 21M65/G/BOX1.
25. HRO 11M59/E2/159643.
26. PCRO 129A/S/3.
27. HRO 11M59/E2/159643, 159644.
28. WPR, p.375.
29. HRO 5M54/64.
30. HRO 11M59/E2/155643, p.114.
31. HRO 11M59/E2/155498, p.163.
32. HRO 11M59/E2/155499, p.544.
33. HRO 21M65/G/BOX 1.

11. The Church

1. *Bishop's Waltham*, report by English Heritage, p.7.
2. *Hampshire Treasures*, pp.48, 49.
3. *Hampshire Treasures*, p.49.
4. Pevsner, N., *op. cit.*, p.105.
5. Hopewell, P., *The Hospital of St Cross* (1995), p.76.
6. *VCH* V, p.281.
7. Sargeant F., *The Story of the Church of St Peter*, p.4.
8. Sargeant, F. *op. cit.*, p.6.
9. HRO 30M77/PO1 list of churchwardens, overseers, surveyors.
10. Hopewell, P., *op. cit.*, p.76.
11. *VCH* V, p.280.
12. HRO 111M94W/N1/17.
13. HRO 21M65/F7/23/1-2.
14. Coleby, A., *Central Government and the Localities*, p.9.
15. Walker, C., *Sufferings of the Clergy*, Vol.1, p.77.
16. Matthews, A.E., *Walker Revised*, p.17.
17. Matthews, A.E., *op. cit.*, p.191.
18. HRO 30M77/PR1.
19. HRO 30M77/PO1.
20. Matthews, A.E., *op. cit.*, p.183.
21. Cal SPD June 1660.
22. HRO 30M77/PR1.
23. Sargeant, F., *op. cit.*, p.13.
24. Sargeant, F., *op. cit.*, p.9.
25. HRO 5M54/73.
26. HRO 11M59/E2/159646.
27. Veck, H.A., *A Selection of Hymns and Anthems for the Use of Bishop's Waltham Church* (1812).
28. HRO 30M77/PV1 20.9.1816.
29. HRO 30M77/PV1 16.4.1828.
30. HRO 30M77/PW1 12.6.1837.
31. Hall, J., *Ironwork Fastenings of the Fourteenth Century*, Newcomen Society, Vol.XVI.
32. HRO 30M77/PV2 14.11.1850.

33. Sargeant, F., *op. cit.*, p.5.
34. HRO 30M77/PV2 7.5.1867.
35. HRO 30M77/PV3 30.3.1875.
36. *St Peter's Parish Magazine*, April 1900.
37. HRO 30M77/PW29.

12. Welfare in Bishop's Waltham
1. HRO 30M77/PO1.
2. Titou, J., *op. cit.*, p.96.
3. HRO 30M77/PO1.

13. The Parish Officers
1. HRO 30M77/PO1.
2. HRO Q1/10.
3. HRO 30M77/PO3 1726.
4. HRO 30M77/PR2,PR3.
5. HRO 30M77/PO1 1.4.1676.
6. HRO 30M77/PO6 15.6.1774.
7. HRO 30M77/PO3 May 1723.
8. HRO 11M59/E2/159643.
9. HRO Q1/17.
10. HRO 30M77/PO5 5.4.61.
11. HRO 30M77/PO6 6.11.67.
12. HRO Q1/18.
13. HRO 30M77/PO6 9.5.1770.
14. HRO 30M77/PO8 22.8.1815.
15. HRO 30M77/PV1 13.11.1818.
16. HRO 30M77/PO8 12.8.1811, 28.5.1814.
17. HRO 30M77/PO3 7.10.1722.
18. HRO 30M77/PO4 22.4.1759.
19. HRO 30M77/PW1 25.7.1825.
20. HRO 30M77/PV3 10.2.1892.
21. HRO 30M77/PV3 6.4.1882.
22. HRO 30M77/PV3 16.2.1872.

14. The Welfare System
1. HRO 30M77/PR3.
2. HRO 30M77/PO4 15.5.1758.
3. HRO 30M77/PO6 18.12.1767.
4. HRO 30M77/PO3 17.8.1723.
5. HRO 30M77/PO6 11.10.1767.
6. Woodforde, J., *The Diary of a Country Parson*, 25.1.1787.
7. HRO 30M77/PO7 23.4.1785.
8. HRO 30M77/PR3.
9. *Burke's Peerage*.
10. HRO 30M77/PO1 May-June 1665.
11. HRO 30M77/PO3 5.6.1725.
12. HRO 30M77/PO3 5.2.1726.
13. HRO 30M77/PO6 17.6.1766.
14. HRO Q1/17.
15. HRO 30M77/PO7 23.5.1775.
16. HRO 30M77/PO3 5.4.1723.
17. HRO 30M77/PO6 8.3.1768.
18. HRO 30M77/PO5,PO6,PO7.

15. The Health Service
1. HRO 30M77/PO1.
2. HRO 30M77/PO2 17.4.1718.
3. HRO 30M77/PO6 18.4.1773.

4. HRO 30M77/PO6 28.7.1766.
5. HRO 30M77/PO6 31.7.1773.
6. HRO 30M77/PO3 9.1.1725.
7. HRO 30M77/PO2 1.1.1724.
8. HRO 30M77/PO7 23.4.1785.
9. HRO 5M63/1.
10. HRO 30M77/PO6 10.10.1772.
11. HRO 30M77/PO7 26.2.1785.
12. HRO 30M77/PO4 9.6.1757.
13. HRO 30M77/PO7 11th month 1789.
14. HRO 30M77/PO7 6th month 1787.
15. HRO 30M77/PO6 Oct 1766-1775.

16. The Pest House
1. HRO 30M77/PO3 5.6.1726.
2. HRO 30M77/PR3.
3. HRO 30M77/PO6 9.5.1769.
4. HRO 30M77/PO6 9.5.1773.
5. HRO 30M77/PR3.
6. HRO 30M77/PO7.
7. HRO 30M77/PV1 22.4.1818.

17. The Workhouse
1. HRO 30M77/PR3.
2. HRO 30M77/PO4 5.5.1756.
3. HRO 30M77/PO4.
4. HRO Q23/2/14.
5. HRO 30M77/PO5 13.5.1761.
6. HRO 30M77/PO5 17.6.1762.
7. HRO 30M77/PO5. May.
8. HRO 30M77/PO6 1.3.1766.
9. HRO 30M77/PO6 9.3.1769.
10. HRO 30M77/PO6 31.3.1774.
11. HRO 30M77/PO7 7.4.1784.
12. HRO 30M77/PO7 2.4.1796, 13.4.1796.
13. *Hampshire Repository*, Vol. 1, 1798; *Transactions of the South Hampshire Agricultural Society*, p.76.
14. HRO 30M77/PO8 10.5.1811, 18.10.1811.
15. Vancouver, C., *op. cit.*, p.505.
16. Reitzel, J., *The Progress of a Plough-Boy to a seat in Parliament* (1933), p.165.
17. HRO 30M77/PV1 9.7.1819.
18. HRO 30M77/PO8 Labour of the Poor 1.3.1822-28.2.1823.
19. HRO 30M77/PV1 2.5.1828.
20. HRO 30M77/PV1 9.3.1832.
21. HRO 30M77/PV1 29.1.1835.
22. Anstruther, I., *The Scandal of the Andover Workhouse*, p.41.

18. The New Poor Law
1. HRO 30M77/PO2, PO9.
2. Anstruther, I., *op. cit.*, p.45.
3. Anstruther, I., *op. cit.*, pp.42, 43.
4. *DNB*.
5. HRO 30M77/PV2 24.3.1835.
6. Anstruther, I., *op. cit.*, p.50.
7. HRO PL3/7/1 12.2.1836.
8. HRO 30M77/PV1 30.3.1827.

9. HRO PL3/7/1, p.49.
10. HRO PL3/7/1, p.30.
11. HRO PL3/7/1, p.361.
12. HRO 30M77/PV2 3.1.1839.

19. Employment and Rates
1. HRO 30M77/PO7 1794 8th month.
2. HRO 30M77/PO7 1787 10th month.
3. HRO 30M77/PO8 10.9.1814.
4. HRO 30M77/PV1 6.6.1817.
5. HRO 30M77/PO8 Labour of the Poor 1.3.1822-28.2.1823.
6. HRO 30M77/PV2 29.11.1833.

20. The Highways
1. WPR 249-259.
2. Tate, W., *The Parish Chest*, p.240.
3. HRO 11M59/E1/155/6.
4. HRO 78M73/DH1 8.11.1864.
5. HRO, *Pigot's Directory*, 1821.
6. Albert, W., *The Turnpike System In England 1633-1840*, p.238.
7. HRO 4M30/1-4.
8. HRO 44M69/91/130.
9. HRO 36M72/A1.
10. HRO 36M72/A1.
11. HRO 30M77/PO7.
12. HRO 36M72/A1.
13. HRO 5M54/111.
14. HRO 5M54/111 15.5.1801.
15. HRO 5M54/111 23.3.1824.
16. HRO 5M54/118 22.3.1853.
17. HRO 5M54/139 7.9.1874.
18. HC 1.1.1810.
19. Nuff XIII.
20. HRO 30M77/PO8 12.2.1815.
21. HRO 30M77/PV1 6.6.1817.
22. HRO 5M54/68 1.10.1821.
23. HRO 30M77/PV2 30.5.1833.
24. HRO 5M54/67 Nov and Dec 1829.
25. HRO 5M54/144 18.2.1833.
26. HRO 5M54/144.
27. HRO 5M54/144 8.3.1833.
28. HRO 5M54/142 25.9.1832.
29. HRO 5M54/144.
30. HRO 5M54/142 2.3.1833.
31. HRO 5M54/67.
32. HRO 5M54/146 10.11.1834.
33. HRO 5M54/67.
34. HRO 30M77/PV2 6.4 1838.
35. HRO 78M73/PV1 14.6.1829.
36. HRO 78M73/DH1 12.9.1871.

21. The Militia
1. HRO 30M77/PO7 13 month 1792.
2. HRO 30M77/PO7 27.3.1795.
3. HRO 30M77/PO4 1757.
4. HRO 30M77/PO8 5th-20th.5.1812.
5. Buckley, R., *The Napoleonic War Journal of Captain Thomas Henry Browne*, p.174.

22. Napoleonic Prisoners
1. Abell, F., *Prisoners of War in Britain 1756-1815*, p.289.
2. PRO ADM99/164 13.1.1806.
3. Abell, F., *op. cit.*, p.34.
4. PRO ADM99/164.
5. PRO ADM103/562.
6. PRO ADM103/563.
7. Melville, L., *The Life and Letters of William Cobbett*, Vol.1, p.291.
8. Abell, F., *op. cit.*, p.445.
9. PRO ADM103/563.
10. Garneray, L., *The French Prisoner*, p.162.
11. HRO 30M77/PR3.
12. HRO 30M77/PO8 22.8.1815.

23. The Last Private Bank in England
1. Richards, R.D., *The Early History of Banking*, 1965.
2. HRO 30M77/PO4.
3. HRO 44M73 BOX149 4.10.1809.
4. Hodgson, R.A., 'Gunners Bank', *Portsmouth Archive Review*, Vol. 2, p.34.
5. HRO 44M73 BOX150 minute book.
6. HRO 44M73 BOX150 20.10.1810.
7. HRO 44M73 BOX150 18.6.1812.
8. HRO 44M73 BOX150 14.9.1813.
9. Hodgson, R.A., *op. cit.*, Vol. 2, p.52.
10. HRO 44M73 BOX148.

24. Health and Drainage
1. PCRO 129A/S/3.
2. HRO 44M73 BOX/132.
3. PCRO 129A/GS/4/1/16.
4. HRO 30M77/PV2 30.5.1833.
5. HRO 30M77/PV2 25.10 1848.
6. *DNB*.
7. HRO 30M77/PV3 14.8.1875.
8. H.I. 9.9.1875.

25. Arthur Helps and the Bishop's Waltham Railway Company
1. HRO 30M77/PV2 24.12.1847.
2. *DNB*.
3. HRO 11M59/E2/155513, p.292.
4. Pitman, T., *Newtown and Clay 1860-1957*.
5. HRO 11M59/E2/155514, p.173.
6. PRO Rail49 BIW/1/1 29.2.1862.
7. PRO Rail49 BIW/1/1 August 1862.
8. Act for making a Railway from Bishop's Waltham to Botley July 1862.
9. PRO Rail49 BIW1/1 29.2.1864.
10. PRO Rail49 BIW1/1 13.10.1863.
11. Pitman, T., *op. cit.*
12. HRO 45M69/23.
13. PRO Rail49 BIW1/1 28.2.1865.
14. PRO Rail49 BIW1/1 11.7.1866.
15. PRO Rail49 BIW1/1 4.8.1881.
16. Pitman, T., *op. cit.*

26. Education

1. HRO 30M77/PK3.
2. HRO 125M85/12.
3. HRO 125M85/12.
4. Jones, M.G., *The Charity School Movement*, 1938.
5. HRO 30M77PK3.
6. HRO 21M65 A2/1.
7. HRO 30M77PK3.
8. HRO 30M77PK3.
9. HRO 5M87/40,41, Charity Commissioners' Report 1819-37, 1878.
10. 30M77/PZ28.
11. HI 6.3.1875.
12. HI 14.7.1875.
13. HRO 125M85/18/6.
14. HI 14.7.1875.
15. HI 23.10.1875.
16. HRO 84M76/PK83.
17. HRO 125M85/18/9.
18. *DNB*.
19. Melville, L., *op. cit.*, Vol. 1, p.265.
20. HRO 125M85/18/5.
21. HRO 5M54/73.
22. Melville, L., *op. cit.*, Vol. 1, p.265.
23. HC 17.7.1809.
24. Cobbett, W., *Cottage Economy* (1926), paras 11-14.
25. HRO 5M54/78.
26. HRO 5M54/71.
27. HI 7.11.1865.

27. The White Fathers

1. Burniol, J., *The White Fathers and their Missions* (1929), p.303.
2. Bosworth, J., *Bishop's Waltham and Newtown, Twenty Five Years of Change*, p.81.

28. The Accounts of William Brown Alexander

1. HRO 30M77/PR2.
2. HRO 30M77/PO4.
3. Pevsner, N., *op. cit.*, p.109.
4. *DNB*.
5. HRO 30M77/PO4.
6. HRO 11M59/E2/159643 16.9.1735.
7. HRO 30M77/PR11, PR3.
8. Bosworth, J., *op. cit.*; *Bishop's Waltham, a Pictorial Record*.
9. Thompson, E.P., *Whigs and Hunters* (1985), p.305.
10. Thompson, E.P., *op. cit.*, p.305.
11. Thompson, E.P., *op. cit.*, p.305.
12. HRO 30M77/PR2.
13. Cruickshanks, E., *Political Untouchables*, p.45.
14. BL Add Ms 28,228 15.4.1730.
15. BL Add Ms 28,229 6.10.1735.
16. Jones, G.H., *The Main Stream of Jacobitism*, pp.186, 187.
17. Cruickshanks, E., p.43.
18. White, G., *The Natural History of Selborne*, letter VII.
19. HRO 30M77/PO4.

29. The Growth of Bishop's Waltham

1. Census returns 1801-1991.
2. *St Peter's Bishop's Waltham parish magazine*, 1892-1900.
3. Willis, A.J., *A Hampshire Miscellany*, Vol. 3, p.144.
4. *St Peter's Bishop's Waltham parish magazine*, 1890-1902.
5. Hodgson, R.A., 'Gunners Bank', *Portsmouth Archive Review*, Vol. 2, p.47.
6. HRO 45M69/23.
7. Lewis, E., *op. cit.*, p.98.
8. *Kelly's Directory*, 1921, 1939.
9. HRO 44M73 BOX 132.
10. HRO 44M73 BOX 148.
11. Bosworth, J., *A Pictorial Record*.
12. *Kelly's Directory*, 1939.
13. Bosworth, J., *op. cit.*, p.57.
14. *Kelly's Directory*, 1939.
15. *St Peter's Bishop's Waltham parish magazine*, June 2001, p.26.
16. Bosworth, J., *Twenty Five Years of Change*, p.52.
17. *Hampshire*, 1966.
18. HRO 5M87/49 Report on Bishop's Waltham by David Lloyd 7.9.71.
19. *St Peter's parish magazine*, December 1971.
20. *St Peter's parish magazine*, 1973.
21. HRO 5M87/49.
22. *St Peter's parish magazine*, September 2001.

Abbreviations and Bibliography

BL   British Library
CSPD *Calendar of State Papers Domestic*
DNB   *Dictionary of National Biography*
HC   *Hampshire Chronicle*
HFCAS *Hampshire Field Club and Archaeological Society*
HI   *Hampshire Independent*
HLRO   House of Lords Record Office
HRO   Hampshire Record Office
PCRO   Portsmouth City Record Office
PRO   Public Record Office
VCH   *Victoria County History of Hampshire and the Isle of Wight* Vol. V, 1908

Albert, W., *The Turnpike System in England 1663-1840*, 1968
Anon, *The History of the Blacks of Waltham in Hampshire*, 1723
Anstruther, I., *The Scandal of the Andover Workhouse*, 1973
Aylmer, G., *The Interregnum*, 1972
Biddle, M., *Wolvesey The Old Bishop's Palace Winchester*, 1986
Bosworth, J., *Bishop's Waltham & Newtown 25 Years of Change*, 1988
Bosworth, J., *Bishop's Waltham, a Pictorial Record*
Buckley, R., *The Napoleonic War Journal of Captain Henry Browne*, 1987
Burniol, J., *The White Fathers and their Missions*, 1929
Chadwick, O., *The Victorian Church*, 1966
Charlesworth, A., *An Atlas of Rural Protest in Britain*
Chapman, J. and Seeliger, S., *Formal & Informal Enclosure in Hampshire 1700-1900*, 1997
Cobbett, W., *Political Register*
Cobbett, W., *Rural Rides*
Cobbett, W., *The Woodlands*, 1825
Coleby, A., *Central Government and the Localities 1649-89*, 1987
Cruickshanks, E., *Political Untouchables*, 1979
English Heritage, *Hampshire Treasures, Bishop's Waltham*, 1999
Ernle, Lord, *English Farming Past and Present*, 1936
Farnham Castle, A Short History, 1993
Gardner, J. and Wenborn, N., *Companion to British History*, 1995
Godwin, G.N., *The Civil War in Hampshire*, 1904
Greatex, J., *Notes from the Register of the Common Seal of the Priory of St Swithins 1347-1497*, 1978
Hall, J., 'Ironwork Fastenings of the Fourteenth Century', *Newcomen Society*, Vol. XVI
Hampshire Notes and Queries, Vols. I & II, 1894
Hampshire Magazine, 1966

Hampshire Repository, Vol. 1, 1798: *Transactions of the South Hampshire Agricultural Society*

Hare, J., *Bishop's Waltham Palace*, 1996

Hare, J., 'Bishop's Waltham Palace, William of Wykeham and Henry Beaufort and the Transformation of a Medieval Episcopal Palace', *Archeological Journal*, 145

Harvey, P.D., *Manorial Records*, 1984

Hewlett, G. and Hassall, J., 'Bishop's Waltham Dikes', *HFCAS*, 1973

Hingston, F., *Deer Parks and Deer of Great Britain*, 1988

Hodgson, R.A., 'Gunners Bank', *Portsmouth Archive Review*, Vols. 2, 3, 4

Hopewell, P., *St Cross*, 1995

Huggins, R.M., 'The Significance of the Place name "Wealdham"', *Medieval Archaeology*, XIX

Hutton, R., *The Royalist War Effort 1643-46*, 1982

James, T., *The Black Death in Hampshire*, Hampshire Papers 18, 1999

Jones, G.H., *The Main Stream of Jacobitism*, 1954

Jones, M., *The Charity School Movement*, 1938

Journal of the House of Commons

Kelly's Directory, 1921, 1939

Lennard, R., *Rural England 1086-1135*, 1959

Lewis, E., 'Excavations in Bishop's Waltham 1967-78', *HFCAS* 41, 1985

Lloyd, D., *Report on Bishop's Waltham*, 7.9.71

Local Acts of Parliament, Vol. 2

Loyn, H.R., *Anglo Saxon England and the Norman Conquest*, 1962

Matthews, A., *Walker Revised*, 1948

Memoirs of the Protectoral House of Cromwell, 1787

Melville, L., *The Life and Letters of William Cobbett*, 1913

Monod, P., 'Dangerous Merchandise: Smuggling, Jacobitism and Commercial Culture in Southeast England, 1680-1760', *Journal of British Studies* 30, 1991

Munby, J., *Domesday Book Vol. 4: Hampshire*, 1982

Oldfield, J., 'Private Schools and Academies in Eighteenth Century Hampshire', *HFCAS* 45

Page, M., *The Pipe Roll of the Bishopric of Winchester 1301-1302*, 1996

Parry, A., *The Carylls of Harting*, 1976

Partridge, R. and Oliver, M., *Napoleonic Army Handbook*, 1999

Petrie, Sir C., *The Jacobite Movement*, 1959

Pevsner, N. and Lloyd, D., *The Buildings of England: Hampshire and the Isle of Wight*, 1967

Pitman, T., *Newtown and Clay 1860-1957*

Poole, A., *Obligations of Society in the XII and XIII Centuries*, 1946

Private Acts of Parliament, 1862

Richards, R., *The Early History of Banking*, 1965

Roberts, E., 'The Bishop of Winchester's Deer Parks in Hampshire 1200-1400', *HFCAS* 42

Roberts, E., 'The Bishop of Winchester's Fish Ponds in Hampshire 1150-1400', *HFCAS* 44

St Peter's Bishop's Waltham, Parish Magazine, 1892-1900, 1971, 1973, 2001

Sargeant, F., *The Story of Bishop's Waltham Ancient and Modern*, 1961

Sargeant, F., *The Story of the Bishop's Palace, Bishop's Waltham*, 1958

Sargeant, F., *The Story of the Church of St Peter Bishop's Waltham*, 1965

State Papers Domestic
Tate, W., *The Parish Chest*, 1951
Thompson, E., *Whigs and Hunters*, 1985
Titow, J., *English Rural Society*, 1969
Vancouver, C., *A General View of the Agriculture of Hampshire and the Isle of Wight*, 1810
Vaughan, J., *Winchester Cathedral*, 1918
Veck, H.A., *A Selection of Hymns and Anthems for the Use of Bishop's Waltham Church*, 1812
Walker, J., *The Sufferings of the Clergy*, 1714
Walters, C., *History of Bishop's Waltham*, 1844
Webb, S. and B., *The Story of the King's Highway*, 1913
Webb, S. and B., *The Parish and the County*, 1906
Western, J.R., *The English Militia in the Eighteenth Century*, 1965
White, G., *The Natural History of Selborne*, 1788
Whitelock, D., *The Anglo Saxon Chronicle*, 1955
Wood, L., *The French Prisoner by Louis Garneray*, 1957
Woodforde, J., *The Diary of a Country Parson*, 1935

Documents referred to in text
HRO

4M30/1-4 Stockbridge to Bishop's Waltham Turnpike minute books 1758-1875
7M49/3 no9 Patent offices 1761
8M49/T5 Walter Long admitted to 170 Acres Commonage Stephen's Castle Down 1898
5M54/57 Manorial customs of Waltham, Bittern, Droxford
5M54/64 Copyhold quit rents
5M54/65 Allotment of land in Ashton common fields
5M54/66 Barfoot's bill re inclosure of Ashton common fields
5M54/67 Minute book of Bishop's Waltham surveyor of the highways 1828-42
5M54/68 Inhabitants presented for cutting down fences 1821
5M54/71 Rector leases market hall upper room for school 1816
5M54/73 Plan and names of those renting seats south gallery of St Peter's 1797
5M54/78 tithe rental 1794-96
5M54/90 letter from Rev J. Bale to Rector 1783
5M54/111 Minute book of Botley to Corhampton turnpike 1801-46
5M54/118 Sale of Northbrook tollhouse 1854
5M54/122 Gunner's bill, Bishop's Waltham to Fishers Pond T.P.
5M54/139 Dissolution of Botley to Corhampton T.P.
5M54/142 letters, Bishop's Waltham to Fishers Pond T.P.
5M54/144 minute book Bishop's Waltham to Fishers Pond T.P.
5M54/146 accounts of Bishop's Waltham to Fishers Pond T.P.
11M59/E1/107/9 court rolls 1772-82
11M59/BP/E/B4 Case against Bishop Duppa
11M59/BP/E/B10 Memorial of Richard Norton 1707
11M59/BP/E/B12 Articles of complaint, Kerby v Heron and Heron's reply
11M59/E1/123/10 manorial court 1653
11M59/E1/124/11 manorial court 1658-60
11M59/E1/155/6 manorial court 1641-44

11M59/E1/157/1 manorial court 1655
11M59/E2/153069 fine books 1787
11M59/E2/210191A Enfranchisement registers
11M59/E2/210191C Enfranchisement registers
11M59/BP/E/B40 Bishop orders removal of encroachments on Waltham Chase 1800, faggott wood etc
11M59/E2/155643 lease register 1660-64
11M59/E2/155498 lease register 1747-83
11M59/E2/155499 lease register 1784-87
11M59/E2/155500 lease register 1788-91
11M59/E2/155501 lease register 1791-95
11M59/E2/155502 lease register 1796-99
11M59/E2/155510 lease register 1842-48
11M59/E2/155513 lease register 1857-62
11M59/E2/155514 lease register 1862-64
11M59/E2/159641 Presentments 1711-17
11M59/E2/159642 Presentments 1718-31
11M59/E2/159643 Presentments 1732-45
11M59/E2/159644 Presentments 1746-55
11M59/E2/159646 Presentments 1768-70
11M59/E2/155472 Survey of Palace property 1855-63
11M59/E2/248950 Surveys of Palace property 1784-1828
11M59/E2/380751 Customs of the manor
5M63/1 Minute book of Winchester Infirmary 1736
21M65/F7/23/1-2 Tithe award and map
21M65/G/BOX1 manorial records
21M65/G/BOX2 manorial records
21M65 A2/1 register of Bishop Hoadley 1742-66
44M69/K1/18 Case for inclosure of Waltham Chase 1826
44M69/91/130 Act for Turnpike Bishop's Waltham-Odiham
45M69/17 Printed Act for inclosure of Ashton Common fields
45M69/23 Sale of Blanchard's brickworks
45M69/28b Droxford Court book 1762-1807
36M72/A1 Account book of treasurer Gosport turnpike 1775-96
36M72/A2 Account book of treasurer Gosport turnpike 1797-1831
44M73 BOX 132 Gunner Papers
44M73 BOX 148 Gunner Papers
44M73 BOX 150 Gunner Papers
78M73/DH1 Minute book of Droxford Highway Board 1863-73
84M76/PK83 Search for Grammar School site 1887
30M77/PD14 Sale of glebe 1907
30M77/PK3 Report of Charity Commissioners on Grammar School 1819-37
30M77/PO1 Poor rate book 1650-85
30M77/PO2 Poor rate book 1687-1718
30M77/PO3 Overseers Account book 1722-27
30M77/PO4 Overseers Account and rate book 1756-60 (abstract 1771-72); Accounts of J.B.Alexander 1734-51
30M77/PO5 Overseers Account and rate book 1759-64

30M77/PO6 Overseers Account and rate book 1765-75
30M77/PO7 Overseers Account and rate book 1775-97
30M77/PO8 Overseers Account book 1809-23
30M77/PO9 Poor rate book 1829-33
30M77/PR1 Register of baptisms marriages burials 1612-68
30M77/PR2 Register of baptisms marriages burials 1669-1737
30M77/PR3 Register of baptisms marriages burials 1737-1812
30M77/PR28 Register of burials 1813-73
30M77/PV1 Vestry minute book 1805-29
30M77/PV2 Vestry minute book 1830-67
30M77/PV3 Vestry minute book 1868-92
30M77/PW1 Churchwardens accounts 1823-79
30M77/PW29 Report by T.J. Jackson on Bishop's Waltham church
30M77/PZ28 The life of the Rev. C. Walters 1784-1844
107M90/96 Stephen's Castle Down sold to Sir Warden Chilcott
125M85/12 will of Robert Kerby
125M85/18/5 extract from will of J Padbury 1898
125M85/18/6 Almshouse charity 1609
125M85/18/9 List of documents in Institute safe, charities 1699-1898
5M87/10 Search of pipe rolls
5M87/11 Transcript from Waltham Account rolls 1493-1501, 1666, 1668
5M87/12 Transcript from a 1464 rental of Bishop's Waltham
5M87/16 Transcript from a 1693 rental
5M87/13-17 relates to ponds gates streets mills parks
5M87/18-19 abstracts from manorial records during Civil Wars and Commonwealth
5M87/36-38 the palace, gates courts, bridges, moats, farm buildings from pipe rolls
5M87/40 Rights of tenants in Horders Wood 1862
5M87/42/1-2 Two Acts of Parliament re leasing of Bishops' land at Bishop's Waltham,
    1663, 1664-5
5M87/49 Report on Bishop's Waltham by David Lloyd
30M87/9 Sir A. Helps estate 1875
111M94W/N1/17 Ashton Manor court
PL317/1 Minute book of Droxford Union workhouse
Q1/9 Quarter Sessions 1717
Q1/10 Quarter Sessions 1722
Q1/17 Quarter Sessions 1761
Q1/18 Quarter Sessions 1770
Q23/2/14 Inclosure of Waltham Chase 1870
Q23/2/33 Inclosure of Curdridge Common 1856

BL
Family of Caryll correspondence, Vol. 2, 1719-31, Add Ms 28,228; Vol. 3, 1732-39, Add
    Ms 28,229

HLRO
LP252/22 Petition presented by T. Hatch and others against the Bill, 29 March 1759
LP252/23 Petition presented by Dr Lynch, Dean of Canterbury and others against the Bill,
    25 April 1759

Proceedings at Committees and other matters 1758-62

PCRO
129A/GS/4/1/16 Sale of Waltham Chase mill property
129A/S/3 Gosport Water Act 1940

PRO
ADM99/164 letters and transactions 1806
ADM103/562 Register of Spanish Prisoners of War on parole in Bishop's Waltham
ADM103/563 Register of French Prisoners of War on Parole in Bishop's Waltham
E113 Box 14 Answer of Sir R.Reynolds to information of Sir G. Palmer, Attorney General
Rail 49 BIW1/1/1 Minute book of Bishop's Waltham Railway Co. 1862-81
Rail 49 BIW/2/1 Lloyds Bondholders of Bishop's Waltham Railway Co

Nuffield College, Oxford
Nuff XIII account book of expenditure at Botley, Jan 1808-June 1810

Index

Page numbers in **bold** refer to illustrations